120

SELLING NAKED

(A REVOLUTIONARY
APPROACH TO
LAUNCHING YOUR
BRAND ONLINE)

SELLING NAKED

JESSE HORWITZ

CURRENCY
NEW YORK

Published in the United States by Currency,
an imprint of Random House, a division of
Penguin Random House LLC, New York.

CURRENCY and its colophon are trademarks
of Penguin Random House LLC.

LIBRARY OF CONGRESS CATALOGING-IN-PUBLICATION DATA
Names: Horwitz, Jesse, author.
Title: Selling naked : a revolutionary approach
to launching your brand online / Jesse Horwitz.
Description: New York : Currency, [2020] |
Includes bibliographical references and index.
Identifiers: LCCN 2019025927 (print) |
LCCN 2019025928 (ebook) | ISBN 9781984826268 (hardcover) |
ISBN 9781984826275 (ebook)
Subjects: LCSH: Direct selling. | Direct marketing. |
Online marketing.
Classification: LCC HF5438.25 .H674 2020 (print) |
LCC HF5438.25 (ebook) | DDC 658.8/72—dc23
LC record available at https://lccn.loc.gov/2019025927
LC ebook record available at https://lccn.loc.gov/2019025928

Printed in Canada on acid-free paper

randomhousebooks.com

9 8 7 6 5 4 3 2 1

First Edition

Book design by Jen Valero

CONTENTS

Introduction   vii

CHAPTER 1:
Don't Bullshit Yourself
About Digital Business   3

CHAPTER 2:
Demonstrate Demand   30

CHAPTER 3:
Tell a Great Story   52

CHAPTER 4:
Compensate Experts and Partners   75

CHAPTER 5:
Worry About the Pie Exploding   97

CHAPTER 6:
Use Third-Party Tools   118

CHAPTER 7:
Frame the Digital Offering   139

CHAPTER 8:
Cut Through the Metrics Bullshit   162

CHAPTER 9:
Know What a Customer Is Worth   185

CHAPTER 10:
Pull Your Financial Model Together—
and Use It!   207

CHAPTER 11:
Beware the Dumpster Fire   228

CHAPTER 12:
Grow Your Own Way   245

Acknowledgments   261

Notes   263

Index   271

INTRODUCTION

IN THE PAST, if you made stuff and wanted to sell it, you had to go through gatekeepers—big-box retailers, department stores, neighborhood convenience stores, retail pharmacies. You played by *their* rules. You submitted to *their* understanding of customers. You relied on *their* shelves to help establish consumer relationships.

Not anymore.

A new crop of companies is selling branded merchandise and services directly to consumers, striking deals with suppliers or manufacturing goods themselves, and saving consumers money. They're eliminating the middleman and putting themselves out there "naked," so to speak. You've probably heard of some of these companies. There's Dollar Shave Club. Casper mattresses. The Honest Company. And ours, Hubble Contacts.

My co-founder, Ben Cogan, and I recognized the potential of this new way of selling and thought that we could make a nice business selling naked on a subscription basis. No brand had sold corrective lenses directly to consumers before, and we believed doing so would simplify the process. So in February 2016, with a few friends, we decided to test whether people really wanted a more consumer-friendly contact lens brand. Our approach, borrowed from Harry's, the shaving subscription company where Ben was working, was to promote a mock product through Facebook and other social media platforms. Harry's had created a simple pre-launch site, which it shared on the hosting service GitHub. On one page, Harry's described its new business offering and asked interested visitors to leave their email addresses. On a second page, Harry's provided visitors who submitted their email addresses with a custom link to share with their friends on Facebook. To entice participation, they dangled freebies for each successful referral. We created a site like that, asking thirty of our friends to share the campaign. Then we sat back and waited. Ben and I were amazed to log more than two thousand signups over a four-day period, including everyone from a major CEO to a New York City cabdriver. With this experiment in hand, we approached a group of enthusiastic investors and in May 2016 raised $3.5 million in seed funding (just *slightly* overshooting our initial $500,000 goal).

Following this initial test, we ran a second set of experiments, collecting consumer email addresses through Facebook lead ads (the kind of easy-to-fill-out forms that pop up as you scroll through your timeline on your mobile device) and connecting these potential customers with a network of optometrists who had agreed to work with our lenses. Our early success had caught us off guard. We didn't have a website or branded packaging yet, or much of anything else. We followed up by sending prospects basic, unformatted Gmail messages, dumping leads into the bcc line, and using stock photos in the ads themselves. We just wanted to see whether people would show up and pay for an eye exam in exchange for two months of free lenses. It turned out they would, and on the strength of that knowledge, we went back to investors. In October 2016 we landed an additional $3.7 million in funding at twice the valuation we had received just a couple of months earlier.

Hubble finally went live on November 1, 2016. During the first several months, our team continued to experiment, tinkering in particular with our advertising. Which photos connected most with consumers? Which channels—Facebook, Instagram, search, television, direct mail—delivered the highest return on our marketing dollars? Should our ads send consumers straight to our landing page, or should we drive them through a blog or quiz first? Some of our experiments failed, but others succeeded. Within a year, we grew from three thousand new subscribers per month to forty thousand, logging $20 million in revenues.

We continue to experiment. What shipping speed will help us best manage the trade-off between affordable shipping costs and speedy delivery? What new products or product extensions might we sell? What tweaks might we make in our site's messaging or user experience? Now that Hubble sells in multiple countries, including Canada, the United Kingdom, the Netherlands, Germany, and Spain, we have geographically distinct test labs for our experiments. The data we accumulate allows us to refine and optimize our business as it grows.

Ben and I were hardly the first to bypass the middleman and hawk our wares directly to consumers. Avon and Mary Kay Cosmetics were doing this before I was in diapers, and although their playbook differed from Hubble's, it really worked. During the 1990s, TV infomercials launched Proactiv and a thousand QVC and Home Shopping Network products, bringing in billions in revenue.[1] More recently, hundreds of digital businesses have popped onto the scene, selling everything from kitchenware to hipster couches to stem cell storage. Breaking with their peers, a few traditional consumer marketers have also experimented with selling direct-to-consumer, hoping to exploit the underlying innovation that companies like mine have harnessed: using the data yielded by customer interactions to optimize their marketing.

As these players recognize, selling naked is not merely the latest marketing fad, but the leading edge of a revolution in how consumer companies market and sell their wares. Because consumer companies have traditionally relied on retailers to sell their products, they haven't been able to access data about the behavior of individual consumers in specific commercial transactions. These companies have long identified broad classes of customers and targeted them with advertising (which they prayed would work), but they haven't understood consumers *as individuals,* and they've certainly never personalized their pitches nor tracked and refined marketing efforts on an individual basis. As a result, they've often taken what media expert and Tatari co-founder Philip Inghelbrecht characterizes as a "spray and pray" approach: "Give me a million dollars and let me see [how it goes]. I'll tell you in three or four months. Let's cross our fingers."[2]

Digital companies that sell direct-to-consumer, whether giants like Netflix or smaller start-ups like Hubble, operate differently. They establish an ongoing feedback loop with customers online, collecting data during the sales process and then using sophisticated algorithms (either built themselves for traffic they own or rented from partners like Facebook and Google) to target consumers individually and in real time. These platforms allow direct-to-consumer marketers like Hubble to show the right online ad at the right time to the right person, so they can create and maintain productive relationships with millions of consumers all at once. As a result, each dollar these marketers spend goes further. They can track the consumer behavior—or lack thereof—that their marketing actions trigger, and tweak or "optimize" those actions.

Digital feedback loops such as I'm describing take many forms. That ad in your Facebook News Feed might zip you over to an article on *BuzzFeed* about seven brands you need to try that month, or to a questionnaire asking you everything you could imagine and more about your fashion preferences, or to a blog post written by the brand expounding on the virtues of their all-natural trash bags. Somewhere in that piece of content (and probably in multiple places), you encounter a link taking you to a purchase checkout on an e-commerce store *owned by the brand*. All along the way, the digital companies with which you interact collect information, which they and others can then use to target you with subsequent advertising and offers fine-tuned to *you*.

Alternatively, let's say you wonder why your legs are itching so much, so you hop onto Google. Scrolling through disturbing images of rashes that you won't soon erase from memory, you realize that the somewhat less repulsive rash you see on your knee is probably poison ivy. Browsing a bit more, you feel relieved to learn that zinc oxide serves as an effective home remedy, so you head out to Walmart. When you get there, you find there's a shelf filled with different brands of zinc oxide, as well as several shelves that stock a number of pricier over-the-counter remedies that specifically treat poison ivy. Without your Google results, you might have purchased an over-the-counter remedy. Or, if you stuck with the zinc oxide, you might have felt confused about what brand to buy. Now, hitting Google again on your smartphone, you learn that you can just go for the cheapest zinc oxide—all the brands are functionally the same.

Although this transaction ultimately occurred in a physical retailer, your use of Google allowed that company to gain information about you and your consumer behavior, even as it served you up a couple of quick ads for branded poison ivy treatments (and booked revenue if you clicked on any of those ads in the course of your research). You saved money by sticking to zinc oxide and going for the cheapest option among the offerings. Walmart kept the sale, but it made much less than it would have if you hadn't had your buddy Google in your back pocket. Google, meanwhile, soaked up more consumer data about you and can now offer you more individually tailored ads and optimize its results for other folks with the same rashy predicament.

Or how about this scenario: You gave your kid a furReal Munchin' Rex dinosaur toy for his birthday, but now you need replacement batteries. It's after nine on a weeknight, and although there's a twenty-four-hour pharmacy ten minutes away, you're feeling lazy. So you kick up your feet, open the Amazon app on your smartphone, and search for batteries. Wow, are they cheap. Not the Energizers or Duracells you're used to, but those AmazonBasics batteries that, lo and behold, are highlighted as "Amazon's Choice." Poor Energizer and Duracell—they still appear at the top of your search results, but only because they're paying Amazon for ad space. Moreover, because they paid for space, they suffer the indignity of the dreaded "sponsored" label above their products. With a few clicks, you arrange for the cheap (and quite possibly lower-quality) AmazonBasics batteries to appear on your doorstep within forty-eight hours. Amazon not only books the ad revenue, but also converts you to another one of its brands and gains new insight into your purchase preferences.

Selling naked incorporates each of these scenarios, and countless others. I think of it broadly as the actual sale of products directly to consumers, or the pursuit of an underlying marketing feedback loop (often called "digital direct-response marketing" or "performance marketing"), or both. Randall Rothenberg, president and CEO of the Interactive Advertising Bureau, argues that "direct brands" (brands that sell naked) "are not curiosities, however interesting they are," nor are they relegated to specific consumer categories. Rather, they represent "a permanent and even epochal shift in the way that supply chains are put together and managed for value."[3] Jack Haber, who formerly oversaw Colgate-Palmolive's digital efforts, likewise observes that "the world is changing, the channels of communication are changing, the distribution channels are changing," and companies must change with them.[4] Such statements represent an important wake-up call for others in the marketing discipline. In the years ahead, marketers across consumer industries simply won't be able to function without at least some understanding of selling direct. Direct-response ads on mobile are where the eyeballs are moving, and marketing budgets must follow.

FOUNDERS AND INCUMBENTS, UNITE!

So, how can a young founder interested in marketing come to master selling naked? It's not easy. As popular as direct-to-consumer is, the vast majority of new digital ventures die, many because their teams struggle with the fundamentals.

They worry too much about building the "perfect" brand or product and don't focus enough on the hard work of actually selling. They fail to get the right experts on board, they focus on the wrong performance metrics, they underfund their businesses, they fail to grasp how their businesses operate in financial terms—to name just a few of the mistakes I've seen teams make.

Through our experiments at Hubble, we keep learning about direct-to-consumer selling, and how to hopefully stay one step ahead on Facebook and the other social media platforms that customers can access through their mobile devices. While many recent direct-to-consumer start-ups have failed, we've developed a framework that has allowed us to launch our company, raise substantial funding, and build it into a decent-size business. We continue to experiment with Hubble and grow, and we've also helped other upstarts and large corporate players sell direct, too.

With *Selling Naked* in hand, this framework is now available to a wider audience of current and aspiring founders. Drawing on our experiences launching Hubble, as well as stories from other direct-to-consumer teams, I describe how to conceive, launch, and grow an e-commerce brand. You don't have to be a twentysomething working out of your apartment, and you don't need millions in seed funding right out of the gate (although it certainly helps). The key is to check your assumptions and ego, unroll a series of low-budget experiments, make your mistakes, and—whether you fail or succeed—keep on experimenting.

But *Selling Naked* isn't just for founders. Many large corporates are intrigued by direct-to-consumer but afraid to jump in, for a variety of reasons. They're uncertain about how to make the model work without cannibalizing their traditional businesses; they can't access the necessary talent (particularly challenging for businesses outside of New York, San Francisco, and Los Angeles); and they're hard pressed to rally shareholders around a strategy that requires substantial up-front investment. In sum, selling naked is a "huge change in business model" for large corporations, and "it's very hard to change how you do business overnight," as McKinsey consumer market expert Ken Fenyo tells me.[5]

And yet, for these companies, direct-to-consumer is essential to master. If you're a midlevel manager or senior executive at a traditional consumer-facing company (manufacturer or retailer), the digitization and quantification of marketing, coupled with the relatively slow change in manufacturing and distribution, pose a quandary. All the growth in your industry is occurring in the digital realm, but the prevailing business strategies are different there. Many digital direct-to-consumer businesses currently lose money, despite their ability to win over customers and build sales. That's because they're still scaling up their supply chains and developing physical distribution to complement their digital offerings. In the minds of entrepreneurs and investors, the customer relationships and data that digital businesses like Hubble can acquire today are so valuable that it's worth running businesses unprofitably in the short term. In theory, digital businesses can sort out the physical economics later by adding self-driving cars, opening more fulfillment centers, bringing on the drones, and building their own factories, where they can finally manufacture products with the economics and number of SKUs that Fortune 500 companies have. What's in play today that won't be tomorrow are customer relationships and the data they generate. Companies must attract customers to their platforms before it's too late.

Fortune 500 companies can't pursue this kind of strategy.

Although their large scale allows them to produce goods more cheaply on a per-unit basis, it costs them about as much to produce and distribute physical goods as it did before Amazon launched. The business models of these companies still must support those costs profitably—investors demand it. If Amazon says it's sacrificing earnings for growth, its stock price rises, so long as the company is actually growing. If Walmart does the same, its price tanks. Beyond the sheer expense of traditional production and distribution, this double standard reflects the glaring talent disparity between digital and traditional companies: most traditional manufacturers and retailers don't have on staff all the young engineers and finance brats that direct-to-consumer companies use to optimize their marketing. Without this army of consultants and former investment bankers, investors won't trust the big companies to pursue growth in digital markets.

Given these structural challenges, traditional brands should pursue *hybridization*—the merging of online and offline, brick-and-mortar and digital. As Scott Galloway, a professor of marketing at New York University's Stern School of Business, notes, "The future of retail is omnichannel. Consumers don't live in isolation in any one medium."[6] A glance at markets today reveals that companies are already getting this message. Within just the last few years, digital and traditional firms have begun to learn from each other. Amazon now owns Whole Foods (and claims that it will roll out thousands of Amazon Go stores over the next couple of years), and digital brand start-ups like SmileDirectClub, Away, Bonobos, Casper, and Warby Parker have opened physical stores of their own. Fortune 500 retailers are stepping up their game, finally mobilizing the massive amounts of consumer data that they have long possessed but not fully exploited. Walmart, for example, acquired

Jet.com in large part so that it could get its hands on the latter's first-class team of quantitative marketers (whatever the ultimate fate of that acquisition).

For Fortune 500 manufacturers of consumer products, the evolution is tougher because Walmart and other big retailers (as well as other distributors like movie theaters and banks) have long owned the consumer relationship. Disney's announcement of its video-on-demand service Disney+ illustrates what can happen when incumbent businesses take selling naked seriously. Disney had been working on a direct-to-consumer content strategy over the course of several years; its 2019 acquisition of 21st Century Fox, for example, allowed it to add the original *Star Wars* films, *The Simpsons, Avatar,* and more to its library. Upon Disney+'s launch, the company communicated its determination to build up the service, initially marking down subscriptions to quickly grow a subscriber base and committing to years of investment. Disney stock rose by more than 10 percent on the news, while shares of competitor Netflix slumped almost 5 percent—an indication of how powerful a direct-to-consumer play can be.

In eyeing potential hybrid business strategies, blue-chip consumer brands are paying greater attention to Facebook as well as to the business models of upstarts that sell naked. At present, Google, Facebook, and Amazon have a lock on digital marketing. Yeah, there are those annoying display ads you encounter while reading articles on websites like *The New York Times* or Fox News. There are those even more annoying full-screen ads that pop up when you're on Snapchat or playing mobile games. But such tactics don't generally work, since consumers regard them as noise and are adept at filtering them out before they even mentally process the ad content. Native ads in Google, Amazon search results, Facebook's News Feed, and

Instagram fuel the vast majority of online purchasing, and in any case, Google and Facebook own most of those spammy display networks. "Native" just means the ad blends into the content around it, making it harder for consumers to disregard. If you're a company trying to move merchandise, you can buy ads in those channels or make content or product offerings that are so compelling that they naturally surface as top results. Those are your two basic moves.

Selling naked and the establishment of a performance marketing capability for Facebook and Instagram (and hopefully other platforms over time) offer an intriguing third option. If big brands could establish data flows and a feedback loop with consumers, whether through actual direct sales or some other arrangement, they could continue to exploit the traditional advantages they enjoy as incumbents while also tapping into the superior marketing capabilities exploited by Amazon, Netflix, and digital upstarts like Hubble.

At present, this opportunity is largely theoretical. Yes, a few brands have dabbled in direct selling, as Unilever did by buying Dollar Shave Club. By and large, however, their efforts have been small-scale, halting, and unsuccessful. Although many digitally native brands have raised $50 million or more in capital, few have been acquired by Fortune 500 consumer companies or formed partnerships with the behemoths. Selling naked just seems too foreign and hard for the large consumer brands to execute.

Traditional consumer brands must engage in much closer and more compelling collaborations with their digitally native counterparts, regarding the discipline of selling naked as a core part of their strategy. As former Procter & Gamble executive and respected marketing consultant Jim Stengel tells me, the trends underlying the rise of direct-to-consumer companies are "irrefutable." If companies "don't participate in this and find [their] way in this, [they're] going to suffer enormously."[7] David Kidder, co-founder and CEO at Bionic, notes that a generation of younger consumers have become accustomed to buying from direct-to-consumer companies for a number of reasons. As time passes, these learned behaviors are "going to be very hard" to change.[8]

If big consumer brands went all in, working with the talent that has come of age in start-ups and devoting the funding required to develop serious direct-to-consumer marketing capabilities, they could marry their superior manufacturing capabilities and the legacy R&D functions and supply chains that underlie them with the upstarts' digital marketing savvy and hustler mentality. With these interlocking strengths, traditional brands would gain access to direct selling and the digital direct marketing they need to continue to grow. They wouldn't necessarily seek to ship as much product as possible themselves, but rather to drive more consumers to their mass retail partners (Target, Walmart, CVS, and so on) by interacting directly with consumers. With this kind of mindset, traditional brands would finally bridge the gap between the online realm and bricks and mortar.

Diving deep into Hubble's inner workings, *Selling Naked* presents principles that current and aspiring corporate marketers can apply to build profitable direct-to-consumer businesses and, more generally, unleash the power of digital direct-response marketing. I can't promise that these principles will yield a successful business every time, but I do believe it's hard to get anywhere in direct-to-consumer and digital direct-response marketing without them. If you're an executive or marketing manager at a large corporate manufacturer, or if you're a business student seeking to prepare for the twenty-first-century marketplace, these principles should prove immensely helpful.

I'm writing *Selling Naked* because I believe Hubble and other direct-to-consumer businesses have happened upon a promising, if still evolving, model for marketing goods and services using digital technologies. I'd like to see more companies of all shapes and sizes embrace this model to sell goods and services, and I'd like to help young marketers advance their careers by giving them an inside peek at the discipline's present and future. If you want to bring a product or service to market, or if you want to become part of a team at a corporate player that's doing so, learning how to sell directly through your own digital property might be worth your time. There's simply no better way to understand customers' preferences and how to serve them than by putting yourself out there and trying to hawk products or services without a middleman. So roll up your sleeves, fire up your social media accounts, and start selling—naked!

SELLING NAKED

(CHAPTER 1)

DON'T BULLSHIT YOURSELF
ABOUT DIGITAL BUSINESS

JOHN FIORENTINO FIRST learned the power of selling products directly to consumers from an unlikely (and Canadian) source: pop superstar Justin Bieber. In 2010, John dropped out of college and took a job working on branded-product launches for "the Bieb." There, he saw up close "how powerful this direct relationship with an audience can be if you have the right brand, the right story, and a product that people are really receptive to."[1] John remembers watching Bieber's manager spend whole days on Twitter engaging with fans, giving Justin "that little pop" that allowed him to break out from the pack of wannabes and go mainstream. "It was just crazy to watch," John says, noting that the music industry seemed to be all about creating products and selling them directly to an audience of devoted fans.

After six months with Bieber, John returned to school, designing and marketing several fashion products of his own on the side. None caught fire, but John wasn't concerned. He continued to mess around with new business ideas after graduating, and by 2016, after several years of subsistence-level living, John raised $1 million to found a tech start-up. Good, right? Not in John's mind. The more John learned about what it would mean to take on venture money, the more he soured on the idea. As he saw it, he'd kill himself running the company for five years and then either sell it for $1 billion or fail and wind up with nothing. Better, he thought, not to get into it at all. So that's what he did. He returned all of the investor money and closed his business.

At this point, you might wonder if John had a psychological complex around success. He had no money—he couldn't afford an apartment and had to couch-surf. But John did have one thing: an enduring drive to make products and sell them to customers. For the next year and a half, he wrote a blog called *Good Ones* about cool new products he encountered, all the while searching for a unique product that he could produce and successfully bring to market without taking on outside capital. For his daily needs, he relied on two credit cards that allowed him to go a year before repaying.

By 2017, *Good Ones* had amassed a following of ten thousand people—not much, but enough to get rolling. John had also hit on an idea he just had to pursue: a weighted blanket that helped with sleep. A few months later, with a single prototype in hand, he launched the blanket on Kickstarter, partnering with a media company to provide publicity. The Gravity Blanket, as John called it, was a success beyond all expectations. Within twenty-four hours, John had raised $400,000. A month in, he had an astounding $4.7 million in preorders. John had to scramble to find a partner to produce tens of thousands of blankets all at once, a task that required three weeks of twenty-hour days, but he was off and running. Today, Grav-

ity Blanket does $20 million in revenue annually and is grow-
ing rapidly.

THE GLITZ AND GLAMOUR OF SELLING NAKED

John's success would seem to validate a prevailing stereotype
about selling naked: that it's a quick and alluring path to riches.
People read about the eye-popping valuation on The Honest
Company, Jessica Alba's all-natural home goods company, or
the $3.35 billion sale of Chewy, the popular online pet retail
store, or the "overnight" success of a company like Kylie Cosmetics, and they think they're just a few keystrokes away from
claiming their digital fortune. Marketers at traditional product
or retail brands see the success of these start-ups and likewise
assume that success will come easily to them and their teams
once they jump in.

On one level, all those budding entrepreneurs and ambitious marketing execs aren't wrong. Although John's story is
an extreme case, it's relatively easy to launch a new direct-to-
consumer product with little capital, or to obtain capital if,
unlike John, you want it. Think of it from a risk/reward standpoint. Since you're entering an established product category,
it's clear that a consumer market exists. People needed and
wanted glasses long before Warby Parker came onto the scene,
and contact lenses before Ben and I started thinking about
Hubble. Further, it's hardly a leap to think that at least some
consumers would love it if these products were cheaper and
delivered right to their door. (I'll offer tips for perfecting your
pitch in Chapter 3.)

As far as building your business goes, we'll see that it's fairly easy to pull off as well, if you know what to do. Most of the thousands of direct-to-consumer businesses operating today are hawking commodity products. An ecosystem of suppliers and vendors exists that makes it easy to start selling naked (discussed in Chapter 6), and with the right incentives you can find experts to help you with manufacturing and other areas that are new to you (Chapter 4). Promoting your product on Facebook and developing a solid financial model (Chapters 8 through 11) aren't rocket science, either.

YEAH, BUT IS SELLING NAKED REALLY ALL THAT?

Maybe not. There's another truth about direct-to-consumer businesses that you don't always hear, and which you should consider as you decide whether to proceed with such a venture. As easy as it can sometimes be to launch one of these companies, it's more than hard to turn them into stable, successful businesses. The several dozen or so companies that have become famous for selling naked pale beside the hundreds that have popped up only to sputter out within a few months or a couple of years. Even when companies do succeed, it's a grind for those involved, and profitability often proves elusive. It's not surprising that John wasn't so keen on sticking around after launching the Gravity Blanket. He'd already lived through the fun part. What lay ahead was a lot of stress and grinding.

As I've discovered while running Hubble, e-commerce companies are kind of like wildcatting in the oil business: those first couple of drops of oil gush out of the earth, but that doesn't mean subsequent drilling and refining will be cheap or easy. Or think about running a conventional retail store. If your store is open nine hours a day, you're on for those nine hours, serving customers, preventing theft, and keeping the shelves stocked. If your store is open twenty-four hours a day, your customers expect—and deserve—that same experience around the clock. You, in turn, can expect far less than the requisite eight hours of sleep. Between 5:00 P.M. Friday and 9:00 A.M. Monday (aka "the weekend"), Hubble gets over twenty-five hundred customers, and those folks want the same level of service as people ordering during normal workday hours.

Despite these challenges, Ben and I have chosen to stick around, and to help others with selling naked as well. Despite all the uncertainty and effort, we believe e-commerce is still an attractive option for brand or retail start-ups that lack the resources to launch any other way, even if they imagine developing a physical retail presence down the line. It's also an area in which incumbent product companies should invest, if only to better understand the brands eating their market share.

If you aspire to a career in marketing at a large brand, you, too, must know what it now takes to directly access consumers. The best way to learn is to sit down and *do it*.

WHY SELLING NAKED CAN SUCK: A CLOSER LOOK

Let's examine the hidden, not-so-pleasant realities of selling naked, considered first from the entrepreneur's perspective. Over the long term, it's by no means preordained that digitally native upstarts will have much of a future on their own. As I suggested in the introduction, many companies that sell direct operate at a loss, and many others barely break even. Direct-to-consumer companies might never work out their economics, building or acquiring the real-world infrastructure they need to manufacture and distribute their products profitably at scale.

In the meantime, companies that sell naked can expect tough competition, precisely because of how easy it is to start such businesses. In many industries, a recent college grad and his friends could launch a competing brand in just a few months by reaching out to the same contract manufacturers that existing direct-to-consumer businesses use for their products. Entrepreneurs appear to be doing exactly that. More than 150 direct-to-consumer mattress brands vie for customers, and parts of the apparel market are almost as crowded.

> The intense competition means you're going to have to do better than the other folks at peddling your wares on platforms like Facebook.

Even if you are better, there's a limit to how big you can get, which means that your business probably won't wind up with the valuation of your dreams. Digital ad markets on platforms such as Facebook and Google are markets like any other. If you spot inefficiencies in these markets, you can exploit them for your own gain, but those inefficiencies will likely be small. If you thought of a clever hack to deploy $10,000 per day and win customers, that's great, but it's infinitely harder to rely on such cleverness to spend $100,000 per day as efficiently, let alone $1 million. Further, subscription businesses (if you choose to embrace that model) have built-in growth limits. At some point, you'll be spending more money to replace customers who leave than you make off new customers whom you convert, assuming a constant rate of churn.[2]

It's hardly a coincidence that in 2017, two of the most notable sales of direct-to-consumer companies—Native deodorant and MVMT watches—involved transactions in the $100 million to $200 million range, not in the billions. The founders of these companies didn't raise money along the way, likely because they didn't want to labor under venture investors' turbocharged expectations. You might be proud of yourself for building a business with $30 million in sales, and at that point you might wish to cash out. Your investors will likely have other ideas: they must achieve a certain return on their investment from a sale, and the price somebody will pay to buy your company based on $30 million in revenue likely won't get them there. To avoid such tension, some founders decline venture money and decide to fund growth themselves. But bootstrapping means they have to grind out every bit of growth on their own, at least until they sell. They also don't get the external validation for themselves and their businesses that comes with a quality venture round. The result, in many cases, is perhaps no sale at all in the end, as well as a whole lot of stress along the way.

YOU'RE NO DON DRAPER

To convey how challenging it is to grind out growth, it helps to go back to the 1960s of Don Draper and *Mad Men*. Coming of age during the heyday of traditional marketing, Draper lived a charmed life. All those three-martini lunches. All those big clients raining down money on Draper for his creative advertising campaigns. Oh, and no pressure on Draper to show that those campaigns actually delivered sales for companies, because reliable metrics didn't exist back then (and arguably still don't for most ad dollars spent on brand channels like television, radio, and billboards). Draper's poor, beleaguered compatriots in the sales departments of large companies were forever hustling and sweating over every lead, selling to customers—mostly other businesses—one by one. But Draper didn't have to. Since he was playing to a mass audience, all he had to do was be "brilliant" once, translate his communications insight into a mass-media ad campaign, sell the campaign for millions of dollars (easy for a charismatic, handsome guy like him), and spend many more millions of the client's money buying ad time for the campaign. Life was good.

In the digital age, marketing looks a lot more like drab old sales, only now algorithms do the selling instead of humans. Specifically, it's Google's and Facebook's algorithms, since these giants now claim the majority of digital ad revenue growth (with Amazon recently bursting into the picture). For each individual customer, these Goliaths relentlessly serve up ads until the customer clicks. If customers don't purchase, the algorithms retarget them on the platform where they initially encountered the ad, follow them around the internet with display ads, and send emails reminding them of the sale they passed up. If customers still don't purchase, the algorithms automatically lower the prices and tweak their offers to get the sale.

Once customers do purchase, the algorithms try to cross-sell customers on other products they didn't know they wanted or upsell them onto more expensive versions of their core offerings. The sale of a membership (as in the case of Amazon Prime or Netflix) is the holy grail, because now the advertiser has acquired a customer relationship it can keep mining for sales, hopefully for years. You can understand why, as I suggested in the introduction, digital businesses are flooring it so aggressively to obtain customers, even if the economics don't yet work. Customers want to manage as few relationships as possible to get what they need. As a result, the available "slots" in the customer's mind are limited and precious.

So why is Don Draper so anachronistic? Can't a cool, creative type today just keep making ads and earning a fat paycheck? No—it's no longer enough just to make ads. Now this creative type has to deal with feedback on his ads generated by the ad platforms—endless reams of data, and much of it negative (because in advertising, as in life, many endeavors fail). His ads on Facebook aren't working, and it costs him $400 to acquire each customer. He tests ad after ad—swaps in a new photo or stitches a few into a GIF, plays around with copy, both on the ad itself and in the text fields around it, and tweaks all the audience-targeting parameters—and finally lands on one that works. He has a good day, and his cost to acquire each customer is only $15. He's figured things out, he thinks, and shown Facebook who's boss. Except the next day, he wakes up and, without any changes on his part, the ad that was winning yesterday now has a cost per acquisition of $1,500.

A week later, this creative type has Facebook under control (for now), but his system for sending emails to customers who chose not to buy has crapped out. Normally, such "email retargeting" produces 15 percent of sales, but now it's only 2 percent. Why? He has no clue. The revenue from those new customers from email costs him nothing to obtain, and he really needs this zero-cost acquisition to subsidize what he has to pay per customer on Facebook. Doing a bit of digging, he realizes that the digital connection between his store and the email app he uses broke down, and his emails haven't been going out for days. He tracks down an engineer on his team to get that fixed—first he sees if anyone's in the office, then Slacks, then texts, then calls, calls, calls until his teammate picks up. Meanwhile, a board member emails telling him that a competitor is outbidding him on his branded search terms (the online searches for his company's own brand name) and is directing search traffic to its site and away from his. Our creative type sends an ALL CAPS missive howling at his performance marketing consultant. Three-martini lunch? Nope.

> My partner, Ben, and I aren't Don Draper, and you, Mr. or Ms. Brave New World, won't get to be, either. Killer brand marketing has given way to the monotonous work of data analytics—the domain of engineers and spreadsheet jockeys like me and Ben.

At Hubble, we and the performance marketers we work with more resemble day traders. And Hubble's operation is relatively simple—it focuses on just a single product. Amazon sells almost *five hundred million* products in the United States, Netflix has almost seven thousand movies and TV shows, and Spotify has more than thirty-five million songs. With their tens or hundreds of millions of customers, these companies resemble quantitative trading funds, deploying thousands of finance people and engineers to determine how to maximize revenue from each individual subscriber while minimizing costs for the company.

If I'm Reed Hastings at Netflix and I can get Adam Sandler's fans to watch a bunch of new, very cheap movies that he made especially for my platform, and as a result I don't have to pay big bucks to the studios that own *Happy Gilmore*, *The Wedding*

Singer, or that newer, more expensive Kevin Hart movie, I've saved a few dollars and improved my economics. If I'm Spotify and I can suggest that a given consumer listen to tracks from Madonna's 1983 debut album instead of from Taylor Swift's latest, I've again saved money, since the royalties I pay for Madonna's are fractions of a penny less. Scaled across millions of transactions, such savings add up and hopefully create a path to profitability. This all puts engineers and finance brats in high demand and Don Draper out of a job.

THERE REALLY IS NO ESCAPE

Thinking about the quantification of marketing, you might wonder if you can buy your way out of this data-saturated hellscape by offloading your Facebook stress onto an agency. Good luck: when you're just starting out, your marketing budget will be too puny to entice a strong performance company to work with you. As your business scales, you can hire such a company, forking over 10 percent of your budget for the privilege. Even then, expect to spend your days obsessively watching numbers like CPA, CTR, CPC, LTV, and LTR (discussed later in this book, in a way that is only as mind-numbing as it needs to be, I promise). The further away you get from these noxious, precious data feeds, the more pleasant your life becomes, but your business pays the price. That data, after all, is instantaneous consumer feedback. If you're not staring at it hour after hour, you can't tweak your marketing efforts in real time, and you soon lose sight of broader trends affecting your business.

Many founders do decide they'd rather step away from the

weeds and delegate, even though it means slower, less efficient growth and more risk to their business. The daily rituals of performance marketing are just that draining.

FIVE TIPS FOR POTENTIAL FOUNDERS

If selling naked isn't a party that will make you a billionaire overnight, developing a direct-to-consumer business is still worth it. As Ben and I can attest, it's possible to build a large, well-funded company that makes a difference in people's lives. Consumers are certainly more open than ever to trying upstart brands online. If they're buying a commodity product like zinc oxide or batteries, they want it at the lowest possible price, and are willing to consider less conventional ways of purchasing in order to get it. The products sold by upstarts might not always be the most cutting-edge. But to many consumers, these products will be good enough, significantly cheaper, and as easy as it gets to purchase and restock.

Let's say you try selling naked and your business flames out. Even then, the experience and knowledge you amass position you well for a career in marketing, digital commerce, entrepreneurship, or related fields. That's because selling naked is, as I've argued, a significant part of marketing's future, and also because it represents commerce in its simplest, purest form.

Think about it: If you bypass the middleman, you have an opportunity to get to know a specific category in depth, as well as the needs of groups of consumers. You also get to experience what it's like to win over and retain consumers, navigating the complexities of digital to do it. Remember how fun it was as a kid to create your first lemonade stand? In some respects, selling naked is just like that on a bigger scale, and it will eventually turn into something great—a sweet job at another company, if not a sustainable business of your own. In fact, as John Fiorentino tells me, when he was first thinking about setting up a direct-to-consumer venture, he imagined calling it Lemonade Stand (good thing he didn't—Gravity Blanket has a better ring to it).

Once you've begun to sell naked, you can increase your odds of success by following the principles and tactics in this book. For now, as you consider whether and how to make the leap, I can offer several pieces of advice based on my experiences at Hubble as well as at several previous ventures that failed to gain traction.

TIP #1: KEEP YOUR DAY JOB

You don't have to work at your new business idea full-time at the start. I grant you that devoting nights and weekends to your idea sucks, but most concepts don't pan out at all, and if yours doesn't, you'll be very happy to look in your bank account every two weeks and still see a new, fat (or not so fat) paycheck. If it's even remotely possible, don't go full-time on a new business until either (a) it's funded by money from professional investors, or at least a credible accelerator like Y Combinator, or (b) it's profitable and you can live off the cash it's generating.

TIP #2: TAKE MANY SHOTS ON GOAL, IN COLLABORATION WITH OTHERS

I don't believe in identifying "great" ideas for businesses. It seems romantic, but it puts too much pressure on you. I believe in working with good folks to try a lot of different ideas until one or more of them hits. Prior to starting Hubble, I participated in a number of failed ventures in collaboration with others. I helped set up a trading fund with a super-talented engineer I met while working at the hedge fund Bridgewater; a dating app with a close friend who'd been at Zynga and wanted to gamify matchmaking; and a job site with another Bridgewater guy who'd been on the recruiting side. Each of these ventures left me anxious, unhappy, and unable to sleep, but at least I had other shoulders around to cry on. More important, working within a larger network of friends and contacts dramatically increased the odds of my eventual success. I could only maintain expertise in a single space, but I could work with friends who were experts in other spaces—like my Hubble co-CEO, Ben, who was working at the direct-to-consumer shaving start-up Harry's. Who in your network can broaden your horizons and perhaps even serve as a partner?

TIP #3: DON'T CONCEIVE OF YOUR DIRECT-TO-CONSUMER BUSINESS AS YOUR LAST STOP

If you assume that selling naked is "it" for you, you'll probably put too much pressure on yourself. Think of this business (or any entrepreneurial venture) as possibly the rest of your career, but also possibly a pathway to future opportunities. If your business fails to gain traction, you can apply what you learned in future ventures or jobs. If it gains even a little bit of traction, all sorts of unexpected opportunities open up. Because of Hubble, I now serve as a board member of, an advisor for, or investor in multiple other e-commerce start-ups, a bone-marrow banking business, and even a subscription app that provides ten-minute "short and sexy" audio clips "designed to turn you on."

TIP #4: BE PREPARED TO HUSTLE

Other books have explored how to raise money and set up new businesses, so I won't say much about that here. Just know that nothing can replace good old-fashioned hustle. ("Hustle" might be the only start-up cliché I really like, with all due apologies to "surprise and delight," "move fast and break things," "dent in the universe," and all the rest.) Ask everyone you know to introduce you to potential investors and experts. Scour your school's alumni network. Message away on LinkedIn. Apply to every relevant start-up accelerator program (Y Combinator, 500 Startups, and Techstars are the three biggest). If hustling fails to bear fruit, take that feedback seriously and consider *why* you're failing to connect with potential investors or partners. Is it something about your idea? Or is it something about you? If it's the idea, toss out that one and find another. If it's you, ask yourself whether being a founder really is right for you. (I understand this is dangerous territory, as it butts up against all sorts of overdue conversations about bias and representation in the venture community.) Alternatively, reflect on other steps you might take that would make you more credible in investors' eyes.

One option to consider here is the nonprofit arena. Fewer people these days are willing to give away their time with no prospect of future gain, even if it's for a good cause. That spells opportunity for you. Working at a nonprofit can be a great way to get your hands dirty building an organization. Prior to Hubble, I helped create the Organ Preservation Alliance, a nonprofit that improves the handling and preservation of organ donations. The work was started by friends from Bridgewater, and I forged relationships with government officials that in turn allowed us to work with the White House Office of Science and Technology Policy to open up new research grant programs from the Department of Defense. This experience gave me the confidence I would need to succeed with Hubble. Although I made my share of mistakes, I discovered that I could build a functioning organization from the ground up, linking people and resources in new ways to produce interesting outcomes in the real world.

TIP #5: DON'T BE AFRAID TO BOOTSTRAP IT

As I'll explain in Chapter 5, I'm a fan of taking on money, both for the credibility it brings as well as for the protection it affords in case your business tanks. But as I've suggested, bootstrapping also has its advantages, making it easier to sell your business if it gains traction, and in general giving you more control over what you're doing. Plenty of venture-backed companies that once commanded huge valuations have either gone bankrupt or been acquired for much less than their peak valuations perhaps in part because venture investors pushed off a sale longer than the founders might have liked. Just look at e-commerce companies like Gilt, Fab, and One Kings Lane. By contrast, the two sales I mentioned previously in this chapter, Native and MVMT, weren't giant, but they represented great deals for the founders, who owned large stakes with minimal dilution. Because these founders hadn't taken on much money, these deals could go through. If venture capitalists (VCs) had been involved, they likely would have nixed these deals in a quest for bigger offers down the road.

GET YOUR BOSS EXCITED ABOUT SELLING NAKED

If you work in the marketing department of a big incumbent, you face another difficult challenge: obtaining and sustaining buy-in from your bosses for a digital direct-to-consumer business.

The arguments against selling naked are many. If you're a product company, skeptics will point out that you're committing a big no-no by cutting your distributors out of the loop— what is known as "channel conflict." These skeptics are correct. When Disney/Fox launches its own streaming service, I'm sure the movie theaters and cable companies that currently serve as the primary points of distribution for Disney/Fox's movies and TV programming won't appreciate the direct competition. Certainly, these same players hate Netflix (although they don't seem to attack Disney quite as much for planning to stream its product in competition with Netflix, perhaps because Disney hasn't stepped into the arena yet and maybe because Disney is a decades-long partner of theirs, providing them with all the Marvel movies and princesses they need). Something similar holds for physical product companies that generally sell through retailers. Walmart doesn't want P&G selling Tide directly, since that might cannibalize sales in its stores. CVS won't be as happy stocking L'Oréal if the latter decides to go it alone, taking a meaningful percentage of its sales along with it. Companies that make consumer products still live and die on the shelves of large retail chains, not on digital, so they can't risk biting the hand that feeds them by selling direct.

Even beyond the problem of channel conflict, selling naked might not seem economically viable. Many large companies have figured out how to squeeze significant margins from their big-name consumer products. But if you're a large consumer goods company, it costs a heck of a lot more to ship individual boxes of toothpaste to customers than it does to ship pallets of it to Walmart, even if you do eliminate Walmart's retail margin.

I'll address channel conflict in a moment, but if your company can't easily sell its current offerings online, point out to your bosses that you would still gain by creating new offerings that insert your brand into digital conversations. If you're already spending money on digital advertising, creating new direct-to-consumer businesses will help you optimize your spend so that you're getting more bang from your digital advertising buck.[3] Also, remind your bosses that it's getting harder to reach consumers through traditional media like TV, radio, and print, or, as available impressions decline, to deploy your marketing allocations on these channels.[4] The eyeballs are going to Facebook, Google, and Amazon, and all the growth in ad inventory is there, so you have to be there, too. Then tell your bosses about what has happened lately in the movie industry. In August 2017, MoviePass announced that it would sell subscriptions allowing consumers to see an unlimited number of movies in theaters at the low, low price of $9.95 per month. For avid moviegoers who were paying $10 and up for a single ticket, it was a nice offer. Consumers snapped up

DON'T BULLSHIT YOURSELF ABOUT DIGITAL BUSINESS   21

$72.4 million worth of subscriptions in the second quarter of 2018, up from $47.1 million the previous quarter.[5]

There was just one problem: MoviePass didn't own the the-ater seat inventory it was selling. The service basically just bought tickets for you from the movie theater chains, inserting itself as a middleman.[6] As a result, MoviePass was booking small subscription revenue with the potential of great losses if customers made heavy use of the subscription, as many did. MoviePass is teetering on the edge of bankruptcy, but since its blaze of glory the big movie chains have intensified their focus on their existing offerings in this space or have launched new ones. AMC has Stubs A-List, Cinemark has Movie Club, and even Alamo Drafthouse is testing a subscription service. These services work like MoviePass, but the companies involved own the theater seat inventory, allowing the services to turn a profit. These companies have concluded that a subscription model is a strong way to drive more revenue and build customer loyalty. Incumbents in other categories should take note and get in as well.

As you might also point out to your bosses, there are other ways your company could mobilize selling naked, even in the face of channel conflict or bad economics. Rather than market your existing products online, you could do what companies like Walmart are doing and create new brands online. Walmart decided it wanted a mattress brand of its own. Rather than buy a company like Casper, it launched Allswell Home in February 2018. With Allswell, Walmart could make use of its existing distribution both online and off to copycat a digital direct brand.

If you're a branded manufacturer, you might try starting new, premium brands that sell direct with price points that can support the higher shipping costs. These new brands would be tiny compared to your big brands, but if they succeed, a three-pronged path to sustained growth would emerge, both online and off. First, you could collect the data that selling naked generates for these new brands, take it to retailers, and obtain top placements in retail stores. Second, direct-to-consumer sales would allow you to optimize your spending on advertising, hopefully driving improved performance in physical stores as your new brands move there, in addition to higher digital sales. Third, as retailers come to perceive how adept you are at direct-to-consumer selling and how valuable e-commerce is to brand-building (and hence, ultimately, to in-store sales), they might suspend their channel conflict concerns, allowing you to sell your existing brands directly to consumers while remaining in their stores (although your company would still face those higher shipping costs on that percentage of your sales).

Alternatively, you might propose to your bosses that you not sell directly per se, but rather create a loyalty program or discount plan online so as to participate in the underlying activity of digital direct-response marketing. A brand like Huggies might try to attract new customers for its diapers by sending out coupons worth $5 off your next purchase. Right now, Huggies sends less generous coupons out to everyone in promotions that cost millions of dollars. Many people who see the coupons might throw them out—maybe they don't have a baby, or maybe they're devoted to another brand. Of those who do redeem the coupons, most might already use and love the brand. So Huggies owner Kimberly-Clark risks losing money on its offer, spending all that money while snaring relatively few new customers. Meanwhile, Huggies promotions might turn off many consumers, barraging them with coupons and other offers they don't want.

By participating in digital direct-response marketing, a brand like Huggies could link specific coupons or other offers with specific consumer behaviors. Gleaning data as to how its marketing efforts are driving sales, Huggies could send digital coupons for diapers only to people who aren't already buying the product and are likely to switch. They could send them to Pampers customers, for instance, or to expecting parents who are loading up on other baby items. Consumers would receive more relevant, valuable, and personalized offers, while brands would spend their massive marketing budgets more efficiently and retailers would see increased sales.

How might brands set up productive digital "feedback loops" with consumers without actually selling products online? Well, just look at Amazon. Even before the company sold its own branded products, it optimized its marketing spend by selling something else online: a chance to enter its "ecosystem" via its Prime subscription service. Rather than tracking how many rolls of paper towels consumers buy when shown specific ads, and then having to shoulder the hassle and expense of shipping all those rolls, Amazon could measure how its enormous ad budget was converting potential customers into Prime members, and then tweak its budget to become more effective.

Big retailers can create similar feedback loops by selling loyalty programs and discount plans online as opposed to physical products. If you want more people in your Walmart stores, advertise offers that will drive people to the stores instead of purchasing online. You can then measure how these offers translate into actual in-store sales, which yield higher margins than online sales. If you're a branded manufacturing company without your own distribution, it's harder to track which consumers are buying your products, since retailers aren't sharing that data with you. Even here, solutions exist. Apps like Ibotta and SavingStar allow consumers to share their purchasing behavior in exchange for rewards and cash back. That data might come in inconvenient forms, such as photographs of receipts and forwarded emails of digital receipts, but brands can still use it as a hack to "close the loop" on their digital offers and optimize their marketing budgets. Some of the best solutions have come from companies like Starbucks and McDonald's that control both product and distribution. These firms have been reaccelerating growth with their loyalty apps, which allow for mobile orders and in-person pickup, and which send you coupons of increasing frequency and generosity the longer you stay away from their stores.

GET YOUR BOSS SCARED
ABOUT *NOT* SELLING NAKED

If these arguments don't convince your bosses to get in on digital, then resort to another tactic: fear. Scare the bejesus out of your bosses by evoking for them just what kind of quandary their businesses are in.

As you might explain, the looming threat isn't just direct-to-consumer businesses like Hubble. It's digital platforms like Amazon. Formerly, retailers like Walmart or Target needed to stock the top brands on their shelves to bring in foot traffic. That gave consumer product brands leverage in the marketplace, allowing them to charge retail stores dearly for the privilege of stocking their products. Today, Amazon is overturning this power dynamic, increasingly subbing its private-label products for Fortune 500 branded products. For a product like toilet paper, Amazon offers you its Presto brand right next to listings for Charmin and Cottonelle. If you want juice, Amazon highlights its 365 Everyday Value brand (obtained through its acquisition of Whole Foods) alongside Tropicana and Mott's. If you need to stock up on batteries, Amazon points you toward its AmazonBasics line as well as Duracell. Who loses? The traditional consumer brands.

Although retailers have offered private-label products for decades, those brands have traditionally accounted for only a stable 15 to 20 percent of sales in their categories.[7] Retailers weren't trying to put big-name brands out of business, but rather to just take a bit of market share. Amazon's private-label brands are getting up to 45 percent market share, depending on the category, suggesting that Jeff Bezos has no qualms about putting Cottonelle, Tropicana, and Duracell out of business.[8] With infinite shelf space, Amazon can stock fancy branded products for those customers who search for the brands by name, while also keeping prices on its own brands so low that the name brands get bumped to the second page of product listings if a consumer searches for a generic category. If the fancy brands wish to stay up on the first page, they can, but they have to pay Amazon to run ads. When the name brands are shoved far enough down in the search results, Amazon can start raising prices on its own brands, achieving the profitable margins that a traditional private label would maintain.

Amazon isn't the only digital company playing these games. Initially, when Netflix made money by renting DVDs to consumers through the mail, it depended entirely on the libraries of the major studios. As it moved to streaming videos online, it found that obtaining rights from the major studios was too

expensive. Its solution: original content.[9] Other media companies have developed similar business models. News aggregators
like *HuffPost* and *Business Insider* offer little original reporting
but lots of cheap, self-produced clickbait that looks very much
like the real thing and generally quotes from others' reporting.
For some operators, the internet has proven an incredible tool
for taking someone else's business, substituting a cheaper product, and reclaiming the business as their own.

If you're an incumbent brand, you're extremely vulnerable
to this strategy. Month after month, Amazon continues to
build its share of both online retail and product search. Many
people these days would rather sit at home clicking on Amazon while snacking on their 365 Everyday Value brand corn
chips than get up and head to a grocery store. Moreover, the
vast majority of all purchases—81 percent—begin with an
online search, so even if e-commerce still accounts for only
14.3 percent of retail spending, the digital world's actual influence on physical retail is much greater.[10] Increasingly locked
out of online commerce and the growth opportunities it affords, incumbent brands face dim prospects. Little by little,
Amazon, Netflix, and Apple TV are sucking the lifeblood out
of them.

The solution, you can tell your bosses, is to set about mastering digital direct-response or performance marketing. Partner with start-up companies that are adept at selling naked.
Buy these companies. Invest in them. Develop your own internal skunkworks. It's true that digital companies like Amazon
might face a reckoning when cheap capital starts to dry up and
they face real pressure to turn a profit. The customer relationships that these companies are trying to capture, even at a loss,
might turn out to be worth less than what these companies are

paying for them. Even in this case, customer data and relation-ships will still have a lot of value, just not as much as it seems right now. An opportunity will exist for big, steady incumbents to swoop in and acquire these relationships at a discount (for instance, by acquiring digital companies once their value has fallen). Incumbent brands will have a far easier time of it if they have already mastered digital direct-response marketing. Also, it could be a while before investors call Amazon and its peers on the carpet for their financial metrics, if they ever do. In the interim, incumbents will need to hang on and compete, and that makes selling naked a strategic imperative.

Mastering digital marketing also allows companies to learn about their customers in ways that help companies grow and evolve. Why don't customers like existing products? What other products would consumers like to see? How might you bundle products together to create larger, more compelling customer experiences, and on your end economize on marketing and shipping expenses? Sure, you can answer some of these questions by conducting surveys, but digital marketing (as well as running an actual e-commerce venture of your own) will yield richer insights into how consumers *actually* spend their money. At Hubble, we've learned how important blogs, earned media, quizzes, and other content are in driving customers to buy, not merely browse. We've learned that photographs of our products work better when we're trying to drive potential customers directly to the site, as opposed to stock imagery, which is more effective if we're trying to get someone to read a post about us. We've learned how to manage customer subscriptions in ways that maximize their value. And this is just the begin-ning.

If you work for a large incumbent, I really do hope these

arguments allow you to persuade your skeptical bosses. Digital direct marketing isn't easy, but your business could be better for all the heartache—possibly much better. And your career will be better if you push digital hard inside your department. Like all of those budding entrepreneurs out there, you have much to learn from selling naked. Remember, this is the present and future of the marketing discipline. Not Don Draper.

(THE NAKED TRUTH)

Selling naked is hot right now. Who wouldn't want to get an idea for a new product and in eighteen months turn it into a $20 million business, like Gravity Blanket's John Fiorentino? Don't kid yourself: creating a direct-to-consumer business isn't all fun and games. Founders might get off to a roaring start only to face the onerous task of actually doing digital direct-response marketing day after painful day. Marketers at the big brands face the formidable challenge of selling the model to their bosses and sustaining corporate enthusiasm over time. Neither of these difficulties should dissuade you from jumping in. Just know what you're getting into, and use the tips and arguments in this chapter to make your initial steps into direct-to-consumer a bit easier.

CHAPTER 2

DEMONSTRATE DEMAND

MELANIE TRAVIS KNOWS start-ups. She started her career working at Foursquare, then moved to Kickstarter, then to Bark-Box, a subscription service that sends dog owners monthly shipments of drool-inducing canine treats and toys. Along the way, she always thought it would be cool to start a company of her own, but she didn't have an idea that really grabbed her.

Then, in 2016, while at a BarkBox retreat in a fun tropical locale, she ran into exactly the kind of trouble on which businesses are built. Swimsuit trouble, that is. As she tells me, "I really struggled to find [a swimsuit to bring] that looked good, that felt good, that was age appropriate, price appropriate, easy to wear."[1] She also didn't like the shopping experience—as a woman, "you have to get completely undressed in a tiny changing room under fluorescent lights. It's just terrible."

A non-fluorescent lightbulb went off in her head. What if she could create a service that sends high-quality, well-designed swimsuits directly to women for them to try on in the comfort of their own homes and keep the ones they like? Melanie queried friends, colleagues, and relatives, and they all agreed:

shopping for swimwear sucked. It was a problem that had existed all along, but the mainstream retail industry had ignored it. Melanie was intrigued—she seemed to have hit on a business idea with real potential.

At this point, another entrepreneur might have immersed herself in the standard kinds of research people do in order to raise initial capital for their businesses. She could have come at it like a McKinsey consultant, doing a market sizing exercise complete with breakdowns by demographic category and geography to show who wants your product and where. She might have conducted focus group or "person on the street" interviews or pulled out data from Experian or Nielsen illustrating consumer desires, and then triangulated among half a dozen different approaches to establish the "total addressable market" for her product. Out of the roughly 125 million adult women in America, a certain number—50 million, say—might have been in the market for a new bathing suit, depending on their age, interests, and other factors. Assuming $100 per bathing suit, that might amount to a $5 billion total market. If her business captured just 1 percent of that, she'd have a $50 million business. Pretty amazing opportunity, right? This is the kind of "top-down" logic that entrepreneurs roll out in pitches all the time.

Instead of trying to wow investors by making a top-down case, Melanie set about trying to determine whether her business was actually viable. Before she even approached venture funders, she wanted to convince the most important "investor" of all—herself—that demand for her business and its products really existed, and that she should proceed. So she ran a few quick, nonscientific tests with actual consumers. Only after those tests succeeded would she work her way to the longest, most expensive test of all—setting up an actual business.

Melanie began by launching a Google survey, throwing together questions about women's swimwear shopping habits so as to "understand the landscape a bit better." It was great that her family and friends seemed frustrated with conventional swimsuit shopping, but did enough other women feel the same way? She posted the survey on her Facebook profile and was stunned by the response. "All these women . . . started telling me about their swimwear shopping stories and their bathing suit stories, their worst bathing suits ever." Can you imagine how embarrassing it would be to take a dip while on vacation with your fiancé's family, only to have a wave knock off your ill-fitting bikini top right in front of your future in-laws? That's the kind of story Melanie read over and over, convincing her that she had "really hit a passion point."

She set about trying to figure out how she would produce a simple, better-fitting swimsuit. Hopping on LinkedIn, she connected with twenty-five freelance swimsuit designers (yes, they're out there), asking them endless questions. Eventually, she found one designer with whom she just "clicked" and who didn't judge her for her lack of experience. This woman mocked up a few quick sketches for a simple, timeless one-piece swimsuit.

Before Melanie quit her job and invested in a production run, she wanted more hard evidence that consumers were game for a new swimsuit and swimsuit purchasing experience. So, much as John Fiorentino did with his Gravity Blanket, she ran a crowdfunding campaign in the fall of 2016 with some preliminary sketches, promising users a chance to buy her new swimsuit in exchange for a $75 commitment. "I believe that doing a crowdfunding campaign is a really good way of measuring interest in something before going too deep," Melanie says. She figured that if she got 150 to 200 orders or more, she would move ahead and produce the swim-suit for these customers. Otherwise, she'd table the idea and move on with her life.

Within two weeks, the campaign generated hundreds of orders, or about $10,000 in capital. Melanie was convinced. "I turned to my wife and I was like, 'Hey, I need to quit my job and do this full-time.'" And that's exactly what she did. She gave notice to BarkBox and founded her new company, AndieSwim.com, on January 1, 2017. A few months later, she raised about $250,000 from family and friends. She was off and swimming.

What Melanie did, and what I advise anyone interested in selling naked to do, is to experiment in a non-attached way. Admit that you have no clue what's going to work, because you really don't! And then commit yourself to learning the truth about your idea and its value. Concoct a boots-on-the-ground experiment to gain some sense of whether your concept might succeed or fail. Kickstarter is one option, but there are many others to consider. You might create a landing page for your product and see how much it actually costs to snare an email lead. You might buy sample inventory and try to sell it. You might create a blog post or video about your product and in-duce people to share it. If these initial experiments fail, don't roll out all those fancy zeroes to try to convince investors to back you anyway. Cut your losses and move on to your next business idea. This is Start-ups 101, but digital direct-response marketing has changed the equation by opening up many more paths to quick, cheap tests—just as it's opened up a path to quick, cheap brand launches.

LEARNERS WANTED

Is a bottoms-up, experimental approach really most likely to get you traction with investors? Don't they *need* to see all that market sizing data to grasp the opportunity as you see it? Yes, they do, but that's by no means all they need. In pitching Hubble, I might have wheeled out a fancy PowerPoint deck showing that everyone on earth has eyeballs, so the total number of eyeballs is roughly 14 billion. At $0.50 per disposable contact lens and one pair of contact lenses per day, that's a potential market of $7 billion per day. If we captured 1 percent of that, we'd sell $70 million worth of our product each and every day.

The problem with that math is that it's too high-level—it says nothing about the complex microeconomic factors that influence people's decision in the real world to buy anything, including contact lenses. Understanding how consumers actually behave takes original research—you can't simply pull reports off the shelf and hope to get much insight. A presentation like this also would have cast me as lazy in investors' eyes—a big, fat zero. If I wasn't willing or able to get off my duff, honestly probe the value of my idea, and figure out creative ways to get inside consumers' heads with a limited budget, how would I ever manage to launch and grow a start-up successfully?

> Investors don't just want to fund passionate and engaged founders. As books like Eric Ries's *The Lean Startup* and Steve Blank's *The Four Steps to the Epiphany* have observed, they want founders who are *learners*.

Investors know the odds are almost zero that the business a founder brings them today will work over the long term. At best, this business might conceivably represent a way to break into a market. Within months or years, the founder or someone else will have to reinvent critical parts of the business to achieve or sustain growth. If you have come up with a single smart move to enter a market but you don't keep iterating from there, you probably won't take the business very far. For this reason, investors feel most comfortable with founders who ask smart questions about their business, who understand what they do and don't know, who are willing to be proven wrong, and who are hell-bent on taking their business in new directions. Investors also know that digital marketing tools have made it easier and cheaper to learn about customer needs. In their eyes, there's no excuse for *not* using these tools. If founders aren't curious, informed, or motivated enough to run digital tests, how will they possibly succeed?

ESTABLISH YOUR LEARNER CRED

Investors have no way of knowing for sure that you possess a learning mindset or, more broadly, that you'll do whatever it takes or learn whatever is required in order to achieve goals. They can look at your life story: Where did you go to school? What prior work experience do you have? Did you gain admission to top schools, score top jobs, and advance successfully through them? Yet inferences from resumes only go so far. To gain additional insight, investors pay close attention to the quality of your pitch itself. Did you bother to muster facts that they couldn't easily obtain on Google or by perusing a Wall Street research report for five minutes? How critically did you *really* look at your new business idea to see if it has a prayer of succeeding?

Founders who wow investors—and corporate marketers who convince their internal bosses to fund direct-to-consumer projects—usually design and perform their own experiments to test potential demand. In the introduction, I described two important experiments we carried out to gauge whether people really would consider buying disposable contact lenses from a company like ours. The first was to promote a mock product through Facebook and other social media platforms. It cost us hardly anything besides a few days of our time. We did that and induced two thousand people to sign up in four days. That was a pretty strong sign of consumer interest, and it played a big role in landing $3.5 million in funding.

The second test was to collect email addresses via Facebook's lead ads feature and connect these potential customers with a network of optometrists we had recruited to fit our lenses. Lead ads allow you to collect email leads without a full website. You throw together some cheap ads using stock images, collect your leads, and then email them. We gathered up a couple of thousand leads, and I started emailing them to see if they would go to one of our partner doctors for a Hubble fitting in exchange for two months' worth of free Hubble lenses. We didn't pay the doctors or subsidize the exam, and, as always, the doctors could prescribe whatever lens they wanted. I spent a full month scheduling (and rescheduling) these opportunities, and before we even had a store or could collect payments, we proved that people would make a special effort to obtain our lenses. Based on this data, we raised money right before we launched at double what our company had been valued at just months earlier.

Many founders of direct-to-consumer companies have told me that they performed similar research and that it helped them commit to their business ideas and obtain funding. Sophia Edelstein, co-founder and CEO of the eyewear brand Pair, began working on her company with her co-founder, Nathan Kondamuri, in college. The two had suspected that eyewear retailers and manufacturers weren't serving children well and that it might be possible to start a business in that space, but they didn't know for certain. So, during their senior year, they set about talking to as many kids and parents as possible about eyewear. "We went everywhere to find these kids," Sophia remembers. "We actually got kicked out of the American Girl store once because we were just talking to random customers, and we were [also] kicked out of the Apple store. We would phone family and friends to see if they knew anyone whom we could talk to. We went to San Francisco. We went to a science museum one day. We did some panels. Anywhere we could think of to just talk to people."[2] Ultimately, Sophia and Nathan talked to about four hundred consumers—not bad for a couple of ambitious undergraduates. They found that, almost universally, neither kids nor parents were "having a good eyewear experience." Eyewear was expensive for parents and a pain to shop for, and nobody was selling it directly, not even adult direct-to-consumer brands like Warby Parker.

That research was enough to spur Sophia and Nathan to create prototype glasses. Using resources available to them at Stanford, they designed an eyeglass frame for kids, embedding it with magnets so kids could attach colorful "tops" according to their personal tastes. By purchasing multiple tops, kids could express their personalities and feel like they had many pairs of glasses for a fraction of the price of a typical pair. With their homemade prototype in hand as well as the market research they had performed, Sophia and Nathan managed to raise $150,000 from friends and family, as well as professional investors who took an interest. Even more impressively, perhaps, they were able to attract a former head of product development at Warby Parker to partner with them on developing the business.

> There aren't any magic tricks to obtaining capital. It's just you and the work that you've done, as well as investors (or your corporate bosses) and the concepts that resonate with them. Good pitches are empirically based. They reflect the weirdness of the world as it is.

The preparatory investigations you perform help you frame richer narratives about your business (more on that in Chapter 3), and they show investors and corporate bosses just how engaged and determined you are to succeed. Best of all, they tell *you* whether your business idea is worth pursuing. If the results of your experiments aren't promising, you'll know this sooner, saving you time and money.

If you work for an incumbent brand, imagine spending $35 million out of your budget to develop a product without knowing whether anyone wants it. Or imagine being an entrepreneur and spending your life savings. It's so much better to run tests to get a sense of demand first. By providing for the possibility of a quick off-ramp, tests allow you to launch more digital projects than you would otherwise, without wasting too much time or cash on your losers. Early flameouts are easy to absorb. Those that don't immediately reveal themselves as failures prove far costlier.

ANSWER THE EASIEST QUESTIONS FIRST

How do you get started with testing? Your goal at first is to learn as much as humanly possible in the shortest possible time about your business idea and its feasibility. As critical as consumer demand is, feasibility depends on other considerations, too, such as:

- Is it technically possible to make the product you wish to sell?
- Is it technically possible to distribute this product?
- Can you make, distribute, and market this product cheaply enough at a large enough scale to build a business?
- Do regulations make it impossible or uneconomical to sell your desired product naked?

Before we raised our first round of funding, we looked into regulations, and we also conducted a ton of legwork in hopes of nailing down our manufacturers. We contacted all 150 contact lens manufacturers globally that had approval from the Food and Drug Administration (FDA), seeking to find one or more to supply us with product. We winnowed the list to about a dozen, and after obtaining samples from them, we paid in-person visits to four. Not only did this exhaustive work help land us a supplier, but it gave us a panoramic view of the industry, which in turn allowed us to conduct more substantive conversations with investors. We could inform them that the four biggest suppliers, which together accounted for 95 percent of contact lens product, wouldn't work with a start-up, and that our supplier, St. Shine, the world's fifth-largest manufacturer, accounted for the bulk of the remaining production. This would protect us from copycats—it wouldn't be easy for them to source production at scale. Investors found this argument persuasive, and they were also happy to see how much work we had done to learn about the industry.

> Whether you're a founder or a corporate marketer, pose a range of questions about your business in addition to those about consumer demand, prioritizing those you can answer most quickly and cheaply. If it will take you only a couple of hours of Google research or a few phone calls to attorney friends of yours to establish that regulations block you from selling a product direct-to-consumer, then there's no need to waste weeks and hundreds or thousands of dollars on a full-fledged pilot. The best course of investigation will vary from business to business, but go after the low-hanging fruit first.

THE WONDERS OF FACEBOOK LEAD ADS

Of course, many entrepreneurs and corporate marketers do start with demand experiments, simply because of those powerful research tools that are available cheaply online. Let's examine a few of these options.

First, as mentioned, there's Facebook lead ads. If you ask me, these little ads are basically the greatest thing in the world for potential founders testing product ideas, precisely because you don't have to spend time or money creating a rich external site. All you need is a landing page and a privacy policy to point Facebook to. The landing page can be a stock image, and free privacy policies are widely available on the Web. Any website you might build requires *some* graphic assets, which will slow you down massively, even if you have chops in development and design. Platforms like Squarespace, while amazing, don't save you from this problem. They provide you with templates, but you still must populate them with high-quality graphics. With lead ads, you can have a new product idea in the morning and your ads up and running before noon. Pretty great.

Unlike click-based market tests, lead ad campaigns give you a two-step "funnel" or process for acquiring customers. Consumers must click on the ad *and* provide you with an email address. If you ran a test solely to see if consumers would click on an ad, you wouldn't know if those clicks reflected any latent interest in the product—consumers might have just clicked accidentally because they were trying to start up a game of Candy Crush. (Interesting—or horrifying?—fact: some 40 percent of clicks on ads are stray or spam clicks.)[3] You could "qualify" the clicks by driving them to a spiffy landing page and seeing how much it costs to convince a consumer to leave their email address there, but now you're back to the problem of needing a spiffy landing page.

Since lead ads require both a click and an email address, I'm ensuring that the consumer clicks I receive aren't accidental, leaving me more confident that consumers would purposefully direct themselves to an actual site if one were available. Lead ads also help because they give you great data from true strangers. With non-paid, organically driven demand tests, you might initially have to rely on your network to spread the word, which means you'll end up with results that reflect a mix of true demand and friendly cheerleading.

Lead ads aren't perfect. You can insert only so much information into the copy itself, so if your offering is complicated or unfamiliar (think Uber before any ride apps existed), or if you want to test questions about pricing or other, more nuanced issues, lead ads might not offer the most helpful feedback. Depending on what information you need, you might try building a single-page email address capture site. This requires more work than lead ads, but it also gives you room to describe the product offering in greater detail.

If you still don't have enough room, that says something about the business. Maybe it's too complicated given the ability of potential customers to absorb information. The cost of leads from an email address capture page will likely exceed the cost of leads from lead ads—consumers have to leave Facebook and go to the site, which adds load time, and they have to actually type in their email addresses (on Facebook, those addresses auto-populate, and all consumers have to do is click "Enter"). That's okay, though. At Hubble, leads coming through on our site cost double what they did on Facebook, but for some questions we wanted the feedback of an on-site experience.

BEYOND LEAD ADS

You can take an email address capture site experiment to the next level and actually sell through proto-versions of your store (although at some point you should just concede that you've set your business live). You could put the e-commerce site up without product and track how many consumers are continuing to click through to the top of your checkout, even if you don't yet have the inventory to actually run through the sale. You can also do preorders for a smaller fee, a tactic that offers additional information.

Although crowdfunding worked for Melanie at Andie and John Fiorentino at Gravity Blanket, I'm not so enamored with the idea of using it to gauge demand. Over time, the quality of the photography, design work, and ad copy in the campaigns on Kickstarter and Indiegogo has risen, so much so that pulling off a successful campaign isn't always that much easier than just launching the business itself. Of course, the relative amount of work required depends on how much development and funding your particular product requires, as well as your own design capabilities. If you happen to be an awesome designer/creative, the demands of a Kickstarter campaign might seem less daunting. And if you don't use these platforms as a demand test, you can still deploy them as a means of building pre-release hype.

Given the range of demand tests available, I find it shocking whenever founders don't do a bunch of testing before committing themselves to a project. And it's equally surprising to me that investors would sign off on a business and a founder who hasn't done this work.

In the corporate world, too, we need to see more demand testing. In 2018, Colgate did a quick-and-dirty digital launch of an AI-enabled toothbrush that feeds data back to your smartphone, while Gillette Labs ran a successful Indiegogo campaign for a heated razor. Such experimentation is a great start, but all you corporate marketers pitching direct-to-consumer business ideas need to keep doing it. You're asking leaders to gamble with money that the company could otherwise reinvest in existing businesses or return to shareholders.

You're also asking leaders to take on reputational risk, since any failures, albeit small, will be visible.

> To convince your bosses, you have to take as much risk as possible off the table. Experiments that demonstrate the existence of demand will go at least part of the way to making your preternaturally risk-averse corporate bosses feel more comfortable. If your attempt at selling direct fails but you and your boss can at least point to lots of high-quality testing that justified your decision to pursue the business in the first place, you'll both look less foolish to higher-ups.

NEVER STOP LEARNING

Once you've conducted your initial batch of research, including those dazzlingly successful demand tests, you might feel a strong, almost instinctual urge to pat yourself on the back and think you're done experimenting. Nope. You're not done experimenting—you're *just beginning.*

> After you launch and are actually selling product, up the ante on your experiments and use the results to rapidly improve your business.

This is nothing less than a matter of survival for young businesses, especially when you're trying not just to generate demand, but also to sustain it. As Melanie Travis notes, "You need to experiment and test things, see what works, see what's resonating [with customers]. Otherwise you won't have a business pretty soon. I think it's the only way to have a business."

Travis would know, because she and her team at Andie experimented at a frenetic pace during their first post-launch year. In one instance, they piloted a home try-on kit containing a collection of swimsuits that the company had selected for the customer. All a customer had to do was click "Buy" on the website and hand over a $10 deposit, and the box would arrive at her door. Women could try on the suits and send back anything they didn't like. In Travis's view, the experiment was marginally successful. Since Andie was the first swimsuit brand to offer a home try-on kit, the effort yielded some great media exposure. Economically, however, the home try-on kit didn't work, since all that shipping back and forth between company and customer bit too deep into Andie's margin. Although the company eventually shut down the experiment, on balance Melanie is "glad we did it."

Andie has also experimented with its product, branching out from its initial offering of one-piece swimsuits to sell a limited collection of bikinis as well. "We're experimenting," Melanie says, "we're throwing some Facebook ads against it, we're seeing how that affects conversion on our website, we're seeing how that affects click-through rates on Facebook and ultimately our [cost to acquire a customer]." As of this writing, the test is still ongoing, but as Melanie notes, the stakes for her business are potentially huge. If the product works, allowing Andie to acquire customers more cheaply, then the company will "make a big investment in two-pieces and no longer be known as a one-piece company. We'll be known as a swimwear company, broadly speaking."

At Hubble, too, we've continued to experiment and learn since our launch in 2016. First, we've experimented with more traditional, offline marketing channels. How much does it cost us to acquire a customer through a TV ad? We'll throw one up (or four) and find out. Will direct mail get us anywhere? How about radio? As of this writing, the only major offline channel that we haven't tested or put real dollars behind is outdoor signs (billboards, phone booth signs, subway placards, and the like), and that's because we doubt that we can track how well signs perform for us. (To be fair, signs are very popular with our peer set. Just think of all those subway ads you see in cities like New York or Boston.)

Within each channel, we've constantly experimented with both our creative and our targeting. Do some images or text in our ads work better than others? Should we target older consumers or college kids? People who live in cities or those who live in suburbs? We've also experimented with what happens when consumers click on our online ads. Instead of sending consumers to our landing page, what if we send them to articles written about our company on various media platforms, or to blog posts about our product?

We're helping out other direct-to-consumer businesses, too, including Andie, and we're learning from their experiences. In conjunction with those companies, we're experimenting with new ways of structuring deals, such as giving manufacturers equity in these businesses in exchange for lower pricing. We're experimenting with corporate partnerships, helping Fortune 500 companies think through their direct-to-consumer strategies. And we're testing new ways of getting our message out about direct-to-consumer, including writing a book about it!

BRIDGING THE CORPORATE-UPSTART DIVIDE

I've focused primarily on start-ups in this chapter, but large corporations can also mobilize direct-to-consumer start-ups as valuable learning opportunities. As anyone who has read Clayton Christensen's *The Innovator's Dilemma* knows, large companies can have much more difficulty than start-ups adapting to change, precisely because they're set up to run and profit from a lucrative, existing business. The whole goal of a giant organization like Pepsi is to manufacture, market, and distribute its products as efficiently as possible, to sell as much of them as possible, and to minimize the risk of errors or problems that might damage the Pepsi brand. A great deal of energy goes into minimizing miscues, because so many of them can crop up: product recalls, product shortages, the hacking of consumer data, bad PR due to unfriendly labor or environmental practices, and poorly conceived marketing. If you have a business that generates billions of dollars every year, then you'll put everything you have into minimizing the risk of losing that franchise. You'll also create big, robust, but cumbersome systems and processes that don't lend themselves at all to experimentation. And you'll incentivize the people you hire to reduce risk on what already exists, not to dream up entirely new businesses from scratch.

The solution, as Christensen argued, is to set up skunk works within the company that can take risks, move quickly, and experiment for the sake of learning. In the direct-to-consumer space, one way to do that is by partnering with start-up teams that are already selling naked. In 2018, I entered into discussions with large consumer package goods (CPG) companies about setting up some scrappy, low-budget, external skunkworks. The goal: to launch businesses that sold some of these companies' existing products directly to consumers. These operations would have more room to adjust or maneuver around these companies' typical vendor, privacy and data, and

compensation policies, but the CPG companies would still retain the right to influence key executional elements of the new
businesses we'd create. I'm working with these companies as of
this writing to determine what kind of arrangement might be
feasible, but it seems possible that partnerships such as this will
bear fruit and allow these companies to sell naked in ways that
would otherwise prove elusive.

I should emphasize that the opportunities here are potentially enormous, benefiting both start-ups and corporates. As
adept as start-ups like Hubble are in experimenting with marketing, they have very limited ability to experiment around
distribution or product. As far as the former is concerned, we
don't have distribution on every shelf in America. Rather, we
have sales channels that feed us back a ton of data that helps us
optimize our marketing budget and figure out how much our
customers are worth. And by running optimized marketing
spend, we get to scoop up the most valuable ad impressions,
keeping them away from incumbent advertisers that are just
bidding to maximize the number of people who see their ads.[4]
Eventually, however, many start-ups that sell naked decide they
need offline distribution somewhere. At this point, they often
run into the same channel conflict issues that kept incumbents
away from selling naked in the first place. Why would Macy's
want to stock your brand of custom-designed T-shirts when
you're already running a competitive channel?[5] A lot of the
time, start-ups end up setting up their own retail. Unfortunately, that strategy doesn't always take them very far, since it's
often hard to generate enough revenue with just one brand to
cover the cost of an entire store, especially given the limited
product catalogs maintained by most start-ups. There's a reason so much product is sold in mass retail with multiple
brands—it's a very efficient way to do business.

If the options for experimenting with distribution aren't great for start-ups, they're even worse when it comes to product design. Most companies that sell naked work with contract manufacturers and have relatively little product expertise on their teams. They can experiment marginally around product, making occasional requests of their manufacturers or sourcing through new manufacturers, but that's all. Meanwhile, of all the experiments that you might run, product experiments are usually the biggest and most meaningful. Marketing experiments tend to be pretty small-bore: Is the new ad strategy in Facebook this month product shots or GIFs? Are those GIFs of your product or of a model? Are longer-format videos working finally? Should you deploy user-generated testimonials about how your product changed someone's life? Can you get more text onto a photo or video than Facebook says is optimal? The experiments you might run in these areas are fast, easy, and cheap to execute, but competitors can perform them, too. As a result, it's hard to ever achieve much of a sustainable advantage. By comparison, a new or enhanced product can transform a business. Remember Andie and how its new bikini would potentially change the very scope of the brand.

By teaming up, corporates and start-ups can run experiments across the entirety of the business. Start-ups can contribute their tactical marketing experiments (and learning). Corporate players can bring their product expertise—and to some extent their relationships with distributors—to the party. The result might be a market-altering business that offers incredible products that consumers want, adapted to a digital environment and affording opportunities for optimized marketing thanks to the establishment of a digital direct-response feedback loop. Few such businesses exist so far, although the success of the streaming service Hulu, a joint venture of several incumbent companies (Walt Disney/21st Century Fox, Comcast, and AT&T), offers some indication of what's possible.

> If you're a corporate marketer, I urge you to consider such a collaboration, whether through an acquisition, a joint venture, or some other mechanism. Get those experiments up and running, and start learning your way to innovation and growth.

If you're a founder whose business is already launched, then put down this book and plot your next experiment. What's the cheapest way you can answer a given question about your business? What's the least amount of inventory you need to buy to run your experiment, the smallest marketing budget you can work with, the least expensive website that will work for your needs? Figure that out and go do it. Investors demand this kind of intellectual ferment. Your success hinges on it. The start-up that experiments the most learns the most—and wins.

(THE NAKED TRUTH)

You've conceived your million-dollar idea and have survived the rude awakening that digital business isn't something you can run for just two hours every Saturday in your sweatpants from your couch. Now you face another important challenge: convincing potential investors or executives in your company that your digital business concept might actually work. The best way to do that is to get your hands dirty and *learn something*. Run a cheap and easy trial or two to see if consumers want what you've got. If they do, fantastic—your business just got that much more compelling to investors or bosses. If not, move on to your next earthshaking business idea. And once you've launched a business, keep the learning coming, either on your own or in partnership with colleagues across the corporate-upstart divide.

CHAPTER 3

TELL A GREAT STORY

EVERY START-UP HAS a story. John Paul DeJoria lived on the streets prior to creating the Paul Mitchell hair care brand.[1] Hewlett-Packard began in Dave Packard's garage with $538 in capital. Seth Goldman of Honest Tea brewed tea in his own kitchen, brought samples of it to a grocery chain, and landed an order for fifteen thousand bottles.

By comparison, Hubble's story isn't so dramatic. Ben and I met as interns at Bridgewater, the hedge fund mentioned in Chapter 1. I stayed at Bridgewater full-time, and then worked for several years on the investment team for Columbia University's endowment. Ben went from Bridgewater to Boston Consulting Group (BCG), taking a secondment (temporary assignment) at Harry's, the men's subscription shaving company. Harry's was in the same building as the glasses start-up Warby Parker, since one of Harry's co-founders was also a co-founder at Warby. Ben ended up staying at Harry's for eighteen months—the longest secondment in BCG's history. Subscription boxes and vision care: this was the perfect background for Ben to come up with the idea for Hubble.

In summer 2015, Ben was still working at Harry's and we were living across the street from each other on Manhattan's Upper West Side—you could see from one apartment into the other. One day he was making his annual purchase of contact lenses on 1-800 Contacts and noticed that the cost of his lenses had skyrocketed. He wasn't looking to start a business at this point; he was just curious why his contact lenses had spiked in price. He did a little digging and learned that the four major manufacturers of contact lenses—Johnson & Johnson, Novartis, Valeant, and Cooper—controlled 95 percent of production in the industry and had colluded through a price-fixing scheme called a unilateral pricing policy. In violation of competition laws, they dictated minimum prices to their retailers, which caused retail prices to rise dramatically. The unilateral-pricing policy would collapse within the next couple of years under legal challenges, but not before drawing Ben's attention to the space. Here, he thought, was an industry in which end users of a product were getting shafted. A company that made an end run around the oligarchy and served consumers better might be able to carve out a nice business for itself.

Ben thought about what it would take for him to start such a company. The first question was obvious: how would he source lenses? Ben talked with friends who were optometrists and ophthalmologists, and they informed him that every contact lens on the market needed formal approval from the FDA before a company could market it. Searching some more, he found a database of every contact lens that had the requisite approval. At about this time, I got involved. Working our way through the database, we researched more than 150 manufacturers of those lenses. Somewhere on that list, we thought, there might be a company from whom we could source a product that we could sell directly to consumers. We continued to develop our business idea in the ways described elsewhere in this book, we secured funding, and we launched our company.

Some people might not be interested in an exhaustive account of how your company came to be. But no matter how dramatic or mundane your story, there is one audience that wants every detail: venture investors. We've started off countless pitch meetings not by piling on facts or data but by weaving a simple narrative about who we are, what we're doing, and how we came to be sitting across the table from the investors in question. From there, we continue to spin out a carefully crafted story about our business, how it works, why competitors have a hard time getting to us, what our goals are, what our vision for the company is (I wish I could avoid the pun, but venture investors love that word), and so on. We recognize that our narrative won't appeal to every investor; no narrative can. But we do hope it will appeal to enough of them to create a market for the business we're pitching, and to get some investors to buy in.

So many potential founders don't appreciate the power of their stories. If you've ever had someone throw a bunch of facts and figures at you without linking them together, you know you get bored really quickly. Soon you're yawning or staring off into space. A few seconds later you're off checking email again. To succeed in pitching a direct-to-consumer company, or probably any venture, you need to weave a series of facts together into a more thoughtful narrative, one that makes sense to your audience and that addresses their primary business concerns. Most of all, you need to muster those facts to show the specifics of how you can execute and win. You don't have to be J. K. Rowling or James Patterson, but you do need to tell a story, and you need to tell it really well. Here are five storytelling lessons we learned raising for Hubble that might help you, too.

STORYTELLING LESSON #1: DON'T TAKE YOURSELF TOO SERIOUSLY

There's a surefire way to *not* tell a story really well, and that's to overblow it. As I alluded to in Chapter 2, many founders waste investors' time by blasting through a bunch of slides on "total addressable market" and why their product is "The Special." In their minds, the business they're proposing is epic, monumental, paradigm-shifting, world-historical. Maybe it is, but potential funders are bound to eye you skeptically. They're smart people. They know that any market is giant if you define it broadly enough, and that the first version of a product, cobbled together with minimal funding and nights and weekend time, probably isn't that great.

> A better strategy when pitching is to identify the *minimally viable product* your business could sell, and focus on that. Make your business goals and ambitions somewhat humbler than you might have initially considered.

Many truly transformative businesses have started with narrower product offerings and then evolved toward greater size and more ambitious undertakings. Netflix mailed you DVDs in red envelopes. Sony sold rice cookers. Counterexamples do exist—think of SpaceX or Palantir, companies with enormous ambitions from day one. But these companies were founded by repeat entrepreneurs—Elon Musk and Peter Thiel, respectively—who already had vast networks, access to massive amounts of capital, and experience to draw on, and as a result were well positioned to take on supersized projects. If you lack resources and experience, you're far better off finding a more digestible business idea, building it, and then applying what you've learned to make something bigger later on.

You're also better off avoiding the temptation to overproduce your pitch itself. While you want your PowerPoint slides to appear professionally done and tasteful, if they look like a J. Crew catalogue, investors might regard them as too slick or "salesy." At the very least, investors might question your judgment, asking why you spent so much time on the wrapper when you could have thought through or researched your business concept a bit more. When Ben and I pitch to investors, we've spent countless hours working through our ideas and questioning the assumptions behind them, but not all that much time working through the pitch itself. It has definitely helped that Ben, with his experience in management consulting, knows how to make really clean, polished decks. But these initially weren't too extensive— short and sweet at fourteen slides, with relatively little macro overview of the industry and just a tight summary of the work we'd done. We also aren't particularly "salesy" when pitching. If we do our research and take the time to understand an industry and how it works, we can talk thoughtfully about key issues that matter to investors, such as how we're going to jimmy our way into the industry, and what we're going to do to protect the business from others trying to come in behind us.

If you're pitching an early-stage venture, a solid presentation should probably run about fifteen slides. It might go a little longer—up to around thirty-five slides—if you're pitching a more mature business, since you'll have more financial results and other data to present.

Graphics, including charts, visualizations, and photos, should take up a meaningful amount of the real estate on your slides. Be careful not to overload your slides with text. You need to make your points, but in a pared-down, digestible fashion. If nothing else, doing so will show that you put in that extra bit of thought required to achieve simplicity.

Simplicity and minimizing the amount of text are also important because they allow you to share the least amount of information possible. The more information you share with investors, the more you tie yourself down, especially at the seed stage, when so much about your business remains unknown. If you specify in your deck that you're seeking to raise $500,000, you can't turn around at the end of the meeting, once you see that it went well, and say you're raising $1 million. If you say in the deck that you think the brand should resemble something in the cosmetics and fashion categories, you have a much harder time shifting if an investor pipes up and says that she thinks the business should feel more medical and clinical in nature. Writing as little as possible gives you the greatest degree of freedom. Also, you seem robotic if you're talking off a deck, and it's boring for the person you're talking with because he or she can read the deck faster than you can talk through it. I don't present this as a golden rule: I realize that some entrepreneurs like to present from a deck, and some investors like to have one read to them. Just be aware of the potential downsides of loading a presentation with lots of dense text.

STORYTELLING LESSON #2: PITCH EVERYONE

When Ben and I started fundraising for our seed, we tried to get in front of as many investors as we could. We applied to every semi-plausible accelerator we could find and emailed every investor in our network. We were lucky to have relationships with a decent number of investors and friends who were willing to introduce us to more. During my time at Columbia, part of my job was to help select the venture capital funds in which the endowment invested, so I had a chance to meet a number of people in that community. Ben also had a lot of friends from college who had ended up on the venture side of the world.

We kept our expectations low at the outset and were pleasantly surprised to receive interviews with every one of the accelerators to which we applied. Our conversations with VCs were also going better than expected. I remember feeling beyond presumptuous at first by saying that we wanted to raise $500,000 in a SAFE (a simple agreement for future equity, a more founder-friendly alternative to the traditional convertible note) with a $5 million cap.[2] Under this arrangement, we wouldn't be valuing the business now, but later, if we raised a "priced round," SAFE investors would get their equity at a valuation of at most $5 million, even if the round priced our company at some higher number. Investors seemed keen to put in $500,000, so we gradually upped the ante—to $1 million, and then to $1.5 million, with our target for the cap creeping up as well. After only five weeks of pitching, we wound up raising $3.5 million at an $11.7 million valuation, blowing away our wildest expectations.

If investors don't give you such a positive reception, the issue might not be the quality of your thinking or your pitch itself. Some business ideas are just not good venture capital business ideas. Some organizations might not stand a chance of ever generating significant returns, and you might be better off structuring them as nonprofits and soliciting funds from private donors. Other businesses might well turn a profit, even a significant one, but on a smaller scale than a venture capital firm would find attractive. Early-stage VCs hope a small number of outsized winners will make up for all of the losers they fund, and accepting VC money commits you to trying to shoot the moon on growth. If you're a master craftsperson, you might command a big premium for your products or services, but you'll never sell millions of units. You won't be a good match for venture funders, and regardless of how well you craft your story, you won't find your audience whipping out their checkbooks. Don't despair, however. You can finance such "small giants," as Bo Burlingham has called them, by bootstrapping and taking out loans.[3] You might also try raising money from the subcommunity of angel investors or from nontraditional funding sources like Assembled Brands or Clearbanc. If you can convince them that the opportunity is less risky than others they're considering, they might be happy receiving a strong but not stratospheric multiple on their money. Here your storytelling efforts will fall on more receptive ears.

STORYTELLING LESSON #3: KNOW YOUR AUDIENCE, AND CATER TO IT

Once you're in front of the right people, you need to craft your narrative to address your audience's specific needs. What in the businesses they fund does your audience truly care about? What do they need to hear woven into the narrative in order to get excited?

> Both investors and corporate executives want to understand the potential upside of your business and how much money you—and they—stand to make over time. But as smart operators, they want to review the opportunity more deeply to un-

derstand exactly how and why you'll manage to break into an industry.

As we've found, investors and corporate executives have a number of questions that they want your narrative to address, including:

- Do consumers really want your product or service, and will the math work the way you claim it will in order for you to turn a profit? How do you know? Here the demand experiments described in Chapter 2 become extremely important.
- Who are your existing competitors, and why will you succeed in taking them on? Investors and bosses want you to lay out the existing supply chain in your industry and show how you'll be able to rearrange it to lower costs and present consumers with a more attractive offering. In our case, we talked about the high wholesale price from the major manufacturers and how we could lower that.
- What is your industry's market structure? For example, if your industry is dominated by just a few large players, that's quite possibly a good thing—those suppliers probably enjoy major pricing power, or even a virtual monopoly, which means that consumers might well be clamoring for a fresh alternative.
- Do many contract manufacturing options exist to supply potential competitors if your business works? More broadly, will competitors find it too easy to pursue the same opportunity you identified once you show it's working?
- Are distribution channels in your industry antiquated or noncompetitive? If so, that's likely another good

thing. Traditionally, most people could buy a mattress only by going to a mattress showroom, a process that took time and frankly was a pain. That created an opening for ambitious entrepreneurs to present selling naked as an alternative—and much welcomed—distribution option.

- Will you appeal to consumers by improving the customer experience in some way, in addition to lowering prices? Melanie Travis could argue that her new company, Andie, would do exactly that—a gold star for her in the minds of investors. In our pitches for Hubble, Ben and I noted that the big manufacturers hadn't revamped their packaging for some time, and that ours would be more attractive and modern, improving the purchase and ownership experience. Dollar Shave Club could say that most pharmacies keep razors under lock and key, making for a burdensome shopping experience that selling naked would much improve.

In weaving these issues into your narrative, examine them in depth; otherwise, investors will come away doubting your knowledge and thoughtfulness. If possible, try to identify one special feature of your business that might strike potential funders as compelling and memorable. What truly makes a pitch story is a hook, a small observation on your part that explains why your business is different than existing businesses— different not just in the sense of "Oh, how interesting," but also in a way that explains why you'll snap up business from existing operators.

As Brad Stone reports in his book *The Upstarts,* Uber wasn't the only ride-sharing app in existence.[4] Others had put out similar apps. But Uber made a big move that distinguished itself from its competitors: it didn't try to partner with various municipalities' taxi and limousine commissions, choosing instead to recruit non-medallion drivers. This shift represented just enough of a difference to make for a compelling business. Unlike the other guys, Uber was planning to compete with medallion drivers by organizing non-medallion drivers in a new way.

WINNING OVER VCS

So far I've been focusing on elements of a business that all potential funders will want to know about. To succeed with your storytelling, it pays to look deeper at the specific investor audience you're addressing as either an entrepreneur or corporate marketer and shape your pitch accordingly. Let's take entrepreneurs first, and their audience of venture capitalists. Where is this audience coming from exactly?

I suggest thinking about venture capitalists not just as investors, but also as operators of their own businesses—venture capital firms. Venture capitalists raise funds from limited partners (pension funds and endowments, as well as some high-net-worth individuals). They generally receive a 2 percent management fee on the money they manage, as well as 20 percent of the returns they generate for the limited partners (their performance fee). Venture capitalists care a lot about the upside of the performance fee, but they don't want to risk their management fee, because that's what they use to pay their team and keep the lights on. The question then becomes: How do venture capitalists maximize their upside while minimizing the risk of true embarrassments that could create risk for their business?

The answer is that they choose investments wisely. Venture capitalists must invest in opportunities that are solid enough to allow them to attract capital for additional funds, and they must also invest their money fast enough so that they can raise additional funds (investing the dollars is what their limited partners pay them to do). To become a successful venture capitalist in the first place, you generally need to notch at least a couple of blockbuster deals. Once those are in place, you can raise new funds off the backs of those deals for a long time, as long as you don't experience any epic wipeouts that others regard as boneheaded, unforced errors. In the investing community, there's a big difference between smart misses and just incinerating cash. As a founder, you need to give your investors a story that they can tell their investors to explain why your business is a good, risk-adjusted bet, one that they can accept if it fails. While venture investors might feel all-powerful when you're pitching to them, remember that they are operators just like you, with stakeholders of their own to report to.

Factoring in this mindset of risk aversion, you can fine-tune your pitch to maximize your chances of success. If your business doesn't happen to be in a hot area, don't despair. You might be able to get a deal, but it might take you longer and require an even more developed, better-researched presentation on your part. The burden is on you to demonstrate that you've already achieved a meaningful amount of traction on your own. If you can do that, then watch out—investors will get crazy excited. Not too long ago, everyone thought artificial intelligence was going nowhere. Then a bunch of researchers made breakthroughs in machine learning and Google wrote a $500 million check for DeepMind. Boom—artificial intelligence was hot again. A while back, nobody was even thinking about investing in ride-sharing. Once Uber ground it out for a year or two and showed that the business could work, money started pouring in. If you've got business ideas that are not in vogue, you probably stand a better chance if you're a serial entrepreneur and not a beginner. Serial entrepreneurs are more likely to have the network and money to push the business ahead for a bit longer before involving investors. Chances are, they'll need every advantage they can get.

If your business is in a hot area, play that up by telling investors a good story that they can convey to their limited partners about why you'll emerge as one of the winners in that category. In 2016 when we pitched Hubble, subscription businesses like ours were big—everyone wanted a piece of them. Harry's was just rolling out in Target stores across the country, and a month or two later Dollar Shave Club sold to Unilever for $1 billion. In this context, we made the case that we would be one of the best new subscription upstarts out there. If you're selling customers a subscription in which they receive a regular shipment of a product, you want that product to be something consumers need to restock regularly. Further, you want margins in that category to be high, for customers to spend a relatively large amount each month, and for the weight of whatever you're shipping to be low, to minimize shipping costs. Daily disposable contact lenses ticked all of those boxes. In investors' eyes, we had a compelling story.

WINNING OVER CORPORATE BOSSES

If you're pitching corporate bosses, not venture investors, on an idea for selling naked, the picture is slightly different. Instead of worrying about how your pitch will help venture investors sell you to their limited partners, you should think about how the bosses you're pitching will sell your project to *their* bosses. First and foremost, these constituencies are likely concerned about how selling naked will affect the legacy business. A large business is part of a broader "ecosystem" that includes suppliers, distributors, consumers, regulators, local communities, and so on. If you present a business plan that yields profits but unsettles other elements of the company's ecosystem, alarm bells will sound in the minds of leaders and investors (and not irrationally). Even if your direct-to-consumer project succeeds, the profit it yields will be infinitesimally small compared to those produced by the company's existing businesses. If that growth creates new risks to the cash-cow existing businesses, your company will likely not let you pursue your ambitions of selling naked.

Imagine you work at Procter & Gamble, and you want to create a direct-to-consumer subscription business for Tide Pods. Tide is a very strong brand, and Tide Pods is a particularly strong product under that brand umbrella. Tide Pods also exists as a pretty strong meme in the digital world, a feature that you could potentially leverage on social media to promote your new, direct-to-consumer (DTC) offering. You could play off the Tide Pod challenge gag and possibly create a sizable DTC business quickly. On the other hand, if your promotional efforts backfire, they could damage the broader Tide brand, which is worth billions. Gambling on DTC will likely make management feel uneasy, and understandably so.

Even if you avoided this dangerous territory and made a successful business of Tide Pods DTC, there's another problem: you're cannibalizing your retail business. Your retailers will get pissed at you because they're possibly losing sales. Not only will their anger make it more difficult to sell Tide at retail, but it might also spill over to affect other Procter & Gamble brands. Tide is quite possibly P&G's strongest brand, so it's one the company can lean on to push for stronger store placement for other brands in its portfolio. Turn retailers off to Tide, and stores might stock P&G's other brands low on the shelf rather than at eye level, causing sales of those brands to decline.

If you're a marketer interested in selling naked, how do you counter such concerns when your audience of corporate funders raises them? It's not easy—as I've noted, selling naked is hard for branded manufacturers. But there are compelling arguments you can make.

To allay concerns about damage to the brand, plan your marketing strategy in advance of your pitch, and explain to your bosses exactly how you've mitigated potential risks. If you can solicit input and buy-in from the brand managers, even better. As far as cannibalization is concerned, arm your bosses with an argument that they can take to the company's affected retail partners to allay their concerns. Yes, the sales from selling naked will likely reduce overall sales volume at retail partners. On the other hand, selling naked will finally allow you to spend efficiently on digital, opening up the 50 percent of ad impressions that you had been forgoing (or might as well have been forgoing, given how ineffective traditional brand advertising is on digital platforms). Currently, all you can do is move brand advertising to the digital arena. If you sell directly to consumers, you own your own checkout, so you can tweak your ad spending to maximize the number of consumer purchases, finally making digital work for you instead of just pouring dollars in and seeing no clear return. (By the way, the data from your own checkout should help you optimize your traditional offline marketing spend as well.) Because you can spend more efficiently on marketing in this way, your overall business will grow. The share of sales that you'll be diverting to direct-to-consumer will come out of a much larger pie, allowing everyone to come out a winner.

Beyond addressing the needs of key partners, your story also needs to work internally, advancing the interests of your boss or sponsor, and that person's boss or sponsor, all the way up the hierarchy to the seniormost person who must sign off.

If you can't figure out how to make this a win for your sponsors, your idea won't proceed. One easy answer: share the credit. You might be tempted to keep all the glory for yourself, especially if the idea is yours. Don't do it. It might have been your idea, but ideas are cheap, and it's your sponsors' political capital that will get this done. Your bosses might have put in years, maybe even decades, working at your organization hoping for just a couple of chances to make an important contribution. If they're using your idea as one of those shots on goal, that's a big deal, and you should treat that with the respect it deserves by letting them claim a large share of the credit for themselves.

You should also think about whether any departments or business units within your organization stand to lose as a result of selling naked. Will your project siphon off budget or revenues that would have gone to other divisions, with the profits accruing only to your division and not theirs? In organizations where everyone is part of the same compensation pool, this problem is less likely to emerge. But if your organization determines compensation separately across its business units, and even subunit by subunit below that, with each unit or subunit maintaining its own profit-and-loss sheet, then the situation is more delicate. You'll have to show that your program will make money for every other unit impacted, and not just for the company overall.

One solution might be to find a new budget pool either inside or outside the company that can cover your project's costs. Would a centralized test marketing budget rather than the marketing function of one of the business units fund your project? Would some external investor foot part of the bill, and what economics would make that worth their while? If your program isn't adding costs to the other business units but is increasing their overall revenue, then they're seeing their profit-and-loss numbers improve and have less reason to complain.

Another issue that might loom large in the minds of potential backers inside your company is whether your organization can pull off selling naked with the talent and processes already on hand. This is a relatively easy concern to handle. Point out that both start-ups and incumbents work with lots of agency partners, and if incumbents need additional partners to help with selling naked, they can easily connect with that talent by attending the many direct-to-consumer conferences organized by investment banks, VC firms, technology media companies, and so on. Beyond this, note that your company probably has plenty of sharp people inside it already who might be able to lend a hand. It's true that your company might have processes and requirements in place (concerning how data is handled, which suppliers you must use, what hours people on your team work, and so on) that prevent people from moving quickly and maximizing the odds that new ventures will succeed. Still, you can create workarounds by arranging for exceptions to corporate policies or creating mechanisms for the direct-to-consumer project to operate outside the company (by setting it up either as a joint venture or as an independent company). And you can always buy or partner with upstarts that have the relevant experience.

In addition to explaining why a direct-to-consumer project

won't hurt existing businesses, wreak havoc internally, or be unrealistic for your company to pull off, go on offense and explain why selling naked might be necessary to protect or defend the strong business you already have. Here the arguments developed in Chapter 1 should prove helpful. Point out that direct-to-consumer upstarts are taking market share away from you, and you must respond. Point out that these upstarts are pioneering a new way to launch brands, and because your business needs to launch new brands at a certain pace, it could benefit from a mastery of selling direct. Finally, point out that large companies like Amazon and Netflix are selling naked with their own brands and products, and you need to step up your digital game so as not to get crushed by these ruthless behemoths.

STORYTELLING LESSON #4: ITERATE TO EXCEL (AND USE EXCEL TO ITERATE)

If telling a great story now seems like a nearly impossible task, bear in mind a couple of points. First, you don't have to do a ton of special research to tell a great story. These stories, as I'm describing them here, flow naturally out of the actual running of your business. Yes, you're breaking away from day-to-day work to organize and perfect your pitch, but you're incorporating insights and knowledge you've gained by working on your business, and you'll also likely be able to take any new insights or knowledge generated in the course of the pitch process and apply them to improve the business.

Second, you don't have to get the story perfect your first time out. There are plenty of potential investors out there, and you can't talk to all of them at once. That means you can approach storytelling as an iterative process.

> When engaging in conversations, notice which ideas and language seem to resonate, and which don't. The next time out, adjust your pitch accordingly. Pay attention as well to recurring themes in the feedback you get. Are investors poking holes in the part of your story that concerns your competitive advantage, say, or the part where you describe how you plan to source your product as you scale? Take note and be prepared to address those concerns going forward.

Renata Black, co-founder of the women's direct-to-consumer undergarment brand EBY, is a firm believer in learning as you go during the pitch process. As she tells me, "You never take the meeting you want the most at the beginning [of the fundraising process]. You've got to pitch and pitch, finding people who will ask you the toughest questions," so that you can learn and be prepared for anything. She goes on: "Take your time, because you're really going to screw up at the beginning. As well versed as you are, or as well educated or confident, as much as you know the numbers, there's going to be so many questions that you're just not going to know how to answer. So you just need to practice beyond belief."[5]

Black estimates that she pitched EBY to investors sixty or seventy times. Early on, the skepticism she encountered and the "no" responses she received dispirited her. After a while, though, she found that she could take the rejection in stride, and she focused on learning from every meeting. She began taking notes on her pitch experiences, recording all that she had learned in an Excel spreadsheet. "I made sure that every meeting counted," she says, even if the encounter didn't produce an investment offer or some other tangible benefit. The spreadsheet also allowed her to track investor responses. That way, if she ever sat across the table from a particular investor again, she'd recall his or her previous concerns and make sure to speak to them. Investors came away dazzled, impressed by her keen memory and listening ability, as well as by her ability to refine her pitch and address what *they* cared about. Over time, her pitch improved, leading to a successful fundraise.

STORYTELLING LESSON #5: DRAW ON YOUR NETWORK . . . AND BEYOND

Even if you dedicate yourself to constantly improving your pitch, getting the story exactly right is still a challenge. But you don't need to do it alone. Draw on your network for help with every part of starting a direct-to-consumer business, including pitch preparation. Eric Osman is the founder and CEO of Mockingbird, a direct-to-consumer baby stroller company. He was "overwhelmed positively" by the amount of support he received from his network.[6] Again and again, friends referred him to people they knew who could help him with some part of his business that he was trying to learn about or master. This support "funnels into your pitches to VCs," Osman says, in effect helping you convey an aura of expertise and competence. "By the time you're talking to [investors], even if there's something in particular you don't know really well yet, simply being able to say you've talked to someone who does can make you much more confident in discussing it."

Certainly, the network around Hubble helped Ben and me assemble key elements of what we'd need when speaking with investors. My best friend from college, Paul Rodgers, a computer engineer, helped set up the test site for our initial marketing test, and later became Hubble's first chief technology officer. Ben's best friend from middle school, Dan Rosen, took care of the graphics for that test, and is now our head of creative. My mom, Amy Genkins, a career general counsel, agreed to do Hubble's trademark search; she later served as our first general counsel. My husband, Mark Severs, was our first head of finance. Ben's dad, Bruce Cogan, helped us brainstorm hundreds of names for our business, including Hubble.

> Don't just rely on your own network. If you need folks with particular perspectives, look them up and approach them, even if you share no previous connection. Be shameless about it! People love new ideas, and many will get excited about working on them.

Questions about manufacturers? We looked at who was filing the FDA approvals for the independents and emailed him. Not every instance of cold outreach will yield a response, not every response will help you, and not everyone will brim with excitement about your new business, but plenty of folks will, especially industry insiders. Chances are many of them have been thinking in very similar terms about how their space needs to change.

So, there you have it: five storytelling lessons that will hopefully work some crazy magic, taking you from someone with an idea and a drive to sell naked into—poof!—someone with an idea, a drive to sell naked, *and* some money in your pocket to help you do it. Many people wave their magic PowerPoint wand and come up short, but you can rise to the occasion. Do your homework. Understand your audience. Preempt their concerns and critiques. Craft a narrative that has them nodding their heads and hanging on your every word. You may not be J. K. Rowling or James Patterson. But an advocate for selling naked who truly gets what will make your business successful, and who can speak articulately about it? Yeah, you can be that.

(THE NAKED TRUTH)

When it comes to pitching a direct-to-consumer business, an array of facts and figures piled high like corned beef in a deli sandwich is not as appetizing to potential investors as you might think. What you need is a narrative that speaks to the simple concerns that investors have about your business: How exactly will you wheedle your way into your industry and make money? And how will you prevent others from doing the same thing? Corporate funders have additional questions on their minds: How will your proposed venture *not* totally screw up our existing, profit-belching dynamo? And can little old *us* really pull this off with the talent and processes we possess? It's not always easy to address these concerns, but if you focus on improving your pitch bit by bit and draw on your network to do it, you'll come ever closer to spinning a story that will leave funders satisfied and reaching for their checkbooks. So, fire up that PowerPoint.

CHAPTER 4

COMPENSATE EXPERTS AND PARTNERS

IF YOU'VE EVER bought nutritional supplements at a drugstore, you know how annoying it can be. You sort through an alphabet soup of vitamin and mineral products just to find the one you need, and then you somehow have to choose from among numerous competing brands you've never heard of before. The underlying science also seems complicated. Should you take vitamin C if you need an immune system boost? Vitamin B_{12}? Both? Something else? Even if you know you need vitamin C, can you trust what's really in that little white pill you're swallowing? How do you know the pills are delivering results after you've taken them?

After years at the direct-to-consumer clothing company Bonobos, Craig Elbert thought he could make life easier for consumers by selling vitamins and other supplements naked. His idea: create a website where consumers could sign up, provide basic information about their health needs, receive guidance on what kinds of supplements to take, and then subscribe to the products, receiving a shipment every month with a personalized pill pack for each day. Taking supplements would never be easier, and if Elbert did it right, consumers would feel more secure that they were taking high-quality supplements that were right for them.

Throughout 2016, Elbert and his partner, Akash Shah, worked on developing an online subscription business for supplements. "There was a huge education period of meeting with doctors and nutritionists," Elbert recalls. "We wanted to understand where more research existed, where there was less, what does the supply chain look like, who should we be talking to, how do we navigate this world."[1] Did Elbert and Shah talk to consumers? Yep, they did. They went deep, interviewing individual consumers, surveying groups of customers, and performing segmentation analyses. As a demand experiment, they built an initial version of their website under a different brand name, "just to see how people interact with it and how [they] would think about our product." While they were performing all this research, they also fleshed out a number of other parts of the business, refining their product, setting up a supply chain, and designing the brand's look and feel.

In Craig's view, one of the most significant challenges he and Akash tackled during their pre-launch year was bringing on board people with expertise in nutrition. Consumers needed to trust the specific purchase recommendations the website was presenting, and they couldn't unless recognized experts stood behind those recommendations, and everything else on the site. Hoping to create a formal scientific advisory board, Craig read a Harvard research report on vitamins and supplements and sent cold emails to the professors who wrote it, asking for a meeting. He heard back, but these experts weren't that thrilled to participate. "It took a full year to really get them to understand that we were serious and credible on this," Craig says. "It took multiple trips up to Boston, meeting with those guys . . . and then also getting connected with a functional medicine doctor via a conference."

Craig and Akash had to show these experts that they were not snake oil salesmen and were going to bring some honesty and transparency to a category that had long lacked it. The founders succeeded, convincing two Tufts University nutrition experts, an expert at Harvard's School of Public Health, a naturopathic physician, and an integrative medicine physician to join their advisory board. But they weren't done soliciting experts for help. Neither Craig nor Akash understood the nuances of sourcing and manufacturing supplements. Sure, they could wing it, but this was a core part of their business, and Craig far preferred to bring in people who had done it before. If he had done the sourcing himself, he "would've screwed it up, and it would've frankly been dangerous because I would not have known the right people to talk to, how to get quality ingredients, what questions to ask." Hopping on LinkedIn (your new best friend, if it isn't already), Craig sent a cold email to two longtime employees of the supplement company New Chapter, which he admired. He drove up to meet the pair in Vermont, where they lived, and "bugged them, tried to show them that this was credible." Within several months, they, too, had signed on.

Craig and Akash's business, Care/of, launched in late 2016. Looking back, Craig reflects on the key role played by these two sets of experts—nutritionists and supply-chain/production veterans. The scientific advisory board not only helped him and Akash determine what products to recommend to consumers, but also provided them with a great deal of general knowledge about the category. Meanwhile, the supply chain experts ensured that the actual product got made. Simply put, Craig says, "we couldn't have created the company without either of them."

YOU, TOO, NEED EXPERTS AND PARTNERS

It's tempting to think you can sell naked all by yourself. How hard can it be to throw up a website and start hawking? But succeeding with your business—that's a different story. You've heard the old expression that the attorney who represents him- or herself has a fool for a client. Something similar holds true for entrepreneurs who try to sell naked by themselves. If you're a product person, you're probably not also a brand or marketing expert. If you're good at branding, that doesn't mean your operations chops are there. It's impossible to know everything about every topic, and as I've seen, it's foolish to try to wing it in areas you don't know. You don't have room to make mistakes in core areas of operations while you're assembling your budding organization and building out your business plan. Some mistakes can kill you—like failing to deliver on ten thousand orders because your product is messed up, or getting hit with a product recall because your packaging breaks the law.

> Do yourself a favor: before your business sputters out or goes off track, bring on people who've done it before and can help you get the job done right.

When Ben and I founded Hubble, we engaged multiple experts—and paid them for the privilege. We didn't know much about contact lenses, but we sure as heck wanted to sell them. That meant we needed to collaborate with industry insiders. Many investors competed to lead our seed round, but the investors who won—Josh Kazam at Two River and Len Potter and Drew Tarlow at Wildcat Capital Management, the family office for TPG Capital founder David Bonderman—were the ones who connected us with the former chief medical officer of Bausch + Lomb, Dr. Brian Levy. Brian helped us come to one of the most important decisions informing our business model: whether to sell daily or monthly lenses. As he explained, medical science had long viewed daily disposable lenses as healthier and more comfortable and convenient, but pricing and the hassles of purchasing daily lenses had kept many consumers from buying them. When we heard that, we knew we had to solve this problem and make daily-wear lenses cheaper and easier than ever to buy. Brian also traveled with us to meet our top potential suppliers, which is why we managed to sign a digital exclusive with our manufacturer, St. Shine. It wasn't two twentysomethings in the room sitting across from their management—it was two twentysomethings and a world-recognized expert.

A consultant who had worked with a couple of dozen international contacts companies on the FDA side gave us a rundown of the supplier landscape—whom we could trust, who had manufacturing scale, and who had good product. He and Brian also helped us verify that potential partners were compliant with FDA regulations, a necessity if we were to do business in the United States. We were still two dumb kids, but at least we were smart enough to ask for help.

We sought out investors who would bring real expertise to our business in later financing rounds as well. It's no coincidence that Rick Heitzmann at FirstMark is on our board and that Ellie Wheeler at Greycroft serves as an observer. First-

Mark was a seed stage investor in Shopify and since then has been a central player in the rise of the direct-to-consumer economy. Over the past decade or so, Greycroft has leveraged old media relationships to become a venture leader in the new media world. As we've found, money isn't just money. Our board relationships have played a key role in helping us drive the business forward.

If you haven't connected with experts yet, get out there! The success of your business really does depend on it. And get your checkbook out or be ready to part with a chunk of equity. The best experts—the ones who will really help you—are seasoned professionals and perhaps even the world's top authorities on their subjects. They need to get paid, or they might not feel great about participating. Writing a check or parting with equity hurts in the moment, but in the long run you'll look back on this decision and feel immensely grateful. I know I do.

A SHORT PEP TALK FOR FOUNDERS

I see some of you out there in book land shaking your heads. Sure, you say, some founders and marketing executives setting up direct-to-consumer ventures might need experts, but not all of them. After all, Hubble and Care/of are special cases: Hubble is in a highly regulated industry, and Care/of is a wellness-related business where credibility among consumers clearly hinges on expertise. But any little kid can set up a successful lemonade stand with a minimum of parental guidance. Likewise, if you're selling something basic like T-shirts, cosmetics, or bathing suits, why can't you save your money and equity and wing it yourself?

I'd bet there are few direct-to-consumer ventures that couldn't benefit from expertise, even those that aren't in "special case" industries. That's because direct-to-consumer is a competitive space. If you're not accessing something special, whether it's industry knowledge, superior manufacturing at lower cost, or special distribution, it's very hard to set yourself apart in consumers' eyes. Since you and your co-founders probably don't have everything you need to pull off this "something special," you'll need to seek it out—and pay for it.

Founders are ambitious and perhaps even delusional. We're not, um, the most *egoless* people in the world. And in some ways, that's a good thing, because what gets everyone excited about our businesses are precisely the stories we tell. Yet our ambition can also cause us to stumble when we attempt to solve problems that exceed our knowledge, abilities, and experience. At some level, we need to ground ourselves, tying our vision to something tangible that we can actually accomplish. One way we do that is by taking on tangible tasks, like finding suppliers, running demand tests, or mapping out a launch. But another way is by partnering with experts who have already worked in the markets we're seeking to enter, have seen all of the pitfalls, and have navigated around them. We might well find that some of these experts are too jaundiced from their past battles, and so a bit of our hubris of ignorance is valuable. But hearing their perspectives can prove valuable as a way of orienting ourselves. And in many cases, their expertise will power our businesses forward in ways we never could on our own.

THE STUFF YOU ABSOLUTELY, POSITIVELY NEED TO KNOW

If you resist the idea of paying for expertise, you might not have fully considered the range of knowledge you'll need to succeed with selling naked. Let's go through it, starting with the more obvious regulatory stuff.

If you're selling a medical device or prescription product, you'd better make sure you're playing by the rules, or you'll be out of business quick. Someone on your team must understand how to deal with the FDA, and you'll also probably need attorneys who have experience dealing with regulators. Think I'm kidding? You need only say "Theranos" to send shivers running up any VC's spine.

More generally, businesses that sell naked are advertising and selling to consumers, which puts them under the purview of the Federal Trade Commission. No, you can't just say anything you want in your ads—the government has measures in place to protect consumers.

State laws might also bear on your business. If you have a great business idea about selling alcoholic beverages, hold up: booze is *highly* regulated under state law. Guns? Highly regulated. Medical marijuana? Highly regulated. It's obvious that states would keep tight control over these areas, but in some states shampooers, funeral attendants, and interior designers require licenses as well.[2] Since you don't have time to make yourself an expert on every last state and local law that applies to your business, have attorneys review what you're doing (or planning to do) and confirm that it's kosher.

Hopefully, competent, experienced attorneys will help you figure out how to operate within existing legal frameworks.

But if they can't, you might try to change the law (something that's more realistic if you're working at the state or municipal level). Here you'll need access to an experienced lobbyist who understands what actions to take and which key political players you'll need to cultivate in order to get the laws changed. Companies in the telemedicine space do a lot of state-level lobbying, as do big-name operations like Airbnb and Uber.

Beyond help navigating regulations, companies that sell naked usually need outside help to secure the products they're selling. What does the supply landscape look like in your industry? Is there an abundance of suppliers, both scaled and independent? If supply is relatively scarce and provided by just a few independent players, which suppliers have the best quality, and what production capacity can these players deliver as opposed to the scaled, best-in-class providers? Can you land exclusive deals to protect you from competitors? Where are these suppliers located? If both domestic and foreign suppliers exist, does it make sense economically to go with cheaper foreign options (and yes, they'll usually be cheaper on a per-unit basis), factoring in higher costs due to tariffs and shipping? How long will shipping take when you place orders? These questions can be difficult to answer fully if you're unfamiliar with the terrain, which is why seasoned professionals in these areas can help you land the best possible deals with the best possible suppliers.

Branding is another big area in which you might wish to invest in expertise if you don't possess it yourself. You'll certainly need a branding agency, but you might also wish to have branding expertise available to you in-house, especially if you're in an industry already teeming with meaningful, highly developed brands. To get your business started, you'll need to come up with a brand name and logo, and you'll need to translate this brand into physical packaging for your product. You'll also need to develop a digital store that is optimized for mobile devices. Getting all of this done is both time-consuming and expensive—it could easily take six months and cost about $150,000–200,000. Since branding is likely your biggest cost outside of inventory before your business goes live, you'll want to choose your agency well, and draw on as much expertise as possible within your own organization. Start-ups that sell naked need not just creative partners, but also, as Carolyn Rush, VP of creative strategy at Worn Creative, notes, "a strategic partner in building the brand. Because when you are building a direct-to-consumer brand, the messaging, the storytelling, the look and feel is super-strategic. It's based on all the business goals."[3]

Beyond these big areas, your business will need help in a number of other operational areas, including performance marketing, fulfillment, information technology, customer service, accounting, and human resources. In many of these cases, consultants and off-the-shelf products and services can get the job done for the time being—no need to obtain special expertise beyond that. I'll talk about how to get the help you need, and the importance of not trying to build every last system your company uses yourself, in Chapter 6.

MOTIVATING EXPERTS

Now that we've covered the areas in which you might wish to secure expertise, we get to the not-so-fun part: paying for it. An obvious approach is to hire experts, but you might not have the cash, and the best experts likely have no interest in working for a humble start-up. If this is the case, then there are several other options to consider.

First, you could offer up-front compensation on a month-to-month or quarterly basis, with no obligation beyond that. The lack of security under this arrangement will incentivize your expert to perform well for you, while limiting your capital requirements. We compensate some of our marketing partners in this way—for instance, adjusting their budgets dramatically over relatively short periods of time based on who's been performing well. We're happy to pay these partners well for strong performance, but we need the ability to shift budget (and compensation) away from them if their performance lags.

To build a closer and potentially more fruitful relationship, you might dispense with an up-front fee and propose a revenue-sharing arrangement. Make your expert a joint venture partner, building the business together and giving him or her a cut of the revenue you generate. The risk here is that you might dramatically overcompensate (or undercompensate) your experts, since you can't predict what kind of margins you'll see as your business matures.

Let's say you enter into a joint venture with a partner assuming 20 percent margins (including marketing spend), and so you take 10 percent of revenue as your share. You know roughly what everything outside marketing will look like. Let's also say the product sells for $100, and 70 percent of that is margin. If your cost to acquire a customer ends up running about $20, you'll feel screwed because you're getting $10 out of $70 in margin. If the cost to acquire a customer ends up running $61, the business isn't totally kaput, but your partner is actually *losing* $1 on every sale.

Striking a profit-sharing agreement might seem like a solution, but this, too, is problematic, as you might get bogged down later on in debates about what you're counting as costs to apply against revenues. If your partner is a large organization like a Hollywood studio, what counts as costs? The days filming, sure. And the special effects as well. But what about the costs of the development team that reads potential scripts? Or the studio executives? Or the auditors the studio uses to examine its books every year? Suddenly your profitable project is a money-loser because you've been loaded with the studio's overhead.

A third option that Hubble has used is to part with a chunk of our equity. Many founders hate that idea, and it's painful as well for venture capitalists, who tend to value equity dearly (or they wouldn't buy it). It's true that if your business is a big hit, you might be paying a heavy price. But if you're trying to motivate an expert to help the business succeed, and you want to align closely with a partner or you just don't have enough cash to throw around, offering an equity stake might well be an option to consider. At Hubble, we valued our expert partners highly, giving them equity grants, and have not regretted it. Having their talent and know-how has allowed us to create a far bigger business, leaving us better off even though we own less of the business ourselves than we otherwise would have.

SHARING EQUITY REALLY CAN MAKE SENSE

Many of the founders profiled in this book have chosen to offer equity stakes to experts and have been extremely happy with the results. When Melanie Travis started Andie, she knew almost nothing about manufacturing swimwear. To work around that gap, she was able to strike deals both with an experienced swimsuit designer and with one of the world's largest swimwear suppliers. In exchange for a portion of her business, this company took care of the entire product side of her business for her, sourcing materials, manufacturing swimsuits, and distributing finished product to her customers at cost. Talk about a partner!

When I spoke with Melanie, she seemed tickled that she didn't have to think about production any longer and could instead "focus exclusively on creating a brand that would continue to thrive online." She partnered closely with her manufacturing expert and supplier, coordinating constantly on production issues, and even working in the same physical location (her partner gave Melanie and her team space in their office).

With this arrangement, Melanie says, "we're able to be really nimble with them and try things." For instance, Melanie might notice that consumers are responding well to a certain color of swimsuit and think of trying out a similar shade. Her manufacturing partner can quickly create a few sample suits in that new color for Melanie to sell, enabling her to move forward with the experiment. "It's really a partnership where I use the digital piece to understand what sells really well, what works, what customers want. They do the product piece to get it out, get it done on time, which is something I never could have done before that." In addition to this, Melanie's deal with her supply-side expert increases Andie's margins, making each customer more profitable. As a result, she can drop her prices, giving the consumer a more attractive deal, and pay a higher cost to acquire customers, further fueling growth. To investors, advantages such as these are attractive, as they increase the likelihood that your business will break free of the pack. On the strength of her supplier partnership, Travis was able to raise $2.1 million in venture funding.

Another entrepreneur who traded equity for expertise is Demetri Karagas, co-founder of Keeps, a subscription service for men's hair loss products. To lend credibility to his brand, Karagas secured the participation of Dr. Jerry Shapiro, a dermatologist who "literally wrote the book" on hair loss and restoration that most dermatologists consult during their training. Shapiro signed on as a medical consultant in exchange for equity and helped Demetri build a diagnostic framework that would allow his company to "understand which treatments we should offer and make sure that we really are living up to [our] mission of providing the highest quality of care."[4]

Demetri went on to work out a similar arrangement with the company's branding agency, partially compensating them in equity so that they would be "invested in the long-term success of the company." The arrangement has been "a great decision," Demetri says, because this agency is now "continually investing in making sure the brand continues to be nurtured and developed over time."

Looking ahead, Demetri anticipates launching other brands (in addition to having launched the migraine brand Cove) and continuing to offer equity in exchange for expertise. "We'll be finding the world's leading experts in the [medical conditions we're addressing]," he says, "and working with them to make sure that we build out a framework for delivering a consistent, high-quality of care to a really large number of people."

Although equity, joint ventures, and profit-sharing work well for founders, marketers inside large corporations might find these arrangements challenging when trying to set up new ventures, as they clash with traditional corporate approaches to compensation. Corporations are more excited to pay generous compensation as a base, with limited upside potential, because their primary goal is to minimize risk to the business. Since employees and executives aren't receiving a big piece of the upside down the road, they have no special incentive to make high-risk decisions that will lead to big future payouts. And they always run the risk of losing their paycheck, so they tend to focus on reducing the risk of a big failure in their area of oversight that will cause the company to fire or demote them.

To some degree, such an incentive structure works well for large incumbents, since its employees work on large businesses with lots of value to protect. At the same time, corporations will have to venture beyond their comfort zones when obtaining expertise, including when that expertise is an entire team from a successful direct-to-consumer business. Corporates can try to establish teams outside the corporate structure with equity-like upside, but ultimately responsibility for the team will devolve to a manager inside the corporate structure whose compensation will incline him or her to avoid risk. If we set up Crazy Go Wild Labs as an independent partner to XYZ Megacorp, Crazy Go Wild Labs needs a human being in place managing the relationship on the XYZ Megacorp side. If something goes wrong on the labs side, that team might be okay with it, since they're the scrappy, go-go start-up folks. But the person at XYZ Megacorp risks getting fired. At some point someone needs to assume responsibility within Megacorp for Megacorp's decisions, and it can be very hard to find a person comfortable taking on that risk. Ultimately, senior executives are often required to sign off on relatively small-budget projects. Not only do they have greater power and autonomy in the organization, but they also have more upside in their compensation.

It behooves companies to try to find ways around this challenge. Expertise matters, and it will be hard to attract the best people to take risks if you don't incentivize them properly. As Demetri reflects, you want to get "the right people who are really going to be able to help the company at those pivotal moments, so you want them to be truly invested. It often makes a lot more sense than just paying someone an hourly rate"—or a regular salary, for that matter. That goes for corporates *and* independent upstarts.

FIVE QUICK-AND-DIRTY TIPS FOR GETTING THE EXPERTISE YOU NEED

Whether you're an entrepreneur or a corporate marketing executive, how do you find the right people, and how do you convince them to help you?

TIP #1: FIGURE OUT YOUR "CAN'T SCREW UPS"

Although every business is unique, all enterprises must handle the same basic functions mentioned earlier—product, fundraising, legal/regulatory, marketing, technology, customer service, and back office. In the context of your business, which of these are absolutely essential to get perfect, either to avoid going out of business or to achieve a decisive advantage in the marketplace?

> Make a list of your top three functions, and then create an inventory of skills, knowledge, and expertise possessed by people on your team. If gaps exist between these two lists, consider paying for expert help.

TIP #2: WORK OFF THE PITCH

Try pitching your company in a few low-pressure meetings, telling your story to long-shot potential investors. What questions do you get? Are there any parts of your story that multiple investors rip into? These might be places where you need expert help. When you're done whining about the critical response, search out experts who can help you strengthen these pieces. You'll improve not only the business, but also your ability to sell yourself the next time you pitch. Finding the information you need educates you and improves your ability to run your business, while showing investors that you're resourceful, that you have hustle, and that you can solve problems. You might not know anything about vitamins, but if you've managed to convince five top experts in the field to share their knowledge and lend their names to your business, you've achieved something.

Investors also like to see credible experts associated with your brand, as in their minds it reduces risk. It certainly made a difference to our investors that we had a heavy hitter from Bausch + Lomb working with us. Similarly, David Heath, cofounder and CEO of the direct-to-consumer sock company Bombas, was lucky enough to have a family friend who ran the venerable sock brand Gold Toe (a fact he discovered only after coming up with the idea for his company). "I think everybody knows the Gold Toe brand," he tells me, "so when you're starting a sock company and saying, 'Hey, I've got a guy in my corner who ran arguably one of the largest sock companies in the world' . . . I think, at least on the product side, it provides a certain amount of legitimacy" for investors.[5]

Think of some big names who could provide your brand with this kind of legitimacy, and then go out there and try to sign them up.

TIP #3: SCOUR YOUR NETWORK

If you've decided that you need an expert and you aren't sure how to find one, get out a blank sheet of paper and jot down the name of every person you've already met since you began working on your business. Much of the time, the right person will be in your network already, unbeknownst to you, or else someone in your network might have useful connections. You'll never know unless you systematically review your contact list. My literary agent on this book, Todd Shuster, was the friend of a friend, someone I saw at regular holiday gatherings. When I realized I needed an agent, my husband, Mark, pointed out that Todd wasn't just a nice guy, but a great agent as well. Turned out he was more than great—he's a top performer in his field. Who knew?

TIP #4: BE SHAMELESS

LinkedIn and other social media are great ways to find and connect with experts, but there are all sorts of other ways to make contact with experts once you've identified them. Sometimes I've guessed their email addresses and sent them unsolicited messages. Other times I've emailed sell-side equity analysts who cover a company and asked them to make an introduction. I've also requested introductions from investors, investment bankers, or consultants who have worked with the experts I'm targeting in the past. If you're an expert and I need your knowledge or experience, make no mistake—I'll get to you! (Insert horror film music.)

This kind of detective work takes time, and some people might brush you off before you find the expert of your dreams, but that's okay. Shameless people build winning companies (so long as they don't generate restraining orders). And while many folks might blow off LinkedIn messages, I've forged some of my most important relationships by cold-messaging LinkedIn members or just going through the cold messages I receive from others.

The shamelessness doesn't end once you've made contact. You also must convince the expert that you're worth the time it takes him or her to respond. My advice: brag. If you went to Harvard Business School, ran a $50 million business in your last corporate job, or are running a venture-backed start-up, don't be afraid to mention these credentials. I had no problem telling people that I had gone to Harvard Law School or ran a venture-backed start-up. I even put these credentials in the subject line of emails: "Harvard Law student curious about XYZ" or "Venture-backed start-up founder looking to know more about XYZ" or "Bridgewater/Harvard Law/venture-backed founder" (just a pure credentials list). Bragging like this might seem a tad douchey, or more than a tad, but it delivers results.

TIP #5: CASUAL CONVERSATIONS COUNT, TOO

I've emphasized paying for expertise in this chapter, but you can access a ton of knowledge at no cost just by chatting with folks.

> If you want to know more about a subject, find someone on LinkedIn with a CV that seems on point and message that person in order to pick his or her brain. You'll be surprised how many people will message you back, happy to.

On one occasion, I wanted to understand how much information advertisers could extract from credit card networks.

Can they see which stores consumers frequented, and what they bought at those stores? I reached out to folks on LinkedIn who worked at Amex and Visa (I happened to know someone who was at MasterCard and pinged him, too). The person at Amex ignored me, but the Visa guy messaged back. I ended up talking with him and then another team in his organization. They referred me to two companies outside Visa doing cool things in the space.

Another time, I read an interesting article about a company looking to do gene therapy in pets. CRISPR gene-editing technology promises to lead to a range of exciting potential medical treatments, but the pathway to approval is incredibly long in humans; it's somewhat shorter in pets. Reaching out to the CEO on LinkedIn, I came away with a more detailed overview of the progress this company had made commercializing gene therapy treatments in animals.

I've advocated bragging, but this chapter has really been about checking your ambition and ego enough to invite some more experienced people to help you launch your business. Experts can make miracles happen for founders selling naked—if you let them. In that regard, here's a final story that I like.

Eric Osman of the stroller company Mockingbird had no special knowledge about his product. He spent four months immersing himself in stroller manufacturing, but as it turned out, that was nothing compared to what the experts he consulted with were able to teach him. One of his investors happened to know people who ran a sizable and successful children's products company. These people, Eric says, "shot us into a level of expertise and knowledge that I think would've taken me a long time to get to, particularly when it came to safety and compliance, which was so important for us since we were entering the stroller category."[6]

Would Eric have managed to launch his business without this contact? Absolutely. But as he reports, having them as a partner has made a huge difference: "With them, we were able to move faster, leverage a lot of the insights and data that they've already had from their prior experience, and walk into this with so much more trust that we were going to get it right."

You need this piece of mind, too. Don't do it alone. Get it right for your customers and investors. Get an expert on your team.

(THE NAKED TRUTH)

Selling naked can be a smart move, but to do it right, you also have to *get smart* by paying for the expertise you lack. Yes, I know you're immensely talented and used to figuring things out as you go. Much of the time, that attitude will be enough. But when it comes to core areas of the business, you can buy yourself out of a ton of heartache by bringing an expert on board. You might compensate experts up front, but revenue-sharing arrangements and equity grants can also work. Corporate players might find these arrangements a little frightening or at least unusual. Try to work around that: you need these experts on your side, and it's worth parting with a bit of upside to get them. Whether you're an entrepreneur or on a corporate team, assess where you most need outside help, and then hustle to get it. It's not hard, but you might have to brag a bit. No harm in that!

CHAPTER 5

WORRY ABOUT THE PIE EXPLODING

LET'S SAY YOU nail your pitch with investors. Congratulations: you're the dog that's caught the fire truck. Now you have to figure out what you want out of investors, and what you're willing to give up to get it.

That's simple, many start-up teams say. In negotiating for funding, don't worry about raising the maximum amount of capital. Your biggest priority is to retain as much ownership as possible. It's all about maximizing upside.

Wrong!

Apologies if that comes across as judgmental, but: wrong, wrong, wrong, wrong, wrong, wrong. (Wrong.)

It's understandable that so many founders fetishize equity. When investors plow money into young companies, they make a relatively large number of bets, knowing that many of the start-ups in their portfolio will flop. All they need to achieve outsized overall returns is for one investment to become the next Twitter or Uber. Founders are in a different position—they don't have as many shots on goal. As a result, when they have an idea that seems born for greatness, they hear these internal voices shouting, "Ride it!" This leads them to hoard equity when negotiating with venture firms. They look at examples like Jeff Bezos, who held on to as much equity as possible at Amazon, and assume that more equity leads to enormous wealth, ignoring companies like Gawker that didn't take outside capital in an effort to maintain high equity stakes and paid the price.

Large ownership stakes come with a serious downside. Equity in a company is tantamount to risk. The more equity you possess, the more risk you shoulder. At the extreme, you might bear so much risk that your company's failure could devastate your personal finances and reputation. The key when fundraising is thus to *mitigate the risk* you're taking on in your shiny new venture. If your pie—your beautiful little pie—winds up exploding, you want to escape with the least amount of damage, so that you can proceed to your next endeavor. Dole out hefty slices of equity to investors in exchange for their money and other good stuff. Let them share in the risk. You might get a smaller hunk of the upside in the event the business takes off, but you'll still have a life if it doesn't.

Want another metaphor? Think about equity as manure. To paraphrase Thornton Wilder, it's not worth a damn unless it's spread around, encouraging young things to grow. So stop hoggin' and start spreadin'!

WAIT, IS HE FULL OF IT?

I assure you that I'm not. Let's say you've self-funded your start-up, plowing $350,000 of your own money into trying to launch your business. You used $150,000 in savings plus $175,000 from cashing out your 401(k) (you've done all right for yourself so far) and an additional $25,000 in credit card debt. In return for that investment, you get 100 percent of your business's upside. Every dollar of valuation goes into your bank account when your business sells or some other liquidity event happens. Great, right?

Nope. If your business sells for $100 million, you get $100 million. But let's say that you sold 50 percent of your business for capital to grow, so that those risky equity dollars didn't all come out of your own pocket. Instead of risking your entire $350,000 in available capital, you got to hold on to your entire 401(k). The business still sells for $100 million, and you get $50 million. Is your life meaningfully worse off with a $50 million payday instead of a $100 million one? What is the incremental value of that additional $50 million to you? To your family?

Now suppose the business doesn't work (news flash: it probably won't). What's the cost of that $350,000 to you? To your family? When you become obsessed with hogging equity, you're hogging all that risk, too. How great does it feel going to your retired parents to tell them you need their help meeting the minimum payments on your credit card bills, since you have no other cash available? This assumes, of course, that you're lucky enough to have parents with the resources to pitch in.

Reputational risks also matter here. Let's say you hog all that precious equity. You bet on yourself and you're right. You now have a business that you're selling for $100 million, and you're a flippin' boss and everyone can bow down. If you gave up 50 percent equity, guess what? You. Are. Still. A. Boss. On the other hand, if you hog all that equity and the business doesn't work out, you're far more screwed than you would have been if you'd parted with 50 percent of that equity. To the rest of the world, you look dumb—dumb as your dumb, dumb idea. You're back on the job market, the real one where you have to turn up at 9:00 A.M. every day, explaining to potential employers why you left your great job to chase a start-up dream that everyone told you was dumb. You're also reassuring potential employers, in turn, that you're not going to quit in six months when another leprechaun whispers in your ear. If you had sold 50 percent of your company to a respected venture firm, then the two of you would look dumb together. But not *that* dumb. To the outside world, it would appear that you had a misadventure, but an understandable one. After all, someone else believed in your idea, too.

MY SOB STORY

I understand the downside scenario, because I've lived it. I committed the mortal sin of failing to spread the risk—not because I screwed up my negotiations with willing investors, but because I couldn't find any investors to begin with. In the fall of 2010, as a first-year student at Harvard Law, I landed an internship at Bridgewater, the world's largest hedge fund. By this time, I'd bounced around a lot—I'd been an aspiring filmmaker, then an aspiring management consultant, then a law student. To the outside world, it looked like I couldn't stick with any pursuit for very long. And then, after just a year at Bridgewater, I took another leap, this time into a start-up venture. A venture capitalist I met made a pitch to me that I should build a hedge fund risk management tool with a piece of software he had invested in. I quit my (then full-time) job at Bridgewater and got started without lining up financing.

I wasn't able to build any useful applications with the software, but in the process of playing with it, I met another recent Bridgewater refugee, a really sharp programmer. We hit it off, and we thought it might be fun to wade into systematic trading together. At this point, I was unemployed, with an unemployed boyfriend (later husband), living off savings from my time at Bridgewater. We cobbled together a proprietary trading strategy and went out to fundraise. We met with Blackstone, Millennium, and some smaller groups. All of them told us to come back in two years when we had a track record.

Believing in our research, we buckled down, passing the hat around to family and friends. We lived off our savings to cover our expenses, but at least we had some cash to trade—and of course, we had that wonderful equity all to ourselves. After month one, we were flat. After month two, we were flat. After month three, we were flat. (You get the idea.) By month seven, we were down a couple of percentage points, and I was almost out of money for living expenses. It was time to look for a job. But at this point, not only was I dead broke, but I looked dumb as hell.

If I'd just stuck it out a couple of years at Bridgewater, I would have had a much easier time at this point convincing someone to hire me. But with my short tenure at Bridgewater, my previous flitting around, and, now, my fruitless year in business, I looked unstable to potential employers, even if I had a degree from Columbia and time served at Harvard Law. When I interviewed, I was forced into a corner, asked to explain why I wasn't going to quit whatever job I was applying for after a few months to pursue some different opportunity that was equal parts quixotic and idiotic. If I'd spread the equity in my trading operation with a name-brand investor, it would have looked as if I had really been on to something big and had seized an opportunity. Upon discovering that no investor was willing to take on some of the risk, I should have just shut the business down—I would have had far less explaining to do. As it turned out, I managed to convince the endowment team at my alma mater to hire me, but the job search experience was much dicier—and more unpleasant—than it had to be. My professional reputation had taken a big hit, and my employment options were limited—all because I was going to show the world I was a unique source of truth.

DON'T WORRY ABOUT CONTROL

Skeptics might protest that by giving away equity/risk, founders are also ceding their ability to make decisions about the company. Shouldn't they keep as much equity as possible to maintain control?

No! Even if founders hoard equity, they're almost guaranteed to lose control. It's extremely difficult to capitalize your business for growth while maintaining over 50 percent of equity. Even if you do, some of your investors will hold shares of stock that give them governing rights, which erodes your control.

> To entrepreneurs obsessed with control, I say: Don't fight a battle you're doomed to lose. Your ownership isn't what protects your leadership role as a founder. Your true power lies in your ability to drive your business successfully. If you can do that while holding on to preferential voting shares (shares that give you special voting rights), you'll stay in charge. If you can't, investors will depose you at some point, or your company will go bankrupt.

Travis Kalanick at Uber can tell you a thing or two about these realities. He had special governance rights but was still forced out as CEO because Uber suffered a wave of PR fiascos. The company needed financing, and investors wouldn't agree to it with him at the helm. Business fundamentals ultimately trump ownership. When accessing capital, forget about maintaining control. It's all about risk mitigation.

MORE CHANCES TO MESS UP

So far, I've focused on the bad stuff that can happen if your start-up tanks and you're left holding the bag all alone. There's also a brighter side. As Harvard Business School professor Noam Wasserman has written, "A founder who gives up more equity to attract cofounders, nonfounding hires, and investors builds a more valuable company than one who parts with less equity. The founder ends up with a more valuable slice, too."[1]

How does giving up more equity help you? Well, for one thing, you'll need capital to make your business a success—lots of it, and probably much more than you think. If you're signing for your seed capital, you don't know for sure if your idea will work or not. Even if you think you do, you don't know exactly *when* it will work. You'll have to experiment a bit to prove and refine your concept, but who knows how much of that experimentation will be enough to get customers buying and revenues and profits flowing? Raising more gives you more "runway" to mess up a couple of times and still find your groove in time for a Series A (as your first large round of venture funding is called). It also gives your reputation a boost. The more initial funding you receive, the more credibility you have in the eyes of potential investors and partners, even if the business flames out on you. The cliché these days (an accurate one) is that it's never been cheaper to start a business, but also never more expensive to scale one.

At Hubble, we applied initially to funds and accelerators like Y Combinator, receiving interviews from all of the ones we applied to, and gaining traction with venture firms as well. We told everyone that we wanted $500,000 on a $5 million "pre-money" valuation (the value of the company before the infusion of new capital)—in other words, we wanted to sell 9 percent of the business. When investors started biting, we upped our request to $1 million of capital on a $6 million valuation (a sale of 14 percent of the company). Then we upped it again to a $1.5 million capital sale on a valuation of $7 million (selling 18 percent of the company). In the end, we sold 30 percent of the company, receiving $3.5 million on a valuation of $8.2 million.

Yes, we sold much more of the company than we had initially wanted. But we got a higher valuation, a better-capitalized business, and a bigger, more prestigious seed round. That in turn would make future fundraising easier. Three months after our launch, when we raised our next round of capital, the Series A round, we still had $4 million in the bank, having raised another $3.7 million right before launch. That represented months of extra time to continue our experiments if we'd needed to. Fortunately, we didn't, but our reserves served us as a fantastic talking point when we were selling our Series A, allowing us to push up our company's valuation. We could credibly say that if we didn't obtain a high valuation for that round, we would just wait and raise more money later, using the cash we had in the bank to grow the business.

As other entrepreneurs find, having as much capital as possible on hand early on is not merely desirable, but essential. In 2012, Renata Black joined up with superstar actress Sofía Vergara to launch EBY, a direct-to-consumer company that sells high-quality seamless undergarments to women of all shapes and sizes on a subscription-based model. At launch, EBY had a tidy sum to play with—$2 million. Good thing, because as Black tells me, the company did "have some hiccups" and required three full months to figure them out. "I think that originally we would have hoped, like I guess any start-up, that you're able to launch and just rip it and kill it," she says. "But that wasn't our reality. . . . It was like putting on a new outfit. [We had] to test it out and see how [our website] was really going to fit us. And how we were going to fit the consumer, and what she was going to react to and what she wanted."[2]

Black wasn't exactly a newbie to the space, either. She had years of experience selling intimate apparel to women, and one of her key employees had built e-commerce businesses for well-known fashion brands like Elie Tahari. Yet she still needed that three months of runway to get the offering and the promotion right before the revenues started really flowing in. As she reflects, "There are some things [about a business] that you can't really foresee, and you're just relying on things to work, and if the technology doesn't work, then there's a [process of] trial and error."

By mid-2018, EBY had proven that a significant market exists—enough for EBY to one day succeed at scale. Sales were growing rapidly, and EBY was in a great position to raise more capital to fuel its future growth. Still, Black notes that if she could do it over, she would have tried to obtain even more capital early on. That initial $2 million gave her about eighteen months to get the business right. Additional funding might have allowed her and her team even more opportunity to generate the data they needed showing that they could retain customers acquired through their now efficient marketing machine. That data might have made her company's next round of funding significantly easier.

Black also observes that women entrepreneurs in particular should aggressively seek out the most funding possible. While it's hard for most entrepreneurs to raise money, female entrepreneurs have an extremely tough time of it. In 2017, they received only about 2 percent of all venture capital funding, despite owning 39 percent of all businesses in the United States.[3] Given that glaring gender bias, women need to grab funding when they can get it—the maximum amount. And by temperament, Black says, women are less inclined than men to aggressively pursue funding, because women tend to be more cautious and circumspect. "I think [that] given the opportunity to raise more money, [female entrepreneurs] can't go wrong . . . definitely lean into that."

KEEP THE EXPERTISE
(AS WELL AS YOUR HAIR)

In addition to buying you more time to experiment, taking on capital can buy you more of what we discussed in Chapter 4: expertise. Demetri Karagas's company Keeps, mentioned in that chapter, is a "full service healthcare company" founded in 2017 that "offers men the easiest way to keep their hair."[4] If you're a guy and you're noticing hair clumps collecting in the bottom of your tub after you take a shower, you can now navigate to the Keeps website, sign up for a consultation with a licensed physician, obtain a prescription, and receive a subscription to the appropriate hair-loss medications at rock-bottom prices (because Keeps has cut out all the retail and distribution middle-men). As Demetri tells me, he and co-founder Steve Gutentag initially were "pretty set on not taking venture funding and scaling."[5] They had some cash on hand from their previous jobs at Google—why not bootstrap it and keep the equity for themselves?

The two believed so heartily in that approach that they initially turned down meetings with venture firm Maveron. But when they took a closer look at Maveron, they realized that this fund, which was focused solely on start-ups that were consumer brands, could contribute valuable knowledge about the "hard-core branding" side of their business. Demetri and Steve were growth and operations guys—they had never really immersed themselves in the intricacies of branding. "We ended up raising more money than we had thought we were going to raise," Demetri says. "I know we would not be here today if we hadn't done that."

Since then, Maveron has become a highly valued partner for Keeps, jumping in and providing feedback and advice when necessary. "They were extremely involved during the process of developing the Keeps brand," Demetri says. "They just have an eye for this stuff, a mind for brand." Demetri sums up his experience by noting that, "if you're going to start a company, the odds are typically not in your favor. However, you can do things like making sure that you have the right partners" on board—including your funders.

CAN YOU SELL SECONDARY? DO IT!

The equity-versus-capital-risk trade-off I've been discussing continues well beyond your seed round. Every time you raise more capital, you'll hopefully face the choice of whether to gobble up more money or less. And if your business is really hitting its marks, you might even have the chance to sell some of your stock holdings on the private secondary market.

"Selling secondary" means that instead of raising additional capital for the business, you cash in some of your own shares, gaining liquidity and taking some of your own money off the table. Such sales gained notoriety about a decade ago in the tech world, and they've become ever more prominent, with payouts in the billions of dollars (to investors as well as founders and employees). In 2014, "secondary sales totaled $47 billion in 2014, up 80 percent from the previous year, according to investment bank Evercore."[6] In 2017, *The Wall Street Journal* reported that SoftBank had "committed $1.3 billion to buy out investors and employees at shared-office-space company WeWork Cos. as part of a $4.4 billion investment" and was poised to buy $10 billion in Uber shares in a secondary transaction.[7]

Secondary works like this: When you're selling equity to investors in a formal round of capitalization, you might find that the round becomes "oversubscribed"—that is, there's more demand for your company's equity than the amount of capital you're seeking to raise. You can approach investors and say, "Hey, you didn't get to buy as much of a stake in the primary round as you wanted, but you're in luck: I'll sell you some of my own common stock at a discount." Common stock are shares that lack all the governance rights and protections of the preferred shares that these investors or others bought in the primary round. Investors might not care that they don't gain governance rights with these shares, since they've already bought these protections (likely the bulk of their stock was acquired in the primary round), and they're getting a deal on the common stock, which typically trades at a discount to the preferred.

Why in the heck would you want to sell secondary shares when you've already raised capital—and parted with a chunk of your equity—in the primary round? Well, how about quality of life? As Oren Charnoff, principal at New York City–based Hanaco Ventures, observes, entrepreneurs work and work and work and work, all the while hopefully building up the value of their company.[8] And yet only when a "liquidity event" occurs (a sale or an initial public offering) do entrepreneurs have a chance to cash out. That could take years, and meanwhile, the entrepreneur has only paper wealth. As a result, in many cases his or her quality of life sucks. By selling a portion of your stock in the company on the secondary market, you lower your potential upside, but you also lower your risk, stabilizing your own finances. If your business doesn't make it, you put yourself in a position where you can more easily experiment with future ventures. Also, selling stock and building some real net worth gives you much more leverage in future conversations with VCs. No longer do you need to do a deal at any price.

THE ARGUMENTS AGAINST SELLING SECONDARY—AND WHY THEY'RE WRONG

Many in the start-up community argue against secondary sales. They take those sales as flashing yellow lights signaling that entrepreneurs don't believe in their businesses. As Bloomberg writer Brad Stone observes, "The conversion of private shares to cash also raises basic questions about how the secondary markets will affect the fabric of the high-tech community. Could they be divesting startups of vital entrepreneurial energy?"[9] The answer, I think, is a big fat no. There's something called risk management, and founders who don't get that concept have no business running a company.

> No matter how great you think your business is, the fact is that you're probably overexposed to your illiquid, private stock. The prudent thing to do is to sell some of that stock. Even if you do, you'll still own plenty.

The other, equally fallacious argument investors sometimes lob against secondary sales is that if founders sell some of their personal stock, they won't be properly incentivized to care about the performance of their business anymore. Let's think about that for a moment. Say you own 20 percent of a company that just raised funds at a $50 million valuation. You convince your board to let you sell $1 million of stock. You have $10 million of stock and you're selling $1 million of it, which means that you still have . . . $9 million in stock. That's nine million reasons to continue to care about the fate of your business. Most people would consider that to be plenty of incentive.

Despite such concerns, secondary sales are an increasingly common phenomenon in the start-up world. Some of this owes to sheer expediency. As venture funds increase in size, investors have a harder time putting all that capital to work. When investors find a business they like, it's as easy for them to write an $11 million check into that company as a $10 million check. That a founder is willing to sell $1 million of his or her own stock only helps investors put more of their money to work.

There are other reasons investors benefit from letting founders take risk off the table. VCs and founders have different

WORRY ABOUT THE PIE EXPLODING

goals because of their different risk profiles. VCs have diversified portfolios consisting of many businesses, and they are trying to generate the best return across that entire portfolio. To do that, they must assume a high level of risk in each individual business. Founders, on the other hand, are overconcentrated in a single business. They have every incentive to try to make that business a double instead of swinging for the home run their investors want. By letting founders sell some of their stock, investors put founders in a position where they can make the high-risk bets that investors want. Arguably, founders whose investors allow secondary sales should follow through on their side of this partnership, managing the business in accordance with their VCs' likely aims. In a world where "time to exit" (the time before a major liquidity event) continues to stretch out for start-ups, secondary sales also help by making founders and their teams feel that their successful start-up is in fact a success.

What's true on the secondary side goes double for primary. (Primary is issuance of new stock to bring additional cash into the business.) A company with more cash on its balance sheet can go bigger and harder when facing off against competitors. Uber, Airbnb, and WeWork can bully or buy start-ups that pose a threat to them. And on the biggest stage (as corporations go, at least), Amazon's incredible access to capital without the need to post profits allows it to beat other players into submission. This dynamic has gotten so extreme that Amazon merely has to intimate that it might be thinking about possibly maybe someday at some point in time entering a space, and every stock in that industry falls off a cliff.

Bottom line: Capital is king. So is liquidity. Why not go out there and get yourself some? Primary or secondary—it's all good!

THE OTHER BIG MISTAKE

Beyond striving to maximize equity at all costs, many entrepreneurs make another massive boo-boo when taking on funding: they aim for a deal that values their company for as much
money as possible. In later rounds of funding, many teams
even agree to highly unfavorable preferred structures, guaran-
teeing investors two to three times their money, just to get an
eye-popping headline valuation number for *TechCrunch.**

That's crazy! Why? Because valuation isn't a grade—it's a
goalpost. If an investor pumps money into your business, valuing it at $100 million, that's because he or she thinks you can
eventually sell the company for at least $500 million. VCs tell
their own investors that they're investing in companies not just
to get a certain percentage return on their money each year, but
also to receive a multiple of their capital investment when the
company sells. Usually they tell their investors that they seek a
minimum of five times their investment. If you plan to try to
sell the business for $200 million and raise at $100 million,
you're setting yourself up for a frosty relationship, or even open

---

* For instance, teams might agree to special liquidation preferences. In a
plain-vanilla preferred structure, an investor gets only what's called a "1×
liquidation preference." If I raise $10 million of equity at a $100 million
valuation, and the company sells for $50 million, the investor gets $10 million
back, not $5 million (to reflect the 50 percent loss). Teams could agree to a
2× or 3× liquidation preference, in which case the investor would receive
$20 million or $30 million, respectively, in this scenario. The greater the
liquidation preference, the greater the valuation investors will be willing to
assign to the business because of the economics they've negotiated independent
of valuation. So a start-up team could have a $200 million valuation instead
of a $100 million valuation, but that valuation could come with a 3×
liquidation preference. In that case, the team might wind up worse off despite
the higher valuation.

conflict, as your most recent investors will typically have a veto on any potential sale.

On the one hand, raising more primary investment (capital that flows into the company instead of into the entrepreneur's own pocket) gives you leverage to push the value of your company even higher. It's a natural deal to strike with your investors to say that you're willing to sell more shares of the company than you wanted—diluting the value of each share—if investors push the share price higher than they wanted. Both sides are doing something they don't like in order to produce a well-capitalized business (everyone being unhappy seems like a roughly accurate definition of compromise). However, that sky-high valuation that feels so exhilarating today could be setting you up for a big fall tomorrow.

BIG PLAYERS SHOULD SHARE THE RISK, TOO

If you work at a large corporation flush with cash, you might think that none of these considerations apply to you. You have billions on your balance sheet and can borrow at 4 percent, so why must you worry about financing? That line of reasoning misses the point. Accessing the appropriate investor base isn't just about having the amount of capital you need. It's about properly allocating risk—something that isn't as easy as it looks even in corporate contexts. If you're a megacap consumer goods company or retailer, you have shareholders. Unless your company's name rhymes with Blamazon, those shareholders will be incredibly averse to actions on your part that might shrink your earnings. And earnings reduction is precisely what happens in the short term when you're building a direct-to-consumer business.

In traditional advertising, I might spend $5 on television this year to get a customer to buy $50 of coffee *this year*. I log the revenues at the same time as the expenses, thus showing a net profit on the income statement. But if I'm selling that same consumer a coffee subscription via Facebook, I'm spending $50 this year to get somebody to buy $75 of coffee a year for the next twenty years. The $50 investment might be a great one over the long run, but the cost this year runs much greater than the $5 of TV spend. In year two, when I don't need to make any additional marketing investment on that customer, the numbers look better—infinitely so. But year two doesn't help me today, and today is what my shareholders are grading me on.

Because of this dynamic, large corporations have more trouble financing direct-to-consumer businesses than you might think, despite all the cash on their balance sheet and their incredibly low borrowing costs. Internal politics also come into play. Let's say you work for a consumer goods company with ten highly profitable brands of deodorant, detergent, and so on, and you are a brand manager trying to launch an eleventh. Who's going to win the internal budgeting process? Little old you with a new brand that shows no revenue and has large capital needs, or the brand manager for one of the existing brands that generates lots of revenue and profits? We both know the answer to that.

As daunting as these problems are, solutions do exist. Those same venture capitalists and growth equity funds backing start-ups would be more than happy to provide capital to joint ventures with large corporations as well. In the pharmaceutical space, these kinds of arrangements are already commonplace, used to finance research and development beyond the loss levels that management believes the public markets will tolerate.

If you're Pfizer and you have a $6.5 billion annual R&D budget, you might have $10 billion worth of projects that you believe merit financing. Every year that you delay investing in that additional $3.5 billion of projects, you waste a precious year when you have those assets on patent. So, what do you do? You bring in a private investment group to finance that extra R&D for you, guaranteeing it a strong return if the drug you're testing is approved.

Analogously, consumer goods companies and retailers could (and should) drop down to minority stakes on high-risk projects, creating room for private capital to come in and finance the businesses that those corporations need for their continued growth. Bringing in a private investor to finance a business pursued internally for a couple of years is a lot cheaper than forgoing the direct-to-consumer project and then jumping in and acquiring an upstart outside the firm that pulled it off. First, by retaining a large minority stake in the business and then purchasing it, the corporation puts itself in the position of already owning a substantial percentage of the acquisition target, which it purchased at a cheaper price early on, when the start-up's viability was unclear. In effect, the corporation gets to purchase the upstart at a discount. Second, an investor takes on much lower risk pumping money into a business that a large corporation has already indicated it wants to buy back. As a result, the corporation can pre-negotiate much more favorable exit terms than it would get if it had just purchased some random start-up, particularly if it's willing to provide investors with downside protection.

The private investment firm Abingworth was one of the first to unveil a biopharma strategy in which it partners with pharma companies, "[providing] financing for late-stage therapeutic assets with the co-development company incurring all the clinical and regulatory risk. The co-development company receives a pre-negotiated return once the drug is approved."[10] As of 2019, Abingworth has raised $2.2 billion for its life sciences funds, with sixty-five of its companies progressing to initial public offerings.[11] Another firm, NovaQuest, has raised funds reaching into the billions. I could imagine similar funds cropping up to service the needs of consumer goods companies as they pursue relatively risky direct-to-consumer ventures. Sharing the risk by opening some of the equity up to private investors is an idea whose time has come!

As I've been arguing, the same is true for the idea of sharing the risk generally. Equity really is like manure, and trust me, you don't want to be the only one who stinks of it. Give up your fixation with being the Big Owner, and your fledgling business just might stand a fighting chance.

(THE NAKED TRUTH)

Forget upside. Forget valuation. Taking on capital is all about reducing risk. Starting a new venture is just about the riskiest thing you can do in a cubicle. If during the first month of your potential new venture you focus on mapping out the idea you're going to roll the dice on, you spend the next *decade* taking the risk out of that concept. You remove that risk in a number of ways: running experiments, lining up partners, and giving yourself as many off-ramps as possible. Aggressively capitalizing your business is one of the most powerful levers available to you to take risk off the table. So, do it!

CHAPTER 6

USE THIRD-PARTY TOOLS

YOU'VE GOT YOUR product, you've got your team, and you've got financing. What's there to stop you?

How about . . . *you?*

Many digital projects flounder from the outset, even if they have the right people on board and adequate financing. The culprit is usually a kind of "writer's block" on the part of founders—procrastination that leads to an inability to execute. We dither endlessly to create the "perfect" product. We tinker interminably with our website. We subject every potential hire to phone calls and interviews and more interviews. We review our pricing options for the umpteenth time. We wimp out on customer acquisition and fail to deploy our advertising budget.

This last form of procrastination is especially dangerous for companies selling naked. Entrepreneurs are terrified of spending their marketing dollars inefficiently, so they wind up spending them much . . . too . . . slowly. At any given time, they don't spend enough to learn from their mistakes and optimize. If they hope to spend $100 acquiring each customer but they're only spending $50 a day on marketing, they'll probably only notch a sale every other day, and they could go weeks without any sales because of normal random variation. That represents a pretty slow learning curve, one that leads to the demise of many a digital venture. What's it like to bleed to death from a paper cut? These companies know.

Even when it doesn't prove fatal, procrastination on a range of fronts can make it harder to establish and grow your business. When one U.S.-based direct-to-consumer firm decided to launch in the United Kingdom, it took them a full year to make it happen. They had to get it perfect, setting up an office with a full-time team and launching a large brand marketing campaign. They had to think through every last cultural difference between Brits and Americans and adjust their offerings and outreach accordingly. By contrast, Hubble launched its U.K. operations in a couple of months, and went on to launch in other countries. Over an eighteen-month period, we launched in seven countries before this other company had done so in three. We didn't do it perfectly, but at least we did it, and as a result, we could start learning.

Sometimes you can find yourself procrastinating because you're stuck waiting for bottlenecks elsewhere in the business. While we waited for the inventory we needed to launch in the United States, our team spent weeks crafting standard emails we would send to customers. We had dozens of these messages covering all possible scenarios: when customers cancelled, when we were about to ship an order, when customers abandoned their shopping cart on our site before ordering, when they created subscriptions, when we had declined their credit cards, when we had updated their addresses, and on and on.

We wound up using very few of these emails, since many of the scenarios we had envisioned never materialized. We wrote these emails because it felt good at the time to be "productive." In truth, we were just making busywork for ourselves, trying to manage our own anxiety.

It's easy to fall into the procrastination trap, which is why even big corporates with strong histories of execution do it. When Gillette saw Dollar Shave and Harry's horning into its market, it could have started its own subscription service in a matter of months. Instead, it took years. Gillette knew what the "good enough" response was—it was kicking Gillette's butt. But executives labored to come up with the perfect response, one that would allow them to take a strong share of the online market without alienating their channel partners. In the meantime, likely because of the delay (or at least partially because of it), Gillette's share of the shaving market declined from 62 percent to 49 percent, while the combined share claimed by Harry's and Dollar Shave climbed to 10 percent.[*]

To beat procrastination once it has taken hold, entrepreneurs should ponder *why* they're stalled. Is it because deep down you know your business isn't viable? Have you been occupying yourself with busywork to stave off this unpleasant reality? Before Hubble, friends and I hatched a plan to launch a company that made it easier for people to apply for jobs and for recruiters to find and interview qualified hires. We had no clue how to start this business, so we spent a few months doing a bunch of fake work. We thought about names. We made a PowerPoint presentation. We mocked up a site. In our hearts, we knew that the task of starting this business was beyond us, but we didn't want to face it. Eventually we shut down the venture and went on to found others, but only after a lot of useless effort.

If you reflect on your business and conclude that it really is viable, then you might be falling prey to your anxieties. Maybe you're obsessing over executional elements, falling into a pattern of perfectionism because you're terrified of getting it wrong. Accept that you can't know many aspects of your business before it launches. You don't need to get it perfect. Good enough really is good enough. If you get something wrong, you can always change it later.

If those options don't work, then I have another solution, one that we've found can make all the difference: hire a third-party service to execute for you. There's no need to bog yourself down with execution for every last part of your business. Fantastic third-party tools and services exist for almost anything a start-up or incumbent needs in e-commerce. Host your site on Amazon Web Services (AWS), or if interfacing with Amazon is too much of a hassle, use an intermediary like Heroku. Build your store on the e-commerce platform Shopify (like nearly a million other business do). Run your payments through a payment processing company like Stripe. Hubble uses all of these and more. As we see it, running a business requires a vast array of executional competencies, and we can't excel at everything. Better to follow the dictum outlined in Courtney Reum and Carter Reum's book *Shortcut Your Startup:* "Do what you do best, and outsource the rest."[1]

YOU REALLY DON'T NEED TO BUILD IT

But wait—shouldn't you try to build the infrastructure behind your operations yourself so as to create the perfect customer experience?

No!

"Perfect" is the wrong bar. Be realistic—you're not going to develop "perfect" internally. Third-party tools will probably outperform what you'd have the funding and bandwidth to develop yourself. These tools have worked for others, so they can take a portion of risk out of your business. Also, these tools afford you flexibility. How much warehouse space will you require, and where should you locate these facilities? How much server capacity will you need? How many customer service reps? At the outset, you probably don't know the answers to these questions, so it's best to keep your options open. If you buy a 10,000-square-foot warehouse space but you suddenly need 50,000 square feet, you'll be scrambling to make up the difference. If you hire thirty customer service reps but it turns out you only have work for twenty, you'll have to lay ten of them off. Do you really want that kind of pain? Add to that, you don't have to maintain a third-party tool, and new features and apps are released for it every day. Can you beat that? If so, at what cost?

If you're a giant company, you might be able to go in-house and beat third-party offerings at a reasonable cost (emphasis on the word "might"—many corporate players are using Amazon Web Services and have long outsourced their marketing to agencies precisely because they're cheaper). If you're a start-up, however, going in-house won't save you much if anything—you don't have enough scale. Meanwhile, you'll waste valuable time on the minutiae of setting up and managing an executional capacity. Every hour you spend on these details is one hour less you're spending on what should be your top priority: finding customers and growing your business. As Dave Heath, CEO and co-founder of the sock company Bombas, reminds us, "Throughout the entire start-up journey, the one thing you can never create more of is time. You can always raise more capital, you can always hire more people, you can always leverage more solutions, you can always get more product, you can always find a way to get more customers. But you can't simply create more time."[2]

As Dave recounts, Bombas relied heavily on third-party vendors in order to save time, especially at the beginning. In August 2013, when Bombas launched its campaign on Indiegogo, Dave and his team expected to receive a couple of hundred orders during their thirty-day campaign. They planned to have the product shipped to Dave's parents' garage, where the team would take a weekend to pack all the orders by hand and ship them out. Imagine everyone's shock when 2,500 orders came in. Packing all of those orders would have taken two full weeks of their time. Hiring an employee for what then was a one-time task didn't make sense. So team members looked into third-party warehouse and logistics services. As they discovered, it would cost about $1.50 per order to have one of these firms pack and ship their 2,500 orders. As Dave recalls, "The four of us in the room looked at one another, and I ultimately decided that we might as well leverage [this service], and get these two weeks back to focus on building the website, continuing to develop the brand, [and] talking about how we're going to launch."

Folks who sell naked should apply this logic to virtually everything their company does. In addition to fulfillment, you can outsource manufacturing, freight forwarding (shipping from your manufacturer to your fulfillment center), and shipping to customers. You can use an external design agency for your initial branding work, and you're better off with third-party services like AWS (maybe packaged by Heroku), Stripe, Shopify, ReCharge, and Twilio instead of building your own tech stack. To manage customer service tickets across multiple agents, try Zendesk. To track customer satisfaction on tickets, there's Stella Connect. Sprout allows you to track consumer comments on Facebook and other social media. To manage email campaigns, try Campaign Monitor. And great new services are coming online every month.

ACHIEVING THE RIGHT BALANCE

In many cases, you need so much expertise from so many sources that it's impossible to do anything *other* than outsource. (Or you need expertise from one key player—like a contact lens manufacturer for us—whose capabilities you would struggle to replicate.) Still, many founders find themselves balancing concerns they might have about quality with the important benefits outsourcing can confer. EBY's Renata Black thinks of outsourcing as a "beautiful dance" between maintaining quality, on the one hand, and outsourcing, on the other, so that you can focus as a company and grow. "You're searching for balance in your life," she says. "How much do you bring in? How much do you outsource?" Relatedly, skeptics might feel that they want to perform a function in-house because they believe they are uniquely competent at it. You have that fancy design degree or the programming skills, so you might as well use them. Maybe, but unless you're comfortable filling that role indefinitely, you'll have to hand it off eventually to someone who doesn't have your self-perceived talents. It might make more sense to call in a third party at the outset.

Some founders might worry that outsourcing marketing and customer service in particular will keep them too distant from consumers. They shouldn't. When engaging third-party vendors, you'll still own access to the performance data generated by marketing activity. You might also still make some of the creative content yourself as you collaborate with outside photographers, editors, and so on. You'll remain quite enmeshed in marketing, even as you share some of the headaches with others. I also wouldn't advise that you outsource marketing entirely. If you know that a particular channel works well for you, you might hire people in-house to run that or to manage external partners as your business grows. For other channels, hiring people is risky. If the channel proves ineffective, you're either stuck with an unproductive team member or forced to fire someone, which is always demoralizing for the rest of your team. Better to outsource that piece of it, bringing it in-house once the channel has proven its mettle.

Customer service can likewise be tricky to outsource, but for different reasons. When we initially launched Hubble, we built up an in-house customer service team, assuming that local service overseen by us was key. We quickly realized that we needed a small army of customer service agents on duty at all hours, and were struggling to find folks willing to provide that kind of coverage. We also noticed that the vast majority of customer service tickets dealt with just a few predictable issues, like updating an address or tracking or rescheduling a shipment. Questions like this didn't require long, elaborate responses, but they did require speedy ones. We couldn't keep up with the volume internally, but when we sought out good third-party options, we couldn't find any that would work without large guaranteed contracts (always a bad sign that a vendor might not believe in their own product).

We had an idea: we could mobilize an army of freelance agents, allowing them to work from home instead of in traditional call centers, and paying them for each ticket they completed rather than on an hourly basis. No call centers meant no commutes for the agents (so higher agent retention) and lower costs, and paying per ticket aligned the agents' incentives with ours—by working hard they could make more per hour with us paying less per ticket. We could use tools like Stella Connect to ensure high quality alongside efficiency. By 2017, almost a hundred freelancers were handling our customer service tickets on a freelance basis, and we were handling more than 90 percent of the customer emails we received within an hour. To ensure quality, we maintained a small internal team (nine employees) that oversaw our agents and their operations. Seeing how successful this solution was, one of Ben's friends started a business of his own providing it as a service to other companies. In 2018, Michael Feinberg launched ResolvedCX, a company that locates, trains, and manages freelance customer service reps. Today, ResolvedCX works with dozens of direct-to-consumer companies, ranging from seed stage to the Fortune 500.

In any executional area, stay alert. If you don't find enticing options, there might be a business opportunity for you if you can improvise a workable solution.

OVERSEEING VENDORS

If you outsource to the extent that I am suggesting, you might wonder what's left for you and your teams to do yourself. The answer is quite a bit. Hiring third-party services doesn't absolve you of responsibility for the business's functioning. You still must coordinate your partners, track their performance, and hold them accountable. Dave and his team at Bombas did plenty of that, bringing on people with expertise in a range of areas to help. For example, nobody on the team had much experience in online marketing, so they hired Kate Huyett, Bombas's current CMO, who had successfully scaled a business across multiple marketing channels. Kate made certain that the company's marketing partners focused on what mattered most to the business, including metrics like cost per acquisition, and lifetime value. "It's important," Dave says, "to make sure that for whatever third-party providers or technologies you're leveraging, you have somebody internally who at least understands what success looks like so you can best utilize and manage those teams." Oisin O'Connor, founder of the third-party subscription management vendor ReCharge, agrees, noting that this person doesn't have to be technically expert in the field in question. "You just need someone on your team, either in-house or an agency, who is strong enough to understand the solutions out there and how they can push the business forward."[3]

More generally, founders and their teams have to function in some sense as the brains of the operation, developing strategies and handling key executional issues in collaboration with vendors. At Bombas, the team initially "leveraged outside agencies to help on the actual execution" of marketing, while Kate "really drove the strategy." Meanwhile, two of Dave's co-founders—Randy Goldberg and Aaron Wolk—helped generate the initial creative strategy for Bombas and oversaw agencies executing against it, having previously worked in agencies themselves. A third co-founder, Dave's brother, Andrew, was an MBA specializing in finance and operations. He oversaw areas of the business that were "numerically and operationally intensive," including third-party logistics and shipping providers. Among other questions, he decided "how many orders are we going to do a day, what kind of turnaround time should we aim for, [and] what should we pay for shipping."

Although your team might divvy up relationships with key vendors like Dave's team did, as a founder, you'll probably involve yourself at least somewhat in all the big operational decisions. When challenges arise, your vendor partners have to understand that as long as they do their job, they have your full faith behind them, and you're not privileging other partners or internal teams. Rivalries can emerge, for instance, when both employees and external partners are handling Facebook marketing for you. Your job is to make everyone feel fairly treated, even if not everyone loves each particular decision. Make external media buyers understand that they have your support, and that they should clarify what they need (such as photos or past performance data) in order to deploy your marketing budget. Make your team understand that competition between them and the agency is good for the business.

BECOME AN ALLOCATOR

Founders should also drive results by serving as efficient allocators of budget dollars. Putting partners in competition with one another, you can shift your budget to the top performers and away from those that fail to meet expectations. Our team actively allocates budget dollars among marketing channels and the third-party teams running them. In late October 2017, for instance, we spent almost half of our marketing budget on television, running spots during the World Series. Afterward, unsure how well television was actually driving sales, we shifted money to other channels, including Facebook, Instagram, Pinterest, Google, Snapchat, and podcasts. By September 2018, having reviewed our site's post-checkout customer survey, we realized that television might have been working well for us after all, so we upped our spend again.

Our vendors would have preferred that we stuck to particular channels longer, but we need performance, and we'll send our marketing dollars wherever we can find it. We also routinely shuffle our budgets around within channels. To manage our Facebook ads, we use multiple third-party buyers, and also have an in-house team. We compiled our list of partners by working with about a dozen third-party providers and disengaging with some along the way if their performance failed to impress. When agencies came up with winning ideas, we took note, flipping our budgets month to month to reward partners who had delivered.

BIGGER ISN'T NECESSARILY BETTER

One implication of this outsourcing mindset is that your core team doesn't have to be very large. This might strike you as anathema—employee count is the most common question you get at cocktail parties when people are trying to gauge the size of your business (it just seems too gauche to ask directly about revenue and valuation). But with outsourcing, you don't need many people to keep the different pieces coordinated and allocated. Plus, small teams offer many benefits. They make it much easier to offer generous compensation packages to your employees. They facilitate tight-knit cultures. They keep salary low as a percentage of your total budget, reducing the risk of layoffs if your business suffers reverses.

It's true that small teams can't operate every business—your head count will likely balloon if you can't outsource production from existing manufacturers, or if your complex supply chain prevents you from using third-party logistics providers. But for many direct-to-consumer companies, a relatively small team will do just fine.

MAKE THIRD-PARTY
RELATIONSHIPS WORK FOR *YOU*

Hopefully I've convinced you by this point. You're mentally ticking through your business functions, identifying areas where third parties might be able to help you up your game. Maybe you've already zipped online and are checking out some of the vendors I've named. If so, I applaud your enthusiasm, but I also wish to sound a note of caution. As attractive as they are, third-party relationships do have their pitfalls, and you'll need to correct for them in order to make these relationships work for you. Here are seven simple guidelines we at Hubble have followed when powering up our executional capacity.

1. VET VENDORS CAREFULLY

You'll want to ask for references, of course, and check out the client lists available on many vendors' websites. But we recommend going much further. Think about the direct-to-consumer companies that you respect. What platforms or third party services do they use? Check out Web forums to see what existing customers are saying about these services. Contact other founders via LinkedIn or through your investors and ask for their feedback on the pros and cons of different options. If the downsides are considerable, can your company create suitable workarounds that might make a given option viable for you? And if founders have chosen to keep a certain function in-house, why is that? Do the factors that gave rise to that decision apply to you and your company?

As ResolvedCX's CEO, Michael Feinberg, notes, so many young founders feel reluctant to consult with others about executional matters. Excited about their business idea and convinced of its unique value, they go into "stealth mode," fearful that others in the entrepreneurial or venture communities will steal it. As a result, they fail to learn as much as they can about the basics of running the business from people who have actually done it. It's "basically impossible to differentiate quality and assess the different models that [vendors offer] by going online," he says.[4]

> The best way to learn about vendors and how best to structure relationships with them is by talking with others.

2. AVOID AGREEMENTS WITH LONG COMMITMENTS

Third-party vendors afford flexibility, but not if you sign a contract locking you into an arrangement for months or years. Opt for short-term deals with clear exit provisions, even if you must pay a slightly higher price. We once committed to buying three months of advertising on CNN at a preferred rate, since the network had performed well for us previously. A few weeks later, we realized we had spent too much and were dealing with diminished returns. We still had two more months locked in, and there was nothing we could do about it. Lesson learned! Month-to-month arrangements are best, but if your vendors require a commitment, try to keep it to under a year. In addition to the flexibility that short-term arrangements afford, they keep your vendors constantly hungry and working to prove their value to you.

3. TEST, TEST, TEST

As a corollary of #2, and in line with your role as an allocator of your budget dollars, perform ongoing testing to ensure that you have the right mix of third-party vendors in place. Testing allows you to grow smarter over time and allocate funds more efficiently. You'll also be in a position to give investors and others better answers when they inquire why you've chosen *not* to go with a particular option. If you don't test, you don't know!

At Hubble, we've tested all of our marketing channels and vendors to see how they perform. Aside from the checkout surveys mentioned earlier, we carefully analyze the reports we receive from Facebook, our TV buyer, Google Analytics, and so on. We also turn channels on and off to gauge their effect. If you shut something off, does your cost per acquisition (CPA) spike or acquisition volume suddenly decline? Then you know the channel made a difference and that you're getting value for your dollar.

To the extent you can, structure contracts to make third-party partners prove their worth on their dime, not yours. Ask vendors if you can sign up for a no-obligation trial with them. (If your customers appreciate offers like this, why wouldn't you?) Give vendors a tiny slice of your marketing budget and see how they do. Create a copy of your site and direct 10 percent of new customers through their checkout, comparing their performance to the checkout you're currently using. If your vendor is a new customer service partner, send a few tickets their way, ramping up the volume if they perform well.

> The best way for a vendor to develop trust is by building a record of performance. Experiments let you try vendors at little risk to you. If one experiment is good, more are better!

4. PAY FOR PERFORMANCE

Some vendors, especially those in the marketing space, prefer to receive a percentage of your spend as compensation. That's great for them—they get paid regardless of whether their service performed for you. For you, it's far better to tie compensation directly to performance. Perhaps vendors receive a bonus for reaching certain performance targets. Perhaps you'll agree to increase their budget if they perform well. In the marketing space, perhaps you ask vendors to acquire customers for you at a particular price, requiring them to take a loss if the actual cost of acquiring a customer runs higher than this target.

Your partners might not accept agreements such as these. If they don't, that's quite possibly a sign that they don't believe in their abilities. Take note!

5. COMMUNICATE

It's vital to remain up to date on your partners and their offerings. If you're ignorant of changes your partner has made to its services, you might suffer unforeseen disruptions to your business. One partner of ours is constantly upgrading its platform, deploying changes without spreading the word. We've written our own code on top of the partner's, so when the company changes its software, ours breaks, and it often takes us time to figure out why. Look to establish close channels of communication at the outset with partners, and to keep these channels open. With many partners, we maintain Slack channels, messaging with them in real time just as we do with full-time members of our team.

6. CONSIDER THE WHOLE SPECTRUM

I've distinguished in this chapter between in-house and outsourced solutions, but work relationships exist on a spectrum. Some partners—your employees—are fully integrated into your business, while some services are external and far removed from your company (Google Analytics, for instance). Between these extremes there's a range of solutions. In some cases you might own an external partner's work product, while in other cases you might not. Some partners collaborate so closely with you they feel like members of your team, even though they're not. Vendors might own a chunk of your business, or you a chunk of theirs. As working arrangements become more flexible and fluid, other, even less conventional possibilities open up. If you have extra office space and an external partner needs it, maybe you give it to them (that way you know you'll have ready access to them if you need it). Think creatively about which exact arrangement might best fit the needs of you and your partners.

7. NEVER STOP EVALUATING YOUR OPTIONS

Just because you've decided to outsource a function today with a certain vendor doesn't mean you should continue to do so indefinitely. Stay current on your vendors' competitors. Have new offerings appeared in the market that might make more sense for your business? And does it still make more sense to outsource this function rather than develop an in-house capacity?

As Bombas has grown, Dave and his team have begun to bring outsourced functions back in-house. In 2017, the company spent millions on Facebook advertising, with its vendor taking a percentage of that as its fee. Dave and his team realized they'd reached the point where they could hire a team of employees to perform this function internally. Within a year, as Bombas's Facebook expenditures soared, relying on an in-house team led to significant savings for the company, while also allowing it to become nimbler. "With Facebook agencies," Dave says, "we would have weekly calls where we would set the budget for the next week based on the previous week's performance. We'd check in and monitor the [key performance indicators] on the marketing spend throughout the week. By handling all of our Facebook strategy and execution in-house, we were not only able to adjust campaigns in real time, but we could also tie the program more organically into the rest of the organization's strategy, which ultimately led to performance improvement."

When Bombas was smaller, it made sense to outsource Facebook marketing in order to provide the small team with additional bandwidth and allow it to focus on other priorities. Now that the company is bigger, moving this function in-house has allowed Bombas to save money and execute more strategically.

Growth doesn't always require you to bring functions in-house. If you have multiple vendors in a space (for instance, multiple media buyers in a channel), you'll potentially sacrifice efficiency by bringing the function in-house, since you'll have a harder time mobilizing full-time employees against one another in competition. You can also contract with multiple fulfillment centers and have them bid against one another for your business—a potential advantage over building and maintaining your own centers.

> At every point, ask yourself what you need out of the business function. Are costs lower if you do it in-house, and are lower costs a priority for the function? Is quality better in-house? Do you need in-house capabilities for the optics (say, for an investor, a partner, or a potential buyer)? Weigh these factors in making your decision.

It's up to you to figure out what degree of outsourcing is right for your business. The most important point is this: just like you don't want to hog all the capital (Chapter 5), you also don't want to hog all the work of operating from day to day. Stop obsessing about execution, hire someone else to do it, and move on. It's worked for us so far and many successful founders we know. Hopefully it'll work for you, too.

(THE NAKED TRUTH)

Procrastination is common among writers, artists, college students working on term papers, taxpayers needing to prepare their returns, and ... founders. Sometimes it's a sign that the business idea you've taken on isn't going to work. Other times it's just good old anxiety-fueled perfectionism rearing its ugly head. Finding external partners can help you cut through a lot of it. You don't need perfect. You need good enough. Instead of doing everything yourself, organize and coordinate your partners. Get them competing to do their very best work. Keep an eye on these relationships to make sure they're continuing to work for you. Regard everything as a test. If you think it might be time to switch these relationships up or perhaps even bring functions back in-house, test that, too.

CHAPTER 7

FRAME THE DIGITAL OFFERING

IN 2018, SOME months after launching Pair, their kids' eyewear brand, Sophia Edelstein and Nathan Kondamuri noticed that customers weren't really "getting" the company's full value proposition. From the founders' view, Pair offered consumers an array of important benefits, including high-quality glasses at an attractive price ($95), the ability to customize the product using colorful "toppers" that sat on top of the base frame, a thirty-day return policy, the ability to test the product at home via an easy-to-use try-on kit, and social purpose (for every pair purchased, the company donated a pair of glasses to children in developing countries). Yet customer surveys on Pair's website revealed that most customers understood only certain of these benefits and not others. In particular, some customers appreciated the ability to test how well glasses fit while remaining oblivious to the attractive pricing, and vice versa.

After a bit of investigation, Sophia and Nathan determined that this communications gap stemmed largely from a test the two were running. Pair had introduced a novel variation on the home try-on kit, sending potential customers inexpensive cardboard cutouts of their glasses to help them find the right fit. Curious about how much customers liked this experience, Sophia and Nathan ran an experiment in which they channeled half of their incoming traffic to a landing page that featured the home try-on kit prominently and half to a landing page that, as Sophia recalls, "didn't emphasize the home try-on kit at all," but rather directed customers to find the perfect pair via their website.[1] The page that emphasized the home try-on kit got customers "super excited about this ordering process, this new experience of getting glasses," but it lacked copy about "a lot of the amazing things about Pair that made us so unique."

Sophia and Nathan decided to improve their communication of the value proposition. Reflecting on their target demographic (parents of kids aged six to fourteen), they realized that two parts of their pitch to consumers stood out above the rest: the $95 price point, and kids' ability to customize their glasses on an ongoing basis. In Sophia's and Nathan's minds, all prospective customers, even those who arrived on the site because they were interested in the home try-on kits, needed to glean these two basic pieces of information. The two founders redesigned their website to make sure they did. Now when customers land on the page that emphasizes the try-on kit page and click the "Learn more" button, they encounter big, bold lettering that reads, "Glasses that change color in a snap." Scrolling down, customers find pricing and other transactional information as well as fun testimonials from happy kids and parents. "Pair sunglasses aren't just any ordinary sunglasses," one parent testimonial reads. "They are *clearly* sunglasses for superheroes. . . . [The child] can change out the frame with a sweep of a hand, instantly transforming his magical powers. . . . Not to mention the frames are super cute, high quality and they give a pair of glasses to a kiddo in need for every pair purchased."[2]

In setting up a direct-to-consumer venture, it's vital to design and structure your digital offering in ways that customers will understand. As Sophia and Nathan recognized, consumers can absorb only a limited amount of information about a business—one or two key concepts at most. Since price matters to most consumers, one of those concepts had better be what a great deal the company's product is. But designing the digital storefront isn't just about conveying the right messages. Businesses like Pair are specialty e-commerce stores that acquire customers via paid social media marketing, most notably on Facebook and Instagram. To close the sale, you'll have to understand how users engage with the social media platforms themselves, and which ad placements will produce your desired results. You'll have to know how these social media sites operate, as well as their "grammar"—common features like intake quizzes, free offers, subscription, bundles, content pieces, referral programs, and so on. You'll also need to optimize the shopping experience on your website for mobile, which is how most consumers today will find you. In this chapter, I'll run through the basics of framing a digital offering, helping you to shape your mobile presence in ways that yield a simple, frictionless shopping experience.

ADVANTAGE, DIRECT-TO-CONSUMER

If you're not excited yet about your digital offering, you should be—this is the stuff that drives direct-to-consumer businesses. Yes, Amazon offers everything under the sun at competitive prices (or lower), but they can't do what you can as a business centered on a single brand. You can offer consumers a simple online experience—just one or a few products, a few webpages to navigate, an easy ordering process—as well as one that works as painlessly as possible on mobile phones, where consumers spend so much of their time. You can also think more carefully about how to sell in your particular product category. Would it work best if you sold via a subscription model? Using at-home try-on? Via a membership structure? Something else? Amazon and large offline retailers like Walmart and Target are marketing products across hundreds of categories, so even if they do pursue multiple selling strategies, their sites will almost inevitably tilt toward one dominant model, like single-order instead of subscription. With your own digital property, you can steer consumers into a purchasing behavior customized to your category and your business.

Since you don't require a template page that works across millions of products, like Amazon does, you can also create a finely tuned purchase funnel (the progression from learning about products, to considering which ones you might purchase, to narrowing down your choice, to actually buying the product) for your category based on the tests you run, and you can optimize the creative that consumers encounter as they proceed down the funnel. Which ads work best for your brand? Are they fun? Playful? Pretty? Clinical? Sophisticated? Some combination of the above? As your learning deepens, you can apply that knowledge to every consumer touchpoint. You don't have Jeff Bezos's headache of creating a consistent retail experience across all the products, and your site design can reflect that reality. You can also keep iterating without having to worry about remaining consistent across millions of other products.

When launching Hubble, we didn't have Amazon to contend with—it wasn't in our category. But we did have other big players selling online, including 1-800 Contacts and Lens.com.

These businesses were "everything stores" for contact lenses, offering virtually every product from the major brands. Competition among these companies was fierce. Much of their business came from search traffic, and often they were bidding on the same search terms. In this context, "winning" generally meant selling the same product as the competition at the lowest price for the least margin. Because of its longer history, greater brand recognition, and reputation for customer service, 1-800 Contacts stood out as the heaviest hitter among this pack, which often translated into a few extra margin dollars per box.

As a single-brand operator, we spotted a couple of potential ways to attack these incumbents. Existing online companies were reselling for the major brands, so they didn't control their packaging. The big contact lens brands all had—to my taste—ugly packaging (with, for some reason, many images of jets of water pulsing into lenses). Maybe this packaging worked for their sales forces, but I didn't think it translated well to social media. The existing resellers were also stuck with the downside of being an "everything store": their online shopping experiences could feel complicated and confusing. Consumers told us they had trouble remembering the difference between brands like Acuvue Moist and Acuvue Oasys, for example, or Biofinity versus Biotrue.

We worked to make Hubble's design fun and our purchasing experience simple. We explained in clear language why consumers should buy from us, and we opted for a subscription model, which none of the existing sites emphasized. We hoped that at least some subset of existing consumers didn't want to buy in bulk. As contact lens users ourselves, Ben and I certainly didn't enjoy tying up hundreds of dollars of our own cash at a time buying contact lens inventory that sat there in our bathroom for months on end waiting to be used.

Think about your product category. What about the way people currently buy is annoying, inefficient, unpleasant, or just plain silly? How are existing big players in your industry failing their customers? And how might you exploit those vulnerabilities to carve out a niche online?

PAID SOCIAL: THE EVER-EXPANDING TOOLBOX

That last question brings us to tactics, and how to get them right. There are many from which to choose, but let's start with the most important: paid social media. Do you run video ads or static images? Do you use square formatting or rectangular? Do you serve ads to Facebook's Audience Network (think of all those display ads trying to draw accidental clicks in Candy Crush)? Do you run ads in Facebook's Stories feature or just its News Feed? Did you remember to exclude your existing customers from your audience? Your success depends on getting every detail right. Ask a digital ad platform for the wrong marketing action—even if you're off by just one checkbox—and instead of sales, you'll get worthless clicks that never translate into paying customers.[3]

The two major levers you can manipulate as a Facebook advertiser are the targeting of ads and the creative content itself. As Facebook's algorithm continues to improve (gorging itself on the data we produce every day), the value of clever ad targeting gradually declines—Facebook can do more of the work itself with no guidance at all from you. Less juice in targeting boosts the value of creative. And creative has become an incredibly competitive game now that Facebook allows anyone to look through every ad that each advertiser on its site is running. While Facebook trumpeted this change as enabling greater advertiser "transparency and accountability," it also facilitates the poaching of creative ideas.[4] As of this writing (early 2019), the consensus is that the most effective ads are generally video—from what we've seen and used, typically short loops of a few seconds. Sound doesn't factor in much, since most social media users watch these ads with their devices on mute. Instagram and Facebook Stories continue to grow in importance, and we're always experimenting with other platforms like Pinterest and Snapchat, with a curious eye on voice-activated platforms like Google Assistant and Amazon's Alexa.

As founder of a direct-to-consumer company, you should pay careful attention to the latest developments in digital marketing to ensure that you're *efficiently* engaging as many consumers as possible.

THE BIG PRICING QUESTION

Another key tactical area—and one of the most important for your business—is pricing. In a number of categories, direct-to-consumer founders face a basic choice: whether to offer subscriptions or sell to customers on a single-order basis. If you opt for a subscription model, your customer is no longer just a customer but a "member" of your service, and a source of recurring revenue. As you begin to understand retention patterns, you can model how much lifetime revenue you can expect to generate from new customers.

The downside of a subscription model is that your business will likely need financing in order to grow. Why? Well, imagine you don't sell by subscription. Say you're an online mattress company with a product that costs $1,000 at retail, with $500 of that representing profit. Since many online mattress companies exist, the market for advertising is very competitive. It might cost you $400 to acquire a customer, leaving you with only $100 to pay for salaries, rent, and other costs of doing business. You're not making much money, but you're not losing it, either. If you can sell more mattresses each month with the same fixed costs, you can grow both revenues and profits. Compare that to a hypothetical subscription business. Let's say it costs you $100 to acquire a customer, and you earn $50 a month of revenue off that person, with $25 of that as profit. If you keep half of those customers over time, you're making $12.50 per customer per month. That is, you're paying $100 today, but walking away only with $12.50. You'll need eight months to break even, which means you'll need cash to plug that gap. If you're looking to acquire more customers each month, your thirst for financing will only increase, which is where venture dollars enter the picture.

Growth might be choppier for a single-order business, since it has to kill what it eats every single month. But these businesses are also better positioned to grow without a lot of capital, as profits can be funneled back into the business, fueling future customer acquisition. So, which model should you choose?

Consider whether a subscription model makes sense for your product. Couches? I don't think so. Contact lenses? We'd argue yes. Consider, too, how much access you have to capital, and how comfortable you feel taking it on. Finally, assess whether you'd be able to deliver well on a subscription model for customers. Has anyone else done it with a product similar to yours? Did they have advantages you lack? If so, how will you make up that gap?

THE ENDURING MAJESTY OF THE FREE TRIAL

Another tactic, free trials, can serve as a great way to turn shoppers into customers. If your product is cheap enough, you could run a subscription with a free period at the outset. For a pricey item like a mattress, you could provide a money-back guarantee for the first couple of months after purchase. At-home try-ons serve much the same function as do "showroom" stores, where you can check out—but not buy—a new brand before the store attendants push you to their website for actual transactions. In each of these cases, a company is displaying how much it believes in its product or service by letting consumers try before they buy.

In the subscription setting, free trials aren't without trade-offs. Most important, they diminish your ability to retain customers. Nestled amidst all those glorious legions of new customers are quite a few who (a) don't really want your product, will never want it, and are just looking for free stuff, or (b) can't really afford your product and in fact submit credit cards that are declined when it's time to bill them for full-price product. If you think a free trial of some sort might help your business, offer it up for a month and see whether it lowers your customer acquisition costs. Then track that cohort for the next few months to ensure that the hit you'll likely see in customer value doesn't overwhelm any benefits on customer acquisition.

A close cousin of the free trial is the referral program. Instead of pushing consumers to try your product, you're incentivizing them to send new customers your way. The meal delivery service Blue Apron was incredibly generous in allowing customers to send "free meals" (offers to redeem free meals) to others to get them on the program. Existing customers didn't realize an actual financial benefit, but they did receive the opportunity to "gift" a free meal to a friend. Other programs, such as those by the personal finance services Wealthfront and Betterment, provide financial incentives to both customers and their referrals.

Referral programs are a great way to generate new customer relationships, and in theory you don't pay anything except the cost of the freebie itself. In practice, such programs can exact a toll on retention, especially for consumable physical goods. It's hard to track who's using referrals to hoover up freebies (for instance, giving ten Blue Apron meals to themselves) and who's actually bringing you new customers. You can set up restrictive rules to catch scammers, but that'll restrict your ability to snag more of the bona fide customers. In the end, these programs might leave you with lots of new customers signing on, very few of whom will stay with you.

CONTENT IS GOLD

Did you get a great piece in *BuzzFeed, GQ,* or *The Wall Street Journal* that resulted in a sales spike? Great—take that article and repurpose it. We took quotations from earned media and turned them into ads, and we also ran ads that sent people to the articles instead of our home page. The result: we acquired customers cheaply for months before the tactic petered out and it was time to find a new one.

Even if you don't see a sales spike from earned media, that content might benefit you in other ways. James LaForce, whose marketing communications firm LaForce counts many direct-to-consumer brands as clients, notes that some entrepreneurs aggressively pursue earned media not because they think it's going to convert customers, but because they need to validate their business models and their own promise as leaders. "There are investors out there that might need reassurance that the business is recognized by the media as a legitimate exercise," LaForce says. He adds that a lot of the most successful direct-to-consumer companies "now say that media coverage was essential to their success," and that "a lot of investors believe that it's an essential piece. They ask to see that in order to stay with a company and believe in it."[5] Earned media also helps validate the quality of your offerings with consumers if they see it during a Google search, or if they spot those fancy "as featured in" media brand logos at the bottom of your own page.

What if you're not getting much earned media, and your customers like content? Simple: Write your own content and publish it as a blog. We've published posts that describe why consumers should sign up for Hubble, and then used ads to drive traffic toward those posts. It's worked great. Or you can sign up bloggers and other influencers to promote your products. You'll need to decide whether to give them free product as an incentive or also provide cash payment. Be careful: once folks hear that you're paying influencers, then all the other influencers out there might want to get paid as well.

EMAIL THEM SOME LOVE

Emails are another great tool that can help you make the most of customers, both potential and existing. Let's take potential customers first. If someone puts his name on your mailing list or abandons his shopping cart on your site, you'll want to keep emailing him to try to get him to complete a transaction. It's a way of retargeting prospects with no advertising spending required. Pretty great!

As for existing customers, there are, of course, all those standard emails you'll want to send confirming a customer's order, announcing that a package is shipping, informing customers of sales or special offers, and so on. But don't limit your emailing to that. Melanie Travis, founder of the women's swimwear company Andie, realized early on that many of her customers were excited not merely about her products, but about supporting a female entrepreneur. Melanie has since used emails as a means of making customers feel like they are maintaining personal contact with her. For months, she sent out a weekly newsletter called "Mel's Musings" in which she recounted "what we've done in the last week to build this business." A few days after customers placed an order, they also received an email from her thanking them for their purchase and telling them a bit about Melanie's motivations in starting the company. "What's been so amazing," Melanie says, "is that many women have written back saying that maybe the swimsuit doesn't quite fit or whatever, but because I reached out and people crave a personal connection these days, they're gonna keep the swimsuit, because they want to support my business. I mean, it's amazing what it's done."

In the age of Amazon, a key appeal of many direct-to-consumer brands is the opportunity they afford to sustain a more intimate or personal relationship with customers. Many people like brands that are small, creative, and focused on them. They're drawn to businesses with a strong sense of purpose, and often a cleanly defined social cause that goes beyond commerce. How can you nurture that relationship using all the tools at your disposal? In particular, how can you craft emails that express your brand identity and invite customers into a relationship?

It's possible to overdo email by sending out too many of them (although I'd argue many folks are too conservative here). Make your emails simple and meaningful, keeping your customers' needs foremost in your mind. You also should tread a bit more carefully with emails if you're a subscription business rather than single-order. When single-order businesses like Andie notch a sale, they've generated revenue but they haven't acquired a lasting customer. To obtain more value from that consumer over time, they need to entice her to come back, and email is a free way to encourage repeat purchasing. With subscription businesses, you run the risk that customers will cancel once you acquire them, and an email bugging them might give them the prodding they need. It might still be worth your while to email if you're seeking to get customers to refer friends to you, or if you're selling other products and want them to upgrade their subscriptions.

MAKE IT GREAT FOR MOBILE

When you're creating your digital experience, it's tempting and natural to spend all your energy critiquing mock-ups of your site (or "wireframes," as we call them) on desktop. Big mistake. Since most of your customers will likely engage with you on their mobile devices, think about mobile first. On desktop, consumers can easily absorb a giant product catalog. The greater the number of relevant items you can present to consumers, the more likely you are to generate sales. On mobile, sorting and filtering through tons of options can be overwhelming—page after page of tiny shots of the products, and tiny buttons that make it hard to navigate, so you accidentally hit every ad or link. If you can free consumers from this experience, you should improve your odds of notching a sale.

One way to facilitate product selection on mobile is to use quizzes or questionnaires. Ask consumers to provide you with relevant information about themselves and their product needs, and use that information to direct them to the products on your site that are right for them. On the fashion site Stitch Fix, consumers complete a seventy-five-item intake form about themselves and their clothing preferences. At the end of this process, Stitch Fix has enough information on hand to choose clothing for them. The pet food site Ollie's does something similar to learn about consumers' pets. What size is your dog? How active? What's your dog's name? They want to know so that they can point you to exactly what you need.

Questionnaires work by creating a flow that begins at a specific point and progresses toward an end goal, with no detours to add friction to the experience. As Craig Elbert, co-founder and CEO of the vitamin company Care/of, notes, quizzes also exploit what he calls "the curiosity gap." When customers divulge information (always a good thing, from the seller's vantage point), they become curious about the personal recommendation they will receive in return. As they type in additional pieces of information, their curiosity mounts until they finally receive the recommendations at the quiz's end. Instead of a boring, rote task, the act of choosing the right product is transformed into a journey with a clear sense of direction, as well as a climactic moment and a nice little "reward."

Quizzes can work both as a vehicle for product selection and for the delivery of technical information about products.

As Craig notes, consumers shopping for health or medical products "need guidance," and it's important to be transparent and provide the relevant facts. Still, nobody likes to read large blocks of text on a tiny phone screen. Traditionally, Craig comments, if you were shopping for a product like vitamins, "you'd have an in-store interaction with an expert who would be asking you things and understanding what you needed." Quizzes can simulate this experience, so long as you adapt them to "fit the attention span and screen size of the modern consumer." In developing a quiz for Care/of, Craig and his team kept it short, designing it so that consumers could complete it in five minutes or less. They also observed "character limits on the questions, on the answers, and if something went too long, we said, 'Okay, this needs to be broken up into two questions.'" Employ a similar discipline when crafting your own quizzes— and, frankly, everything else about your digital offering. Respect your consumers *and* their screen sizes.

In addition to quizzes, here are some other tips you might consider:

- Get the basics right. Are the buttons on your site as large as possible, so that customers can easily click on them using their mobile screens? Is the text large enough, and are the fonts easy to read? Is the navigational scheme of your site simple and clear to users? And are the look and feel of your site attractive, with nice photography and engaging design schemes?

- Make sure your Facebook and Instagram advertising looks good on mobile. Think about which ad units will take up the most screen space on mobile, and make creative that fully utilizes the dimensions of the ad unit. Also, when previewing ads, don't do so in desktop mode, but rather in mobile mode, or better yet, just on your phone. The display space is smaller, so ads will format differently. Pay attention as well to copy, since the number of words that ad platforms display often varies between desktop and mobile.

- Design multiple flows for consumers, depending on their point of origination. If a consumer clicks on an ad and goes straight to your site, you could direct him or her to a different place than you would a consumer who comes to your site from a blog post. Different ads might also direct consumers to different pages. Think about how many different ways you can rearrange the pages you have. For example, if you're an apparel site selling a variety of different products, it might work better to take consumers directly from an ad for the product to the product page, bypassing the landing page and overall product catalog entirely.

- Keep shopping simple by limiting the number or kinds of products you offer. As Melanie from Andie related, she and her team offered just a few items for sale on their site to eliminate "decision fatigue." "We're certainly not trying to compete with Amazon," she notes. "We actually want to offer basically the complete opposite—a very curated site experience. You land on a swimsuit, you buy it, it comes in a great package, and you're done." Andie also minimizes the number of clicks it takes consumers to get to the checkout once they click on an ad. If consumers have to think too hard to make too many decisions, they'll get impatient and possibly abandon their shopping quest.

- If you must offer complexity, do so on an "opt-in" basis. Just because consumers like the idea of transparency doesn't mean they want to read every last data point or scientific study you provide on your site. And just because they can customize an order doesn't mean they'll want to go to the trouble to do that. Organize the site so that consumers can opt in if they wish, but enjoy a streamlined experience otherwise. A simple "Read more" button is all you need to give consumers the comfort of knowing that information is there if they want it. And if you do offer customization, also allow customers to select standardized bundles of products. Craig at Care/of notes that many of his vitamin customers like knowing that they have the option to customize their monthly vitamin packs, "even if they didn't actually wind up adjusting the pack."

- Use visuals to your advantage. On a landing page, high-quality photography might make an impact when standing alone, while illustrations can give a page a friendlier, more approachable feel, fitting in more naturally with text elements. In quizzes and questionnaires, imagery can serve to help simplify the experience. If you're asking consumers what patterns they like, you could say "(a) solids, (b) checks, (c) polka dots, or (d) stripes," or you could just illustrate the four options instead.

THINK HOLISTICALLY

With so much to consider, founders often make the mistake of focusing on one or two pieces of the flow and losing sight of the bigger picture. And yet everything you do ultimately comes together in the only metric you really care about: how much profit you earn per dollar of marketing that you spend. Running a *BuzzFeed* article might drive lots of traffic, but is it driving actual sales? A new campaign with an affiliate partner might convince lots of consumers to sign up for subscriptions on your site, but will those subscribers cancel at a higher rate or have lower credit scores?[*] Killing a free trial program could improve retention, but what damage will that do to your cost per acquisition?

> When running new creative campaigns, it pays to broaden your perspective and think holistically about the campaign in the context of your entire business. What are the campaign's strengths and weaknesses, and what net impact will it yield? Compare the net impact against that of other campaigns you might run or marketing actions you might take, taking into account the cost of each. Will this campaign outperform relative to these other options, and at an attractive price? Will you actually make more money? If so, how much?

START SIMPLE AND MODIFY AS YOU GO

As important as it is to be thoughtful, don't go too far and assume you have everything about your digital offering figured out from the very beginning. That's what experimentation is for. Work on getting your site selling. If you're happy with the sales you're seeing, push them even higher by spending more on marketing. If you're not happy, start tinkering. Watch closely as your initial customers move through the marketing funnel. How is it working? Are certain aspects of your digital experience alienating customers? What steps might you simplify or eliminate to make life for customers easier? Can you take customers from your ad to your landing page, or do you

---

[*] An affiliate partner is a marketing partner whom you pay per sale, and who often requests special pricing deals from you. For example, I could run a deal on Groupon and pay Groupon $2 for every sale they drive to me as an affiliate, offering Groupon's customers a 20 percent discount.

need to tailor the flow more carefully, taking them to a specific product page matching the particular product advertised? Pay attention as well to the quality of your customers. How valuable are they? If you sell on a subscription basis, what proportion of your initial customers are sticking with you over time? If you sell products individually, how often are customers returning to purchase from you, and how much are they spending for an average order? In either situation, how many customers are requesting refunds? How many are entering credit cards that are declined?

Once you feel you have a workable digital offering, start to scale it. Add additional media channels beyond Facebook and Instagram, such as television or radio. Move into search engine advertising (Google and Bing), cultivate influencers, place ads on Web advertising platforms like Taboola and Outbrain, and test other social media sites like Pinterest and Snapchat. Don't expect every channel you test to work for you, but the more channels that do, the easier you'll sleep at night. Start building more complex Facebook and Instagram funnels, running ads and sending customers to blog postings, earned media, or quizzes as well as to your website. See how high you can push your monthly spending while still hitting your CPA and customer lifetime value (LTV) goals (covered in Chapters 8 and 9, respectively). From there, expand your business by adding additional products and launching in different countries. You might also try selling through new distribution channels. Can you get your products into a mass retailer? What about opening your own stores?

There's so much to do when it comes to marketing and your digital offering, and different businesses will move at different paces. You might zoom through the process of optimizing your online selling and begin expanding into new products, countries, and channels within just a year or two. Or it might take you five years or more. Push hard, but be realistic. You can only go as fast as your customers—and your own understanding of those customers—will let you. Focus on solving problems for customers and making some money off that. And know when to call it a day. If you're not getting customers to buy, you can lower prices or change the offering. You can make new Facebook ads until your fingers bleed and then redesign the site and retool the product. The goal is to learn, and sometimes the lesson is an unhappy one: folks really don't want what you're selling. That's fine. Better to move on than to ignore the feedback.

STAY FOCUSED ON YOUR CUSTOMER

The best direct-to-consumer businesses thrive because the founders understand their customers well and design their offerings accordingly. But it's not enough to amass customer knowledge at the outset, design a great online experience, and then move on to other parts of the business. You have to stay sharply focused on the customer as you move through the steps I've just described, adjusting your digital offering as you gain additional insights, and in general doing everything in your power to remain relevant.

Renata Black, co-founder of the women's underwear brand EBY, personally reviews every customer cancellation as well as the feedback customers give about how the company's apparel fits. If her product isn't working for customers, she wants to know about it! But her concern for customers goes beyond product to encompass other key marketing dimensions. "We have a full-time customer service person," Renata says. "I work very, very closely with her on how she responds to customers, what that voice and tone is like, and tracking all of her responses so that we can be more responsive, rather than reactive."[6] Since women's empowerment and community are a big part of the EBY brand (the company gives 10 percent of its net sales to "empower women out of poverty and into business through microfinance"), Renata also makes sure on an ongoing basis that "at every touchpoint the customer has, she understands that she's part of something bigger. Every touchpoint should remind her that she's actually having an impact with the choice that she's made, and that she's part of a movement." And she means *every* touchpoint: the first email a customer receives confirming her EBY order, her shipping email, the email informing her that her order is about to arrive, EBY's Instagram posts, and its advertising.

At Hubble, we likewise spend a great deal of time thinking about our customers. We keep tabs on them through the emails they send, the comments they share on social media, and the surveys they fill out for us. Inspired by this feedback, we constantly brainstorm and test improvements to our service. Do we offer the first two weeks for $3, or do we reduce that to only $1? Would we be better off lowering the price on our monthly shipments? How should we adjust our pricing policy in different countries? We also investigate how we might serve customers better by offering new products. Should we offer contact lenses from other manufacturers for special conditions like astigmatism, which our own contact lenses don't correct? Should we add a telemedicine eye exam on our site? What about a weekly or monthly lens?

Framing the digital offering is a big job, and this chapter has just provided a quick overview. Yet for many founders, it's one of the most interesting and rewarding parts of selling direct. You can tweak your core product all you want. You can spend all day long building your team or cultivating investors. But the digital offering is where you live or die. If you don't have customers, you don't have a business. And the way to get customers in a retail environment populated by a voracious monster and a bevy of older but still fearsome beasts (from an upstart's point of view) is to nail your digital offering and keep iterating on it over time. Do that, and haul ass to deliver. It's as simple as that.

(THE NAKED TRUTH)

It's not just kids' eyewear companies that need to "frame" their digital offerings (get it?). All direct-to-consumer businesses do, if they want to have any hope of carving out a niche for themselves. So, immerse yourself in the array of digital marketing tactics available to you. Figure out if you're a subscription business or not. Test free trials. Hustle some earned media. Optimize your site for mobile devices. You don't have to do everything at once. Start small and proceed from there, keeping an eye on the customer at all times (make that two eyes, preferably wearing Hubble contacts). Framing the digital offering is a big job, but hey, it beats managing Facebook ads all day long. And it's absolutely vital. If you don't have a strong digital offering, you probably won't have customers—or a business.

CHAPTER 8

CUT THROUGH
THE METRICS BULLSHIT

THE YEAR WAS 2013. Twenty-two-year-old Jake Kassan was broke, a college dropout, and fresh off not one but two failed start-ups. Still, he and a buddy of his, Kramer LaPlante, had big dreams. Inspired by brands like Nike, Adidas, and Supreme, they wanted to create a lifestyle brand with global reach. They looked around for a corner of the fashion market they might break into, and thought they'd found it: watches. Although the world was saturated with watch brands, none of them seemed geared specifically to the tastes of younger consumers, and their products were also way too expensive.[1]

Jake and Kramer decided to create MVMT, a new watch brand targeted to millennials. Maxing out their credit cards, they spent a year and about "four or five thousand dollars" designing sleek, minimalist timepieces, obtaining samples from suppliers, and creating a promotional video. They launched in June 2013, having raised $300,000 on Indiegogo. Within a year, they'd notched $1 million in sales, including the Indiegogo presales. The second year, they grew sales to $7 million, marketing primarily on Facebook and Instagram—

massive channels that other watch companies were largely ignoring. By year three, sales reached $30 million, and by 2017, $71 million. In 2018, the watch company Movado acquired MVMT for a reported $200 million.[2]

How did Jake and Kramer sustain such explosive growth year after year? Clearly smart marketing was critical. By selling direct, they could profitably offer watches for between $95 and $130, a fraction of the price other brands charged at retail. By advertising the brand on social media, MVMT could connect with younger consumers where *they* were. MVMT's creative also evoked an "aspirational, fashion-forward kind of lifestyle" that resonated with millennials, one that depicted travel and adventure "or just people who are really passionate about their life and living [it] on their terms."

But MVMT's success went beyond consumer-facing aspects of marketing to include close scrutiny of both demand-related metrics and revenues. As Jake reflects, he and his team monitored how much it cost them to snag customers. "What's our cost per acquisition by channel?" they asked themselves. "If you spend $1,000 on Facebook and you get ten orders, it costs $100 to acquire each customer. How much is the watch you're selling? How much does it cost? In general, are you making money on each order?" The team also considered how much each order was worth, on average, but that was about it—customer acquisition costs and revenues. "You try to keep [metrics] as simple as that," Jake says. "Being a profitable boot-strap business, we weren't losing money to acquire customers, basically because we didn't have runway to do that. It was very disciplined. Every dollar I spend, I need at least one dollar, preferably two, three, or more." This fiscal discipline—enabled by attention to just a couple of metrics—was extremely power-ful, allowing MVMT to grow steadily without any outside capital beyond what the founders initially generated from their maxed-out credit cards and orders on Indiegogo.

Some founders downplay the importance of demand-related metrics, talking about how the personal, one-on-one relationships they foster with customers matter most. Don't believe them. Metrics are everything to a direct-to-consumer business. You can't have a one-on-one relationship with everyone, so if you aspire to be a mass business, you need some easy means of gauging how well you're doing at acquiring large pools of consumers. Are you getting your money's worth on Facebook, Snapchat, and other channels? What creative works best? And, most important, are you *making money* overall given how much you're spending to acquire customers? Answering this last question requires precise information about the revenues you derive from customers, not just the costs of acquiring them, and you also must know your fixed costs. We'll bring in the revenue side of the equation and connect it with customer acquisition in Chapters 9 and 10, on our way toward helping you build a workable financial model for your digital effort. For now, let's focus in on how best to track in financial terms the progress you're making toward that all-important goal of getting people to buy what you're selling.

KNOW YOUR DATA

Our first task is to get a handle on the quantitative information available to us. There's an old joke among marketers that they know 50 percent of their budget is working—just not which half. Thankfully, founders who sell naked don't have that problem, or at least not nearly to the same degree. Remember that consumer feedback loop described in earlier chapters? Selling direct does indeed generate a ton of data that you can use to track your progress and optimize your marketing spend. By tracking data from your website, you know how many customers are knocking on your door, proverbially speaking, and how much cash you're generating from them.

What you don't know from your website alone is how many of these customers are coming from each particular marketing partner or channel you're using. In some cases, your partners step in (or claim to), sharing with you their data on how many customers they are delivering individually. Facebook tells you how many people who viewed or clicked on your ad "converted" into customers on your site.* Google has Google Analytics, which allows you to monitor traffic coming in off every channel.

In other channels, you can create your own rough metrics. With television and radio, for instance, you can compare average traffic on your site before and after an ad airs to determine how many site visits the ad drives. If you send out direct mailings to consumers, you can perform "matchback" analyses to figure out how many people who received a mailer ultimately bought (you have to baseline this properly for what rate of purchases you'd otherwise expect from this pool). A lot of companies will also use custom discount codes for ad spend on channels like billboards, radios, and podcasts.

None of these metrics are perfect. You can't be certain that other factors unrelated to your television or radio ad didn't also contribute to that nice post-airing spike you're seeing. You should also regard Facebook and Google's metrics with some skepticism. Since these companies' lifeblood is ad sales, they

---

* Facebook can track you if you logged into the app on the device you're using to make an online purchase. It also tries to buy as much data as possible to track you across other devices you might be using.

have a vested interest in making their contribution to your business seem as great as possible. We've shied away from matchback analyses from direct mailings. Once you create different offerings for different groups, you have to track how long customers in each of these groups stay with you in order to determine if these customers are truly valuable. That can be quite a headache. As for discount codes, these often leak onto sites like Reddit. This isn't that bad if the leaked code drives additional sales, which is, after all, your primary goal. But leaks do invalidate your analysis of the channel's performance. It's not that podcast XYZ performed so well, but just that the discount code from that podcast got out on the Web.

So what can you do? One option that I don't particularly recommend is to sign up for one of the sophisticated multi-touch attribution offerings out there that purport to track which customers of yours come from where across the internet and beyond. Theoretically, these services determine which advertising works by statistically analyzing data about groups of consumers to understand how many pieces of which kind of advertising each consumer has received. If you and I both purchased from a site, and you saw four television spots, one Facebook ad, and one mailer and I saw three Google ads and five Facebook ads, these services would analyze all of this data and allocate credit for the consumer's purchase among the four channels in question. Such methodologies are imperfect, to say the least. If you saw four television spots, one Facebook ad, and one mailer before buying a product, and you saw the last of those ads several days before you finally decided to make that purchase, then the question of which ad drove your decision seems impossible to answer—not in a data sense, but in an actual philosophical sense. Such an analysis is an inquiry into a subjective state within your own mind on which even you don't have a clear perspective.

A much simpler technique that really does help is fielding good old-fashioned customer surveys. Simply ask customers at your checkout how they heard about your website. Some percentage of customers won't fill these surveys out, and you don't know if the responses you do get are entirely accurate. But as we've seen at Hubble, these surveys do help us document general trends related to the relative performance of individual channels. We can also glean information about the *quality* of customers these channels give us. For instance, our checkout survey might reveal that customers who come to us because they saw our television ad cancel at a higher rate than those who come to us from Facebook. That's valuable information, helping us to shift our spending to where it's most effective and economical.

You might also try running time-based and geographic tests. Stop advertising on television for a month or two, and see whether sales rise or fall and if your cost to acquire customers rises or falls. Run ads in one market and not others, and compare sales and customer acquisition costs. Frequent testing coupled with customer surveys and data from your channel partners (taken with a grain of salt) will help you understand what marketing spend is working for you and what isn't.

GOING BEYOND THE ALPHABET SOUP

Once you understand where demand-related data comes from, you're left with the seemingly unenviable task of figuring out how best to slice it in operating your business. Direct-to-consumer businesses give rise to an alphabet soup of marketing-related metrics that on the surface seems quite confusing. There's CTR (click-through rate, the percentage of customers who actually click on an ad), CPC (cost per click, the price you pay for each click in your marketing campaign), CPM (cost per thousand impressions, referring to advertising bought on the basis of the number of impressions), CPV (cost per view, the price you pay for video views or interactions), CVR (conversion rate, the percentage of people visiting your site who become customers), and bounce rate (the percentage of people who navigate away when they come to your site). (Hey, they can't all be acronyms starting with *C*.) What do you do with all these metrics? Which are important and which aren't?

Marketing metrics are not quite as complicated as they seem. You don't have to worry so much about most of these metrics day to day, since they don't help you very much in making decisions. To understand why, let's take a step back. If you're selling naked, there is really only one metric that truly matters: how much profit you reap for each dollar you spend on marketing. As Gravity Blanket's John Fiorentino observes, "The strongest indicator of success with a direct-to-consumer business is, can you acquire a customer profitably? . . . Is there some channel you can find where you're spending a dollar and getting three back? If the answer's yes, then you probably have a pretty interesting direct-to-consumer business."[3]

As true as Fiorentino's insight is, you can't just focus on profit per dollar of marketing when operating your business and forget the rest of the alphabet soup. That's because profit per dollar of marketing is simply too high-level to give you meaningful feedback about how specific functions in your business are operating. A number of factors influence the amount of profit per dollar of marketing, so your team can't use this number to know, say, whether a tweak to a marketing campaign is bearing fruit, or if a new channel is working. The revenue side of the equation also evolves slowly. If you make a marketing tweak today, you won't know for months how it impacted lifetime revenue (and hence profit) for a customer.*

Operationally, you need to specify business goals in enough detail that different parts of the business can work on them every day and have some sense of how they're doing. Of course, if you make goals too specific, then team members might strive to reach the goal in ways that hurt the overall organization. If I were to tell you, for instance, to take action to reduce the cost per click as much as possible, you could do that. But you'd be buying up cheap traffic that doesn't actually attract many customers. Your CPC numbers would be fantastic. The business would be hurting.

The most important metrics to monitor closely are those that are specific enough to help you day to day, but broad enough so that delivering on those metrics would likely move the business in the right direction. If we move down a level of abstraction and look at what factors contribute to the profit earned per dollar spent on marketing, we encounter just three

---

* It's a bit easier to track this in businesses with little repeat purchasing. The more that lifetime value accrues at the beginning of a relationship, the easier it is to measure it. If you have a subscription business that garners most of the lifetime value after year one, and you make a marketing tweak today, you won't really know the total impact it has on CPA and LTV for months. You'll need to collect enough data to see changes not only in CPA, but also in retention. After all, your CPA might decline, but the customers you're buying might be of lower quality and retention could degrade meaningfully, leading to net negative impact on LTV/CPA despite the CPA improvement. On the other hand, if you're selling a mattress, and a marketing tweak you make causes the CPA to go down, you can feel pretty comfortable assuming right away that the change is for the positive, absent a spike in refunds, which you would also see pretty quickly.

metrics: CPA (cost per acquisition—the amount it costs you on average to acquire an individual customer),* LTR (lifetime revenue—how much cash a customer pays the business over time), and your margin (how much you make after you subtract the variable costs of doing business from revenues).

We'll talk about a fourth, related metric, LTV (lifetime value, the product of LTR and margin), in Chapter 9, when we cover the revenue side of your operations. For now, let's note that of these metrics, CPA and margin are the easiest to work with operationally. Information about lifetime value only comes in over time. If you make a change hoping to increase lifetime value (by improving the quality of your product, say, or changing your pricing policies), you won't know for months if you've actually improved your business. On the other hand, if you make a move that results in lower shipping costs—thus improving your margins—that's an immediate improvement you can model in. Likewise, if you experiment with a change to your marketing (running different kinds of ads, say, or a change in the customer's flow through your website), you'll know in a matter of days or weeks if it's costing you less to acquire a customer, although it might take a bit longer (especially if you're running a subscription business) to tell if you've also improved the quality of the customers you're acquiring.

THE WONDERS OF CPA

Of these two metrics, CPA and margin, CPA is generally the more important to monitor every day. There aren't many ac-

---

* Another commonly used metric, CAC (customer acquisition cost), overlaps heavily with CPA. For the purposes of simplicity, I'll just talk about CPA.

tions you can take day to day to improve your margins. You could find different vendors for shipping, call center management, and other functions that generate costs, but these are generally not daily decisions. You might sign a contract binding you to a vendor for months or years. Even if you don't, you're not going to be switching vendors weekly or even monthly to cut costs. Imagine moving your inventory from one fulfillment center to another every couple of weeks—that would be crazy! By contrast, there are many moves you could make day to day to keep your cost per acquisition as low as possible. You could put up new ads on your existing marketing channels. You could buy advertising on new marketing channels, or change how you're allocating your budget between channels. You could change where your Facebook ads send traffic—to a blog, a quiz, a landing page, a product page. You could tinker with your site itself, introducing new options at checkout or a new look and feel.

Most of what will impact CPA occurs in the digital realm, where you are at your nimblest and can test your actions most quickly. This is also the area where founders hold their greatest advantage over incumbents. On the flip side, the areas where you can generally hope to make the biggest impact on margin manufacturing and distribution—are strong points for incumbents. To focus on maximizing your advantage, pay the closest attention to optimizing CPA.

It's true that most of the other "alphabet soup" metrics mentioned earlier contribute to CPA in some way. CPM, CTR, CPC, and CVR will all affect how much it costs you, in the end, to acquire customers. But these measurements are so specific that taking their optimization as your ultimate goal might create big headaches. If you put a team member in charge of your marketing funnel, for instance, you could think to evaluate that person based on how your conversion rate (the percentage of people visiting your site who become customers) changes. Seeking to deliver amazing results, this team member might decide to buy higher-quality traffic that has a higher chance of converting into customers. Sounds great—except that this traffic is more expensive. This team member might also try to make your online offers more generous or offer bigger incentives to customers for referrals. You'll get more customers, but you'll do it by wrecking your revenue per customer. If you're looking only at conversion rate, you don't care about the cost—but if you want to run a profitable business, you do. The broader CPA metric accounts for customer conversion and your cost. It's thus a better metric to help you drive daily operations.

Similar logic holds for the other metrics feeding into CPA. You could try to minimize your cost per click or your cost per impression, but the traffic you're buying could be garbage, leading your bounce rate to spike and your customer acquisition to dry up. You could try to maximize your click-through rate by providing engaging content, but you might not be driving to the site consumers who would consider making a purchase. As a result, your overall cost to acquire a customer could skyrocket. By capturing the cost, quality, and relevance of traffic, CPA will keep you focused on what really matters to drive sales. Concentrate on optimizing CPA and you'll take actions that over time strike a better balance between cost and quality. When you factor in revenues, these actions will make for a profitable and sustainable business.

SOME CAVEATS

That isn't to say that you should ignore the metrics that contribute to CPA. These numbers can help you troubleshoot when things break down. If sales flag or CPA spikes, you might want to investigate these other metrics for signs of weakness. If your cost per click is ten times higher today than it was yesterday, for instance, then that's a sign that a significant issue might exist in your marketing funnel.

There are a couple of other caveats to bear in mind. As helpful as CPA is, you don't necessarily want to minimize it. That's because many of the actions that lower CPA (and that also improve your margins) will hurt the other metric that really matters, customer lifetime value (LTV). If I dangle a free trial, my cost of acquiring customers will likely drop right away, but I might also acquire customers who won't stick around (because they're interested in the freebie, but not in paying full price). In that case, my LTV will decline. If I increase my spend on affiliate platforms (sites like Groupon that present consumers with special offers), I might obtain low CPAs, but also a bunch of bargain-hunting customers who aren't seeking a relationship with my brand and thus might not stick with me very long. It is true, as Nick Shah of the digital marketing firm Ampush says, that "early on you want your CPA, you always want your cost per acquisition as low as possible."[4] But in working to keep CPA low, consider the impact on customer loyalty and spending over time. Optimizing CPA entails keeping it as low as possible while still attracting high-quality customers who will stick around to spend with you.

A second caveat concerns scale. You might find a way to deploy your marketing budget that dramatically lowers your

CPA and improves your margins. That's fantastic, but can you scale it? If your enviable results only work with a tiny amount of spend, they don't help you very much. Look for marketing actions that deliver a big payoff and which you can sustain with larger amounts of spend. Pinterest, Snapchat, and services like Outbrain and Taboola (which provide those spammy links you see at the bottom of articles) have a fraction of the ad inventory of Facebook, Instagram, or TV, so you can spend only so much in those channels before your ability to acquire customers diminishes and your CPA skyrockets. Podcast or blog endorsements can accommodate more spending, but working with podcasters or bloggers can prove quite time-consuming. For us at least, the highest yield has come from focusing on the big, "vanilla" paid acquisition channels of Facebook, Instagram, and television.

OPTIMIZING CPA BY CHANNEL

If CPA is so important, how do you optimize it? Think on a channel-by-channel basis. Facebook and Instagram are the most important channels for us (and many others) for acquiring customers. Twitter and Snapchat are promising, but in our experience they don't generally work as well yet, perhaps because the algorithms and tools they use to match different brands to consumers aren't as well developed and functional as Facebook's and Instagram's. Recent tests with Pinterest have been much more encouraging, perhaps reflecting investments the company has been making on its ad delivery platform.

A number of other channels available online might allow you to acquire customers cheaply, but those customers might not prove all that valuable. Search engine advertising, for instance, will usually allow you to acquire customers who want your product and are ready to make a purchase. After all, these customers are actively searching for your product online. What search engine advertising won't do, however, is allow you to build your brand among consumers who might not know yet that they want or need you or your product. In practice, folks generally buy the search terms applying to their own brand simply to prevent competition from using their search traffic to poach sales. Affiliate channels like Groupon can generate sales, but as I've suggested, the quality of these customers generally isn't great (their lifetime value is low).

Other online channels are even less useful. Video and music streaming sites like YouTube and Spotify have lots of cheap ad inventory to sell, but as we've seen at Hubble, most of the traffic they send doesn't convert into paying customers. As a result, CPAs tend to be abysmally high. Email marketing likewise doesn't work terribly well if you're buying email addresses, as these tend to be of very low quality. (Emailing people who have visited your site and shared their addresses will generate more sales and lower CPA, but you're not attracting new customers to your site, only retargeting those who have already been there.)

As for offline channels, television is the biggest and has been for decades. It's a good option, in our experience; while CPAs are generally higher than on Facebook and Instagram, the customers you attract are worth more. Radio and podcasts can generate attractive CPAs for you if your product appeals to the consumer demographics that these channels serve (radio listeners tend to skew older and male, while podcasts skew younger and male). If you target largely female consumers, as Hubble does, you might dabble in these channels, but you won't invest in them like you might in TV. Direct mail is generally an effective strategy, albeit an expensive one. If you try to lower the cost by bundling your mailing with those of other brands (using a service like ValuPak, for instance), you'll attract fewer customers. If you're selling a product where customers stick around for a while and deliver large amounts of value (like credit card or insurance companies do), the high cost of effective direct mailing might be economical. Otherwise, you might want to steer clear.

> Think about your business, and assess the available marketing channels. What kinds of CPA does each give you, and which channels give the most loyal, highest-spending customers? Adjust your CPA targets for each channel accordingly. You might be willing to spend more to acquire customers in television, say, than you would in radio because the customers will tend to stick around longer.

> Pay attention, too, to scale. Most of the time, marketing ends up being a trade-off between CPA and scale. If you can eat a higher CPA, you can very likely increase your new subscriber count, but you might not be able to afford to do that for very long. In practice, you only have a rough sense of scale dynamics, so you're basically just looking to cut spend from channels that are wildly inefficient and scale it in those that are strongly outperforming.

IF YOU'RE YOUNG, GO DIGITAL

Digital channels are vital for getting your business up and running. These channels are a form of ad inventory that incumbents still don't know how to utilize, making it a marketing playground for you. They allow you to iterate frequently, spend in very small dollar increments, and scale up your spending very quickly.

As your focus turns to scaling, offline channels grow in importance. In general (at least for us), these channels have somewhat higher (though still acceptable) CPAs and generate worse and slower attribution data. Despite their drawbacks, they're still critical for deploying larger advertising budgets. The only major offline channel that we haven't at least tested is public signage (for instance, billboards, subway), because we're skeptical that we can mobilize it effectively. Folks always tell us that they've seen ads for Hubble on the subway, when in fact we haven't appeared there. To us, that's a warning sign that the dollars we might spend on public signage won't have the kind of impact we desire, and that we won't be able to track reliably the relationship between our ad spend and sales.

Lesson for founders: Start with social media first, taking advantage of the nimbleness they allow. As time passes, test television and other offline channels.

BEWARE THE ZYNGA EFFECT

Experimenting with additional channels as you grow—offline or not—can help you for another reason. There's a danger to relying too heavily on one or two channels, something I'll call the Zynga effect. As Candid founder Nick Greenfield notes, the games developer Zynga got into big trouble a number of years ago because almost all of its traffic originated on Facebook and it hadn't figured out a way to profitably acquire customers via other channels. When Facebook changed its policies in unforeseen ways, Zynga's cost of acquisition spiked considerably. Yelp was similarly vulnerable. Relying on Google for its customers, it saw its costs rise overnight when the search engine changed its algorithms.

For marketers, it pays to aim for channel diversity. "We think about it as a portfolio," Greenfield says. "We don't want to be overindexed to any one [channel] more than 30 percent."[5] Greenfield notes that as of late 2018, his team is spending close to 70 percent of its marketing budget on online channels. Going forward, they'll seek to shift their marketing mix so that it is more evenly spread across channels, even if it means that "the blended mix of our acquisition cost is maybe 10 or 20 percent higher." The safety afforded by channel diversity is worth the extra cost.

How do you feel about the risk posed by relying on a single channel? And what premium are you willing to pay to avoid it? Aim for a diversified mix, but don't force it. Some businesses just don't have diversified marketing mixes, no matter how hard founders might try. If just a couple of channels are really working to generate sales and the rest aren't, be honest about that and accept it as a risk inherent in your business. The alternative—wasting money in other channels as you try to trick yourself into believing you have a diversified mix—won't get you very far.

FRAMING A CPA TARGET FOR YOUR BUSINESS

What about CPA for your business as a whole? How should you calculate a reasonable goal to drive your overall marketing efforts, given the economics of your business?

Work backward. First figure out how valuable an individual customer is to you, on average. Then decide how much return you need to see on marketing spend for your business to break even or turn a profit.

Let's say your company sells lingerie online. Each customer buys only a single piece, the items cost $100, and you don't offer customer refunds. It costs you $20 to make the product, and fixed costs like salary, rent, and so on come to $10 per item. Your profits, before considering marketing spend, are $70 per unit. In this case, the most you should pay to acquire a customer is $70. If your CPA surges higher than that, you're losing money.

> To ensure that you're turning a profit, you'll want to set your CPA target considerably lower than $70. And you'll also want to set your CPA target lower still, to account for a not-so-curious phenomenon: CPA rises as your business scales.

In general, increasing scale allows you to realize efficiencies, reduce costs, and improve your margins. The cost of manufacturing your product is liable to decline as you grow—if you make and sell widgets, it's usually cheaper to make 1 million than 100,000. Yet marketing gets *more* expensive as you look to acquire more customers over a fixed period. Only a certain number of folks are potential buyers of your

product at any given time, and you're not the only player in
town competing for those prospects. As you and others strive
to grab more customers, the law of supply and demand means
that the cost of acquiring them will rise. Certainly the auc-
tions for Facebook advertising have only grown more expensive over time as more advertisers have moved onto the
platform and as competition for customers in specific markets
has grown fiercer.

These rising costs don't prevent you from achieving significant growth while still making money. As your brand becomes
better known, you can get more customers each month without additional spending. Some of these customers will arrive at
your doorstep thanks to word of mouth, while others will have
seen an ad a while ago and only now decide to buy. You'll also
get smarter about marketing over time. But because CPA rises
with scale, ceilings to growth exist. As you expand, and as
competition in your business mounts, you will eventually reach
a point at which you can no longer acquire incremental customers and still turn a profit. At that point, stop increasing
your marketing budget. Until then, go for it! And set your initial CPA target a bit lower than you otherwise would, accounting for rising CPA with the passage of time while still building
in room for you to turn a profit.

Adam Lovallo, co-founder of Grow.co and founder at the
landing page platform company Thesis, sees the failure to an-
ticipate growing customer acquisition costs as a major cause of
distress for founders. If they've raised money from venture
capitalists, the growth targets they must achieve require them
to spend aggressively on marketing. As they do, they find that
the overall costs of acquiring customers "are way higher than
they ever thought they possibly could be, so high that it's basically uneconomical."[6] It isn't just a question of CPAs rising

over time. Founders might assume that for every customer they pay to acquire, they will acquire two customers for free through so-called organic means (word of mouth referrals, for instance). But when they get to the point of spending $1 million a month on marketing, they might find that they are acquiring only one customer for free for every customer they pay to acquire. That pushes the overall cost of acquiring customers higher. If you haven't planned for that, you're in trouble.

To avoid a nasty surprise, Lovallo's recommendation is that founders track not merely their CPAs over time across individual channels, but also their "blended" customer acquisition costs (the overall amount you're spending to acquire customers, including through organic means). Understand the relationship between your marketing spend and the "blended" costs, and test it to make sure that this relationship will hold up as you grow.

MARKETING ISN'T ROCKET SCIENCE

Thanks to our quantitative-ish backgrounds, Ben and I were comfortable dealing with marketing metrics, critically analyzing them, throwing out the ones that seemed stupid to us, and working on the ones that helped us drive our business. When we spotted limitations in the data, it wasn't much of a stretch for us to invent workarounds, like the post-checkout survey mentioned earlier.

What if you don't have a quantitative background? Can you succeed with selling naked? Absolutely. Any reasonably diligent person can master this stuff, and it won't take you that long. Jake from MVMT hadn't spent years working for a hedge fund or investment bank, nor had he even finished college. As the de facto CMO, he immersed himself in Facebook and other digital platforms, teaching himself the nuances of digital acquisition and advertising as he went. He learned about CPA early on, since it turned up on a great number of marketing-related sites he visited online. With very low overhead and only a couple of channels to worry about, it wasn't hard to track how effective his marketing was. "I looked at our marketing channel that we spent on," he says. "As long as we were making money based off of what the average order value of the typical order was, you do the simple math and move on from there." Over time, as the business grew, it became more complicated, and required more insight and attention. Today "we have forecasts and projections and CPA targets. As you get bigger, you have to be more disciplined, but in the early days, you're hoping the business gets off the ground and that you don't make any wrong moves."

As Jake also notes, optimizing your marketing expenditures takes time, and founders might have to cut themselves some slack early on. "You may need a couple months of inefficient spending just to learn who your customer is, and hopefully every day and every month it's getting better and better and better." Some businesses have more wiggle room than others, given their price points and margins. Jake was lucky: since his watches had fairly high price points and margins, "we had the ability to acquire customers at a reasonable CPA, to scale the business." With a lower-priced product, it might have been more difficult. But Jake also made his own luck by choosing a category with high prices and margins, and by making sure to grow at a pace he and his co-founder could handle. As his business grew, so did his knowledge and sophistication about marketing metrics and how to deploy them.

You never do achieve perfect mastery—and that certainly keeps the work engaging (a double-edged sword, given the daily grind I described in Chapter 1). At Hubble we're constantly refining our understanding of our advertising channels. Is the incremental customer we attract on Facebook cheaper than the first customer we can attract via a television spot? Is our spending on television subsidizing Facebook by increasing brand awareness and perceptions of brand quality, in effect driving down the cost of acquiring customers on Facebook? What can we afford per customer, and should we slash the high-cost channels entirely (sorry, direct mail and podcasts) and shoot for fewer new subscribers each month? Such questions fill our days and not infrequently our nights, and they should consume yours, too.

(THE NAKED TRUTH)

To operate a direct-to-consumer business, you need a reliable financial model. The first step is to get a handle on marketing-related metrics—and by that I mean cut through the metrics bullshit. So many metrics out there won't give you the information you need to make sound decisions on a daily basis. Cost per acquisition is what matters, and trying to optimize your margin helps, too. Analyze CPA channel by channel, remembering to also consider the quality of customer that each channel provides you for the money. Set realistic CPA targets for your business, understanding that CPA will naturally rise as your business scales. You don't have to be a quant genius to succeed with CPA. Anyone can do it, so long as you're willing to immerse yourself in the nuances of marketing, be patient, and learn over time. Social media marketing can be exhausting, but over the long term it also has its moments of discovery. And those are their own, strange sort of satisfying.

(CHAPTER 9)

KNOW WHAT
A CUSTOMER IS WORTH

IN 2014, WHEN Simon Enever and Bill May determined how they would price their initial electric toothbrush and toothpaste offering for Quip, their subscription oral care brand, they didn't have every last element of their financial model in place. Seeking to build a comprehensive brand, they saw their initial products as a worthwhile first step and didn't feel compelled to analyze every last part of the business to generate an "extra two cents, five cents, two dollars" of margin, as Simon put it.[1] Better, they thought, to focus on creating a great product that fulfilled consumers' needs to secure them as paying customers. Simon and Bill needed to pay enough attention to the numbers to ensure that they were operating profitably, but they didn't have to work obsessively to optimize their margins.

Simon and Bill did appreciate the need to frame their pricing with an eye toward generating as much cash as possible up front, while also attempting to acquire customers, retain them, and maximize their lifetime value (LTV). With these considerations in mind, they priced a non-subscription toothbrush at

$35—a big increase for consumers accustomed to manual toothbrushes, but a much lower cost than most other electric toothbrushes in the marketplace (especially when you consider their product's enhanced design aesthetic). To encourage customers to sign on as subscribers (paying $5 every three months for replacement brush heads and batteries), they offered a $5 discount off the toothbrush. If customers subscribed to toothpaste as well, they received a $10 discount off the initial $35 package, creating a $25 advertised starting price. "You need to maximize what customers pay on day one," Simon says, "and what they pay every cycle after that" in order to maximize LTV. "You build your company and maybe your system in a way that tries to keep your customer around as long as possible. And then it's just that versus what you have to pay to acquire that customer." Their goal was to incentivize people to subscribe, "at a cost that didn't mean we were just losing loads of money on marketing and taking six years to pay it back."

To further drive subscription retention, Simon and Bill offered them a small discount if they paid for a year's subscription up front. "That was a huge win for us," he says, "because you've got at least a year guaranteed of that customer, and you have a year to offer them more products and services." Up-front subscription sales also made sense because they reduced how much Simon and Bill would have to spend initially to grow their customer base. As a "very underfunded" start-up (the two had only about $300,000 in capital to work with during their early days), every dollar they could save mattered. The more "we could do to bring that revenue forward in the customer life cycle was great for us," because the company didn't have "millions of dollars a month" to spend up front "just to aimlessly get people into the pipeline."

As Simon and Bill's experience suggests, it's just as important to understand revenue as it is to understand acquisition costs when building and scaling a profitable direct-to-consumer business. You can't build a viable financial model without calculating LTV and, in the process, the value that an individual customer order actually creates for you. In the next chapter, we'll explore how founders can use estimates of lifetime value and acquisition cost (CPA) to drive operational decision-making day to day. For now, let's run through how to calculate LTV. There will be some math in this chapter, but it's worth the effort—LTV really is critically important to get a handle on. You might be able to launch successfully without a clear model, but it's very difficult to stabilize the business, get funded, and grow if you don't understand clearly what value an individual customer contributes, what it costs to obtain a customer, and how those numbers come together into a usable financial model.

HOW MUCH IS AN ORDER WORTH?

The first step when calculating LTV is to determine how much revenue an average customer order contributes. Your average order is exactly that—how much a customer purchases on average—and it's the same whether you sell by subscription or by individual purchase.

If you sell just one product, you simply figure out how many units you've sold and divide it by the number of orders. There you go—average order value. If you sell multiple products, then you have to factor in those products' different price points. Let's say you sell apparel. Your trendy-looking shorts cost $25, your slacks cost $35, and your polo shirts cost $45. To calculate average order value, consider first how much of each product consumers buy on average by dividing unit sales of each product by total consumer orders. Your math runs as follows:

> **Average Order Value** = (average purchase of product #1 × cost of product #1) + (average purchase of product #2 × cost of product #2) + (average purchase of product #3 × cost of product #3) . . . and so on

Let's say you determine that the average customer buys 0.5 pairs of shorts, 0.25 pairs of slacks, and 1.25 shirts. Your average order value calculation is the following: $(0.5 \times \$25) + (0.25 \times \$35) + (1.25 \times \$45) = \$77.50$.

DID YOU REMEMBER THE UPSELLS, ADD-ONS, AND SPECIAL OFFERS?

You're not done yet calculating average order value. Factor in *upsells, add-ons,* and *special offers.* Think of upsells as a higher revenue offering in the same category. It could be more of a product (a set of three shirts, in the previous example, sold at a higher price point) or a premium product (shorts made of higher-end fabric that sell for $55). Add-ons are products added on to the main offering. Perhaps your clothing store decides to start selling sunglasses or leather belts to complement an outfit. Special offers include free or faster shipping, discounts if customers place orders above a certain size, and discounts if consumers buy bundles of different products ("buy shorts, a shirt, and a belt together, and get $20 off"). Such offers can drive revenue higher but reduce margins, producing an indeterminate net effect.

The Honest Company has done a good job of selling add-ons, expanding beyond its core diaper products to offer a variety of products in other categories, like personal care, vitamins, cleaning, and beauty. Dollar Shave Club offers upsells in the form of premium razors, which customers can purchase in place of the dollar versions. The company also offers add-ons like body cleanser, shave butter, shampoo, toothbrushes, and toothpaste. Willow, which sells adult disposable incontinence underwear by subscription, offers volume-based upsell options. Consumers can order four pairs per day (shipping every two weeks), two per day (shipping every month), and one per day (shipping every six weeks). It's all the same product, but the consumer pays more to get more.

> If you've calculated average order value for your company, go back and make sure you've covered any upsells, add-ons, and special orders. Your average order might be higher or lower than you think.

Let's say a pair of shorts costs $25 on your website, but the customer took advantage of an add-on offer and got two leather belts at $20 each and a pair of sunglasses at $15—a total order valued at $80. Every order above $75 gets free shipping, so I give up the $3 I would've booked on that front. The total order value would have been $83, but it is now only $80.

HOW MUCH ARE YOU MAKING ON THAT AVERAGE ORDER?

We've calculated average order value, but that doesn't reflect the profit you're making on each order. You're going to need to know that in order to calculate the number you really care about: the lifetime value of your customer.

The *contribution margin* per order is the percentage of revenue from your order that constitutes profit. To calculate contribution margin, take your average order value and subtract not just the cost of goods from your supplier (or cost of production if you aren't using a contract manufacturer), but *all* of your variable costs, including tariffs, freight forwarding, fulfillment center costs, shipping, and credit card processing fees. Don't include your back-end technology fees (payments to services like Shopify, for instance), since those are usually fixed, not variable. Customer services costs generally are not counted as variable costs, either.

Let's say you sell mattresses online. You buy the mattress from an international factory for $400. Having it shipped to your fulfillment center in Duluth, Minnesota, costs about $100 (what is called freight forwarding). In addition, you have to pay a 5 percent tariff on this imported product at the border. That 5 percent is calculated on the $400 cost of the mattress, amounting to $20. Picking and packing at the fulfillment center costs you maybe $10, while it costs you $75 to ship the mattress to the consumer. Credit card fees cost you 3 percent of the $1,000 sales price to the customer, so $30. Let's add up all of these costs:

Cost of goods sold: $400
Freight forwarding: $100
Tariff: $20
Fulfillment center: $10
Shipping to customer: $75
Credit card fees: $30

Total variable costs per mattress: $635

The revenue you generate from this sale, minus any refunds or chargebacks (customer disputes of charges on their credit cards), is $1,000. So your contribution margin is as follows:

$$($1,000 - $635) / $1,000 = 36.5\%$$

In other words, 36.5 percent of the revenue generated by this sale constitutes profit. That might sound like a decent profit margin, but in many investors' eyes, it isn't. Many investors want to see at least 50 percent of your revenue as profit. Bear in mind that I've simplified this calculation a bit. Most businesses would have discounts, refunds, or chargebacks to factor in that would lower the amount of revenue from an average sale. If your mattresses sell for $1,000, average net revenue per order might amount to more like $900 (in other words, 10 percent of your gross revenue might be lost to refunds or disputes with customers). In a category like mattresses, you'd have to pay some significant shipping costs on those refunded mattresses to bring them back to the fulfillment center. This might be another $75 on those 10 percent of orders, or $7.50 on average for all orders. Your revenue per order would be more like $900 − $7.50 − $892.50, and your contribution margin would be as follows:

$$($892.50 - $635) / $892.50 = 28.9\%$$

If you sell many products, you'll have to perform these calculations for each item, and then average the contribution margin for the items you stock, weighting it based on how many of each product are being purchased and how much each product costs. High-cost items and those that consumers purchase at a high frequency would have a greater impact on the weighted average.

KNOW YOUR VARIABLE COSTS

In presenting these calculations, I threw out a list of variable costs that businesses usually assume when selling naked. Since these costs reflect your business's basic operational realities, it's worth examining each of these costs in turn. Here are some brief explanations for each cost, as well as some tips to keep in mind to help you keep the costs to a minimum:

MANUFACTURING COSTS

Every direct-to-consumer business will have a manufacturer or supplier that produces the products you sell (and you could fill that role yourself). In some categories, the number of suppliers available is small, and forging an exclusive relationship becomes one of your top goals. In other categories such as cosmetics or apparel, many suppliers compete in the market, and you're more likely to want to stay flexible so that you can play suppliers against one another over time.

When negotiating with suppliers, the two terms you care most about are the cost per item and your payment terms (in other words, when you have to pay your supplier). The longer your supplier lets you wait before paying (for instance, you can pay sixty days after you take possession of your order as opposed to sixty days prior), the less working capital you need. And that's a good thing! Working capital is money that gets tied up in your business, primarily in inventory. The less working capital you need, the less you'll have to borrow or raise from investors.

FREIGHT FORWARDING

Your product has been manufactured and is ready for you to take possession. So, what do you do? You hire a freight forwarding company to get the product to your fulfillment center (also generally an outsourced service provider). Initially, you might need to ship by air, rushing product to your fulfillment center to send customer orders on time. Over time, as demand for your products becomes more predictable, you might want to ship it in an actual ship on an actual ocean. It's a lot cheaper, and in some categories where air transport would be prohibitively expensive, it's the only real option. Shipping costs vary depending on how much your product weighs and how bulky it is, and you'll also be responsible for any tariffs levied at the border.* While price is almost certainly the biggest driver in selecting a freight forwarding company, reputation matters as well (this partner could be carrying millions of dollars of inventory for you). You might also factor in technological capabilities. You'll have an easier time tracking your systems if you use a freight forwarder whose systems are already well integrated with the others you use.

Some suppliers will offer drop shipping. This means they'll

---

* Note that tariffs are not the same as sales tax or value-added tax. The latter applies mostly to orders in Europe, so if you're selling there, you'll want to talk to an accountant or tax attorney to ensure that you're handling this tax properly (same to make sure you're handling sales tax in the United States properly). When calculating revenue, you don't include any sales or value-added tax, since you're passing these taxes on to the governments in question. You don't book them as an expense, either, since customers are paying these taxes, not you.

ship directly to the end customer. Pretty awesome, if you can get it. Drop shipping frees you from paying and managing a freight forwarder and a fulfillment center. It might also free you from having to hold inventory (which, again, ties up working capital), although sometimes shippers should logically charge you (either explicitly or implicitly) for maintaining inventory in their facilities.

FULFILLMENT

Your freight forwarder gets your product to a fulfillment center, a place where you store inventory, and where it is picked and packed for shipment to your customers. Selecting a fulfillment center is similar to choosing a freight forwarder. Although reputation and technological compatibility are important, cost matters most. How much does a fulfillment center charge per shipment from the freight forwarder? And how close is a fulfillment center to your customers, thus minimizing shipping costs? You'll generally have to arrange for "outer shippers" at your fulfillment center (the cardboard boxes that your product gets shipped in). You'll need a separate vendor to manufacture these for you, and you'll probably want a supplier located near your fulfillment center to make restocking inventory as quick and easy as possible.

SHIPPING TO THE END CUSTOMER

This piece is fairly familiar to most founders—who hasn't rushed to the door to find someone from UPS, DHL, the U.S. Postal Service, or FedEx standing there with a package? Each of these providers has its own unique offerings and pricing structures. Smart founders will solicit quotes from all of them

regularly to make sure they're using the most cost-effective solutions. Also, play them off one another as aggressively as you
can while negotiating. Who wants to pay more than you have
to for shipping? Not me!

INVENTORY MANAGEMENT

As part of this process, you'll have to manage inventory, making sure you have enough product on hand to fulfill customer
demand while tying up as little as possible of your precious
cash as working capital. At the outset, you might want to
manage inventory conservatively if your stash of cash allows
it, ensuring that you won't run out of product and therefore
waste your investment in marketing. Consumers that hop
onto your site only to find that the products they want are
backordered might go somewhere else, and any money you
spent to drive them to the site is wasted. Some founders think
differently: in their view, the presence of backordered items
helps with brand-building, as it makes your product look desirable in consumers' eyes. I tend to think customers will come
away frustrated rather than impressed when they can't order
what they want. If I can, I want to have generous amounts of
inventory on hand. But you'll have to judge this one for yourself.

CREDIT CARD PROCESSING

To process credit cards through your site, you'll need to work
with a vendor like Stripe or Braintree. These guys charge you a
fee per transaction, generally around 3 percent of the transaction value, a bit less as you scale. One portion of that rate is
typically a flat fee per transaction, while another is a percentage

of revenue. Here again, solicit quotes regularly to get the lowest possible rates.

TWO DIFFERENT LENSES

As your business grows, variable costs tend to decline over time on a per-unit basis. Increasing volumes give you more leverage over your partners, allowing you to negotiate better rates. Your partners in turn experience lower costs as your volumes rise, since they can service accounts more efficiently. For instance, if my suppliers are manufacturing contact lenses for me, it costs them money to switch their production lines to make lenses of different powers. If I'm ordering ten times as many contact lenses, they don't have to switch their production lines as frequently, dropping what it costs them to make each lens.

Your working capital also generally declines on a per-customer basis, for a number of reasons. First, if you have 100 customers, you'll need to carry more product per customer than if you have 100,000. The larger your customer base, the less vulnerable you are to random variations in order flow. In a category like contact lenses, for instance, you're primarily worried about how many lenses of each power to keep on hand. Having more customers means we can hold less inventory per customer while minimizing the risk of stocking out on less common powers. Inventory ties up cash, so less inventory per customer means a decline (in relative terms) in working capital. Also, you can frequently negotiate better payment terms with suppliers as you scale, along with lower costs. If I don't have to pay until sixty days after I get my order from a supplier, as opposed to sixty days before receiving it, I have less cash tied up in inventory, leading to a further reduction in working capital.[*] Finally, you become less risky to investors as your business grows, so you can usually obtain more favorable borrowing or investment terms, which also reduces your overall capital costs (including the opportunity cost of the working capital you've tied up).

Think about your digital efforts through two very different lenses: what an order yields in profit today thanks to your existing variable cost structure, and what it will yield when your project matures. Both perspectives matter. The former affects how fast you burn through your cash, and the latter drives the business case for additional investment to unlock scale efficiencies. Ultimately, very few parts of your business are truly knowable ahead of time, and it pays to be very clear about them. When launching Hubble, we knew our product was lightweight, high-margin, highly replenishable, and relatively high-spend for consumers (as compared with products like razors or tampons). Laying all of this out was critical in attracting investor capital, and it also figured in our initial models of customer value, giving us more confidence that we would have a reasonable amount of cash on hand to spend for each customer that we wanted to acquire.

---

[*] Let's say I want to hold four months' inventory, and payment is due sixty days before an order. We'll assume, for simplicity's sake, that I receive the inventory in my fulfillment center the same day that I order it. To hold four months of inventory, I must pay for six months—the four months I have, plus the two months on order. If payment terms swing to sixty days after an order, I'm tying up only two months of cash for the same stock. Instead of me fronting my supplier two months of inventory, my supplier is doing that for me.

CALCULATING LTV
FOR SINGLE-ORDER BUSINESSES

Average order value and contribution margin allow you to determine how much profit you're generating per customer order. To calculate lifetime value, you'll need to understand how many times you get to collect that profit per customer you acquire.

Let's look at this first on the level of the individual customer. Say for a given customer, I logged $20 in revenue in month one, $15 in month four, $10 in month seven, and $5 in month ten. That would add up to $50 (as we'll see in Chapter 10, it's a little more complicated than this, but let's go with this for now). If your contribution margin on that revenue is 50 percent, meaning that half of what you collected in revenue was profit, then your LTV is $25. Now, let's factor in marketing costs. Any customer you can acquire for less than $25 is profitable for you.

> You can now see why LTV is so important: It allows you to determine what CPA you can profitably sustain, allowing for a bit of cushion to account for your fixed costs, like rent, salaries, and so on. Put differently, if you know how much a customer is worth, you can figure out how much you can afford to pay for one—knowledge that in turn enables you to make better marketing decisions.

Quantifying customer value can also give you an edge when trying to access capital. How can investors value a company like Netflix so highly (Netflix trades at a price-to-earnings ratio of 183, with $107 billion in market capitalization) despite its puny profits (only $178 million in 2017)? The answer lies in Netflix's robust customer retention data, which inspires investors' confidence in the company's future, rightly or wrongly. Netflix possesses more than two decades of data demonstrating its customers' loyalty. Based on this data, Netflix's investors can feel comfortable that as Netflix continues to upgrade its services, these customers will tolerate price increases, allowing the company to become a profit-making beast.

Of course, your business doesn't just have one customer—it has, hopefully, a great many of them. How do you calculate LTV for a crowd of customers? It varies depending on whether your business is subscription-based or not. Let's say you're a single-order business. You know what your average order is, so the question becomes how many times, on average, a customer places that average order. A key quantity to determine is the rate or frequency at which customers make repeat purchases, or their *repurchase rate*. Repurchase rate is something you only learn slowly over time. Once your business has been around for a while, you can look back at early customers and see how many additional orders they placed and what those orders were worth. You'll also need to model how their order sizes vary with each repurchase. You can take the same average order value logic and extend it out across all orders over an average customer's life, discounting orders that come further in the future because you'd rather have the money today than tomorrow. We'll walk through the discounting piece in Chapter 10.

With repurchase rate and order size in hand, you can calculate lifetime revenue. Let's say for the apparel company discussed earlier the value of the initial order is still $77.50. But we also see that half of customers come back to make a second purchase, generally an extra pair of shorts and half a pair of slacks (again, shorts are $25 and slacks are $35). Also, a quarter of customers return to make a third purchase—one more pair of slacks. Doing the math, we have our lifetime revenue of $77.50 from order 1, plus 0.5 × ((1 × $25) + (0.5 × $35)) from order 2, plus 0.25 × (1 × $35). This gives us average lifetime revenue of $107.50. For simplicity's sake, let's assume that all the products in this store have the same contribution margin of 60 percent. Our LTV then would be $107.50 × 0.6 = $64.50.

As you might imagine, if you can boost the repurchase rate, you increase the overall value of customers during their lifetime. The same holds true for order sizes. Get customers to buy more during their repeat purchases, and the LTV will rise.

CALCULATING LTV FOR SUBSCRIPTION BUSINESSES

For subscription businesses, calculating LTV is a bit different. Again, you know how much profit you make per customer order, since you know the average order value and the contribution margin. Now you have to figure out how many orders per customer you have at any given point in time. In theory, this is pretty simple: look at how quickly customers churn, and quantify your active customer cohort at each point in time (active customers are those that have subscribed to the service, have upcoming orders pending, and have a working charge card on file).

Here's the reality we discovered at Hubble: many customers aren't active or inactive, but somewhere in between. Some customers have declined credit cards that will be updated. Some haven't cancelled their subscription but are planning to do so before their next order—and you don't know that yet. Some are inactive and planning to reactivate. Others are active but skipping half their shipments. If you're not a subscription business, the challenge is even greater, as it takes a long time to obtain good data on repurchase rates. And refunds, disputes, and free orders (to address issues with earlier shipments) will mess with your data even more. So, what do you do to calculate LTV?

As a baseline, let's assume your customers don't cancel right away, their credit card is never declined, they never skip or reschedule their orders, and they never change the frequency of their orders. This ideal subscription curve can serve you as a measuring stick, recognizing that reality is never quite so simple and that most customers are not these "gold-standard" customers.

On the basis of these assumptions, we can calculate our *revenue retention,* which reflects how many orders are actually coming our way per customer per cohort.* You might think that your pure customer retention numbers—what percentage of customers are active at a given number of days after they subscribed or first purchased—are pivotal in determining retention. Although investors and other stakeholders care about customer retention, revenue retention is actually more important for calculating LTV, since it combines how many customers are active at a given time with how much they're ordering. Revenue retention does the job of accounting for skipped orders, customer changes in the cadence of orders (from every

---

* The cohort just reflects how long ago a customer subscribed. All else being equal, you should expect fewer orders per month from a cohort that's twelve months old than one that's six months old.

month to every other month, for example), declined credit cards, and all the rest.

To calculate revenue retention, take all the revenue you made from a cohort in a given month and divide that by how many customers you originally acquired for that cohort. This yields revenue per customer from a given cohort in a given month. Compare this to the revenues you generated per customer from that same cohort in month one, and you have revenue retention. All the customers who subscribed in October 2017 (or, in the case of a non-subscription business, placed initial orders) constitute your October 2017 cohort. If this cohort made you $3,000 in month twelve, and there were 100 customers in that cohort, then you made $30 per customer. If your gold-standard customers drive $100 in revenue each per month, then your revenue retention for that cohort is 30 percent.[*]

Let's say that we have a cosmetics subscription business where the monthly shipment costs the consumer $30, with a 50 percent contribution margin (i.e., profit per month of $15). If all customers get their first shipment, then 70 percent get a shipment in the second month (in other words, 70 percent revenue retention, accounting for cancellations, skips, card declines, and so on), 56 percent the third month (56 percent revenue retention), 48 percent the fourth month, 43 percent the fifth month, and 5 percent churn month over month through the rest of the life of the average customer (so 41 percent in month six, 39 percent in month seven, and so on). In this case, LTV would be:

---

[*] This is simplifying a bit, as it ignores factors such as premium subscriptions and upsells in subscription.

$$(1 \times \$15) + (0.7 \times \$15) + (0.56 \times \$15) + (0.48 \times \$15) + (0.43 \times \$15) + (0.41 \times \$15) + (0.39 \times \$15) \ldots = \$164.55$$

WHY YOUR FIRST CUSTOMERS ARE LIKELY YOUR BEST

Just as variable costs and the cost of capital tend to decline as a business grows, so does a customer's lifetime value. Most digital businesses hoover up their most passionate customers first, as early adopters. By contrast, later customers tend to be more expensive to acquire, and they also tend to hang around for fewer orders, leaving you with less value. Some network-based businesses have countermeasures built in. Although later customers at Facebook or Uber may be less excited about the offering, the value these companies are providing has improved over time because the network has grown (more of your friends are online, more cars are available, and so on). Companies that sell naked generally can't draw on super-powerful network effects to add value as they grow. Still, they're not necessarily doomed to declining LTV. As we'll see in Chapter 10, you can sustain or add value for customers by offering more or higher-quality products and services and improving customer experience. Give your later customers more reason to stick around, and they just might.

Although declining LTV and climbing CPAs might seem like downers, they don't have to hurt your business. Just make sure you've budgeted for it from the outset in projecting what you expect to pay to acquire customers. That in turn means being as clear as you can about what you'll need to spend as you grow to acquire customers. As Quip's Simon Enever remarks, founders have "a fiduciary duty to not just grow for the sake of growing." Companies that don't have an adequate handle on their costs blow up at some point because founders realize "that there's no way this will ever work as it [was working]."

> To get a handle on your future marketing costs, think about building your business from the outset using paid acquisition rather than so-called organic means, like word of mouth or referrals. Many businesses can grow organically to a certain extent, but at a certain point founders will likely need to pump in marketing dollars for the growth to continue. If you pay to acquire most of your customers from the outset, you'll have a more realistic sense of what it costs to acquire them. If you push word of mouth as far as it will go before spending to acquire customers, you might find that your paid acquisition costs are much greater than you could have ever imagined, and that you can't turn a profit. It's much better to find this out early and decide then whether you're still excited about the business.

At Hubble, we built our business by consistently paying for the customers we acquired. Of course, getting your business going and growing in this way, without the sugar high of front-loaded organic or referral acquisition, is expensive, but we've already dealt with that by overcapitalizing (Chapter 5).

As we've seen in this chapter, LTV matters because it determines what you can profitably spend on marketing. Ultimately, businesses that sell naked are marketing-driven, and your job as an operator is to spend marketing dollars as efficiently as possible to drive as much revenue as possible. You might think that if you build a brand that's awesome enough, consumers will flock to your doors without any special attention to acquisition on your part. I don't know any direct-to-consumer business of any scale that has found this to be the case. Word of mouth and viral buzz might give your ego a good stroking, but it's paid advertising that almost always ends up driving acquisition at some point. This reality in turn means that numbers like CPA and LTV matter.

(THE NAKED TRUTH)

If you want to build a thriving direct-to-consumer business, you can't content yourself with knowing how much it costs you to obtain customers—you also have to understand as precisely as possible how much cash each customer puts in your wallet. By cash, I mean not how much customers spend on a single order, but how much money they spend over the *lifetime* of their relationship with you. To calculate LTV, figure out how much an average order is worth, how much it costs you to fulfill an average order, and how much profit it brings you. Then it's a question of determining how many times you collect that profit per customer you acquire. These numbers tell you how much you can afford to pay to acquire a customer. Plants won't grow beyond a certain point if you don't water them, and businesses won't either unless you "water" them with marketing dollars. As your business scales, water thoughtfully!

CHAPTER 10

PULL YOUR FINANCIAL MODEL TOGETHER—AND USE IT!

IN OCTOBER 2018, when my research team sat down to speak with Sergei Gusev, co-founder and COO of the subscription perfume company Scentbird, he and his co-founders Mariya Nurislamova, Andrei Rebrov, and Rachel ten Brink had just raised another $8 million of funding for their company, bringing their total to about $20 million.[1] Investors were excited by the team's vision of expanding beyond perfumes to offer a full range of beauty products, all available in small, trial sizes for $14.95 a month. The goal was to become the digital Sephora, serving millennials who liked to try out many brands rather than committing to just a few by paying hefty prices for big bottles. But as important as the plan was, investors also had to see that the team was capable of operating profitably. As Gusev comments, that meant keeping a close watch on lifetime value and making sure that customer acquisition cost (CPA) didn't exceed one-third of LTV.

There are two ways to improve that ratio and keep it where it needs to be: reduce CPA or increase LTV. Since 2016, the team had made a strong push to affect both sides of this equation. To increase LTV, the team tried to improve their contribution margin, wrenching cost out at every opportunity: "We are trying to get our packaging more cheaply. We are constantly looking for new suppliers. We are getting bulk product, like perfume, from different brands at a cheaper rate. We are negotiating price all the time." Scentbird also tried to upsell its user base of 260,000 customers, launching private-label products like scented hand creams, lip balm, shower gels, and candles. Finally, the team focused on keeping customers happy and engaged, improving customer service and on-time delivery and working to drive as many customers as possible back to the website every month to fill their queue of perfumes (customers cancelled more often, they found, when they hadn't taken the time to choose their perfume each month and so received a "surprise" fragrance that they perhaps didn't like).

To lower customer acquisition costs, the team did everything it could to create an efficient marketing funnel. "We do a lot of conversion optimization," Sergei says. "We have a team of people who constantly work on our landing pages. They make sure that we have a best-in-class conversion rate. We make a couple of changes every week—to our payment pages, register page, the whole site . . . just moving our conversion rates up every month." Another way the team tried to lower CPA was to constantly iterate on and improve their advertising. "We have a team of experienced marketers who do a lot of Facebook advertising; they have different channels, affiliate marketing, Snapchat, Pinterest, Twitter, direct mail, TV commercials." The more channels the team used, the more diverse the marketing mix was, "the healthier the CPA is, and the higher our lifetime value." The ratio of LTV to CPA improved as well.

All of this constant, thoughtful effort paid off. Over the past two years, the team increased LTV by an impressive 30 percent. That was especially significant given how cheap Scentbird's product was—again, only $14.95 a month. Consumers were visiting the site looking for bargains—they didn't necessarily have lots of cash to burn. And yet the team had managed to convince many consumers to buy an array of products beyond perfume and to maintain their subscriptions for longer.

To succeed with direct-to-consumer, it's not enough to just know your LTV and CPA. You also have to *work* with these numbers, using them to drive your daily decision-making, especially around marketing. Sergei and his team had created a financial model of their business, and were ~ ·...u by that model and the goal of a 3:1 LTV/CPA ratio. Taking our cue from them, let's examine how you can use the relationship between LTV and CPA to ensure that your business is working. This chapter shows you how to go backward from your LTV to figure out what CPA you can afford. We'll then review tactics you can deploy to improve both sides of the LTV/CPA ratio and hopefully wind up with a fundraising and financial success story of your own.

WORKING THE 3:1 RATIO

Actually, I'm going to describe two methods for figuring out what CPA you can afford—the one most people use, which is faster to calculate, and another that's a bit more work but more accurate and useful. The most commonly used method is the

3:1 LTV/CPA ratio. Firms that sell naked calculate their LTV
on either a three- or five-year basis. That is, they model out how
much value their customers give them within three or five years
of acquisition using the methods described in Chapter 9. Di-
viding this number by 3, they set this as their CPA cap—the
limit on how much their company can spend to acquire customers. They spend their marketing budget across an array of
channels, allocating it based on where they are acquiring customers most efficiently, all constrained by the 3:1 LTV/CPA
target. This doesn't mean they give this target to their Facebook buyers or their buyers in other channels. Much of the
time that target will exceed the CPA target, and that's because
you also have to factor in organic acquisition, or the customers
you acquire that you can't attribute to any particular paid marketing channel.

Let's say my CPA target for the business is $100. Let's also
say I can't attribute 20 percent of my customers to any channel
using my post-checkout survey (or whatever tool you're using).
These mystery customers might have come to me through word
of mouth, or from people who saw my ads six months ago and
are only now making a purchase (thanks to the time lag, such
customers are considered "unattributable"). That 20 percent
figure means that my paid CPA target—the one I would give
my media buyers—would be $100 / (1 − 0.2) = $125. My *overall* CPA target is $100, but because I can spread that money
across only 80 percent of my customers, my effective paid CPA
can be 25 percent higher.

How does this $125 target translate into day-to-day opera-
tions for specific marketing channels? Let's take Facebook.
On that platform, the metric I pay attention to is the one-day
click CPA, which is based on my spend in Facebook and the

number of folks acquired within twenty-four hours of clicking on an ad. I'm not interested in consumers who simply
viewed the ad and then purchased, since I don't know that
they processed the ad or were influenced by it to buy. It's the
click that counts.* The question I have to answer is what CPA
I need on a one-day click basis in Facebook to get to my effective paid CPA target of $125. I answer this question by turn-
ing to my post-checkout survey. Let's say 90 percent of my
customers respond to the survey, and 100 of them report coming to me from Facebook. To determine how many customers
responding to the survey come from Facebook, I take 100 and
divide it by 0.9, giving me 111. For simplicity's sake, I assume
that channel attribution among the 10 percent of customers
who didn't respond to the survey breaks down according to
the same proportions as among the 90 percent who did respond.

Let's then say that Facebook reports to me that I had 74
one-day click purchases. To create a one-day click target for my
Facebook buyers, I would take the number of Facebook customers on my survey, divide it by my Facebook one-click pur-
chasers, and multiply that by $125. Here's the math:

$$(111 / 74) \times \$125 = \$187.50$$

This number, in sum, is my CPA target adjusted to account for
my overall survey response rate, and applied to my Facebook
channel.

---

* Imagine a customer saw a TV spot and was planning to buy already, and
Facebook happened to serve her an ad with which she didn't really engage.
Facebook can try to take credit, but the odds that this ad shaped this customer's
decision are lower than if she had actually clicked on the Facebook ad.

IS THE 3:1 LTV/CPA RATIO
REALLY WORTH ANYTHING?

Venture capitalists pay a great deal of attention to the LTV/ CPA ratio, prompting founders to pay attention to it, too. But this convention isn't the best way to model what is actually happening in a direct-to-consumer business. Critically, the ratio doesn't factor in the passage of time. Let's say I'm selling suitcases, and let's also assume that I make only one sale per customer, so my business reaps its entire LTV for each customer on day one. If my suitcase costs $300, and if 60 percent of that (or $180) represents profit, I should be happy with any CPA that comes in under $180. Imagine how crazy it would be if I said that I wouldn't accept a CPA above $60, keeping to the 3:1 ratio. I would be turning down a great number of profitable transactions that in turn would help me cover my fixed costs and move my overall business to profitability. I don't think any VCs would disagree here; the 3:1 ratio applies more to subscription businesses. In that case, the ratio represents a version of time-weighting, albeit one that is crude bordering on idiotic. By mandating that CPA can't exceed one-third of LTV, you're allowing for the fact that money in your pocket now is more valuable to you than money you receive from subscriptions years down the road. But the ratio of one-third is arbitrary, and barring a somewhat extraordinary coincidence, it will lead you to the wrong CPA target.

Another arbitrary measuring stick deployed by VCs, the concept of "payback," also yields illogical outcomes. The idea here is that any given direct-to-consumer business should turn a profit on a consumer relationship after a certain number of months, typically twelve (so-called twelve-month payback). In other words, my CPA should equal my twelve-month contribution margin, taking the lower of either your twelve-month payback target or your 3:1 target as your CPA cap. How does that make sense?

Let's say I have two subscription businesses. One of them is a meal kit business where I'm losing customers at such a pace that 80 percent of my LTV occurs in the first twelve months. For such a business, it might be that by the end of year one, only 15 percent of my customers are still active. Or I could have a bathroom-products subscription business where only 40 percent of my LTV occurs in the first twelve months, and 45 percent of my customers are still active after year one. The idea that I would apply the same twelve-month payback standard to both businesses is silly. Since my customers stick around longer in the bathroom subscription business, I should be willing to wait longer to break even on a customer there than I would in the meal kit business. Profitability at twelve months might be too long a payback goal for the meal kit business to operate economically, and too short for the bathroom one to grow as fast as it profitably can.

ANOTHER METHOD: INTERNAL RATE OF RETURN

In knocking the 3:1 margin, payback, and three- and five-year LTVs, let me emphasize that investors really do care about these metrics. Because they do, potential acquirers and public market investors have increasingly focused on them, prompting venture investors to care about them even more. This means that, as a founder, you can't help but care about them, too. Ultimately, your business is being evaluated on what it's being evaluated on, and you need to respect that, whether that basis for evaluation is appropriate or not. That said, there's another, much sounder method for time-weighting the value you receive from customers, and for connecting this to customer acquisition costs. Internal rate of return, or IRR, is the return on investment you get on cash flows, time-adjusted to reflect their *present* value. The equation connecting CPA and IRR is:

$$\text{CPA} = \frac{\text{revenue period 1} \times \text{contribution margin}}{(1 + \text{IRR})^1} +$$
$$\frac{\text{revenue period 2} \times \text{contribution margin}}{(1 + \text{IRR})^2} +$$
$$\frac{\text{revenue period 3} \times \text{contribution margin}}{(1 + \text{IRR})^3} \ldots$$
$$\frac{\text{revenue period } n \times \text{contribution margin}}{(1 + \text{IRR})^n},$$

where 1, 2, 3 . . . n are the discrete time periods in question

Because you know the CPA, contribution margin, and revenue for each period (or at least have made some reasonably sound assumptions about these), you can use this equation to identify a target for the IRR. The IRR, in other words, is just an interest rate that makes this equation work. You can use this equation to calculate IRR for any time period you wish, although if you're calculating the periods on a monthly or quarterly basis, you would need to annualize your results at the end.

Using IRR to calculate your return reflects the reality that dollars you earn today benefit you more than dollars you earn tomorrow (because you can reinvest today's dollars to generate even more future profit). Put differently, IRR charges tomorrow's dollars for their opportunity cost. IRR incorporates everything we talked about in Chapters 8 and 9—CPA, lifetime revenue, and margin—into one number. If CPA goes down, IRR goes up. If average order value goes up or churn goes down (the two components of lifetime value), IRR goes up. If margin goes up, IRR goes up.

In theory, the IRR concept gives you a clean and clear framework to use when talking with your board. Just ask board members what return they want to see on the dollars they're giving you, and then manage to that. Concepts like 3:1 and the twelve-month payback become unnecessary. Of course, this assumes that the bulk of your budget is in marketing and not fixed costs like salaries. That is true generally of direct-to-consumer businesses, or it should be if you're keeping your operations lean.

Operationally, you can use the IRR equation to set your CPA target. As your business grows and you gather more data, update your contribution margin (profit per order) and your retention curve (the percentage of your initial customers who stick around as time passes). Doing so will allow you to calculate a cash flow stream for you to discount back. Given your IRR target, you can then solve for the CPA that your business can support. Your CPA in turn determines how much you spend acquiring customers on specific channels like Facebook or television. Does your developing retention picture sometimes exceed your expectations? Then your CPA shifts up a bit. Or, if average order value trends downward for a month or two, CPA follows in turn. With these moving CPA targets go the rest of your business—marketing mix between lower-cost channels (probably Facebook or Instagram) and higher-cost ones (maybe television) and, consequently, how many new sub-scribers you're targeting per month. Everything just becomes an output of the IRR model.

While use of IRR is fairly rare in the direct-to-consumer space, in the finance world it's as basic as it gets. Managing to an IRR target eliminates all the issues I previously identified:

- There's no need to worry about choosing between a three-year and five-year LTV. The weights assigned to the later years in your customer life are minimal, so whether you go with a three-, five-, or fifty-year LTV, your IRR will remain more or less the same. On the other hand, if you didn't discount these cash flows, LTV would swing wildly based on how many years you chose.
- The issues created by a 3:1 LTV:CPA ratio also disap-pear. The IRR for any LTV greater than your CPA that's realized today is infinite, so in the suitcase example, for instance, you get the right answer—which is to spend on any customer that's profitable.
- The meal-kit/bathroom-product subscription problem is resolved as well. Your CPA target is driven by an IRR target, so the strange and arbitrary results that can arise with a twelve-month payback target disappear.

IRR also gives you an easy way to adjust your CPA target as your cost of capital decreases over the life of your business. Initially, your cost of capital is crazy high, whether it's your own cash (or maybe even your own borrowing off a credit card) or expensive seed dollars. As your business matures, your understanding of your LTV improves, and you demon-strate an ability to scale, your cost of capital decreases, since investors become more comfortable that your business can support its fixed costs. Your IRR target is just your cost of capital, so this model gives you an easy way to reflect progress on this front.

Overall, IRR can simplify your life tremendously. The core question confronting anyone who sells naked is: What rate of return do I require on a marketing dollar invested today? This question should determine in turn whether it's worth it or not for you to buy a customer at a specific price. Given the desired rate of return and the cash flows I expect from a customer, let me discount back each of them based on how far in the future they are to figure out what the highest amount is that I should be willing to pay for a customer. That's what the IRR equation has you do. All you have to do is choose your IRR, and the rest shakes out from there. That's because everything else—all the future cash flows—are already defined, and CPA is the only remaining variable.

In effect, the IRR concept prompts you to think of each marketing dollar you deploy as an investment that will generate a certain number of customers. Those customers will in turn produce a series of cash flows—the margin dollars from each order they end up purchasing. Let's say we started a subscription business for anti-acne products. We're pumping marketing dollars in, primarily directing that investment toward Facebook and Instagram, targeting one new subscriber for every $80 we spend on marketing. For every hundred subscribers we acquire, almost all will receive the first-two-weeks-free offer we provide up front. After that, some portion of these subscribers will cancel before the first paid month, some more before the second, and so on. Adding this all up, we can say that a customer costs us $80 to acquire and will generate lifetime revenue of about $600 and profits of $300. Even with corporate overhead, paying $80 for $300 of profit is math that works. Of course, like any investment exercise, this one reflects assumptions around future cash flows, and the output is only as good as the assumptions.

As useful as IRR is, we at Hubble don't rely on it nearly as much as I wish we did. We, too, must hold to the venture community's conventions. I hope that this will change. If you're a member of the investor community, please consider taking a closer look at IRR. And if you're an entrepreneur or a marketing executive at a large company, take it seriously as a way of driving your marketing efforts. The math is something first-year investment bankers at any firm anywhere in the world have to do in their sleep, and the day-to-day guidance that the IRR equation provides is more than worth the small additional effort.

WHAT ABOUT FIXED COSTS?

Fixed costs don't factor directly into the IRR calculation or any other metric discussed in this chapter. Venture capitalists aren't so worried about those costs, since they reason that if your business hits it big, it will scale massively and your fixed costs will become much lower as a percentage of revenues. Still, you must account for fixed costs eventually under the IRR model. You do so by choosing your IRR target and then figuring out how large your business can scale based on the biggest marketing budget you can deploy while sticking to your IRR target. For a subscription business, your peak scale will be the point at which 100 percent of the marketing budget that you can deploy profitably is just going to replacing customer churn. For a single-order business, peak scale would be the point at which the CPA on your next customer would be higher than that customer's expected LTV. If at this point of peak scale you're operating at your IRR target and your monthly profit isn't enough to cover your fixed costs, you should shut down, or at least try to either reduce fixed costs, lower CPA, or improve margins.

GO HIGH ON IRR

You might wonder what IRR target to pick for your business when using the IRR equation. I would suggest picking a high target, at least at the beginning. One way to think about IRR—probably the most logical way—is that it helps you understand whether it makes sense to invest a single additional dollar in marketing. Is the return on your dollar investment in marketing high enough (think back to your cost of capital)? If you're bootstrapping the business and have only a few months' worth of savings and credit to burn through, then you should make your return expectations high to justify the stupid amount of risk. On the other hand, if you're at a Fortune 100 company with a 4 percent cost of capital and a shortage of investment opportunities, maybe it's worth pushing your management to choose a more modest return target. (Or maybe this is considered a high-risk project within a low-risk company and still gets assigned a high cost of capital for internal budgeting purposes despite the corporation's low overall financing costs.)

> In most cases, as I've mentioned, businesses labor under much higher capital costs when they first start, so they should choose a high IRR target. As the project develops over time and

the amount of revenue grows, the IRR target should decrease because (a) you'll feel more confident in the model's assumptions, so the project is lower-risk, and (b) you're spreading your fixed costs across more revenue dollars.

Another reason to choose a high IRR is that the value you extract from customers generally diminishes over time, and acquisition costs tend to increase. Choosing a high IRR target gives you a built-in cushion to handle this degradation. Since your margins will likely improve over time as well, you might wish to calculate what they will be at scale and use that in the IRR equation. In general, it's important to think about your business at maturity. On the margin side, you can often make reasonable assumptions here, and manage to those, assuming that investors will finance you on that basis. When it comes to CPA and LTV, it's hard to assume much more than that CPAs will climb and LTVs will fall as you try to push acquisition volume harder and move past those initial, highly enthusiastic customers into the broader population.

A big decision to make in choosing your IRR target is where in the spectrum you fall between setting a very high target return at the outset and gradually lowering it, or choosing a figure closer to what it should be for the project at maturity. The former runs the risk of killing projects that could have worked with scale. The latter might leave you overly optimistic, believing that the economics of your business will work at some future point in what turns out to be an ever-receding horizon.

While you probably want to leave some space for your CPA to grow into when setting your initial target, you eventually do want to push your CPA as high as you can possibly afford—right up to the limit implied by your IRR model (or your 3:1 or twelve-month payback model if you're working off one of those). Going above those limits is too aggressive because it's pushing you into unprofitable customer acquisition, but keeping your CPA below that target is too conservative. Think about it this way: every month, you're stuck with all your fixed costs—salaries, rent, inventory, and, most of all, the opportunity cost of your time. Spending below your CPA target means you're spreading out these fixed costs across a smaller number of customers, paying more fixed cost per dollar of revenue than you could be. Also, your business is growing more slowly, which means it looks even less impressive to just about every stakeholder that matters.

> To think through the question of how high to go with your initial IRR target, consider how confident you are that the numbers will improve, proceeding assumption by assumption. Most likely, cost-related variables will improve. At greater scales, manufacturing and fulfillment costs decline, as do credit card fees, all in a fairly mechanical way. Beyond costs, I'd be cautious about modeling improvement in other variables, and it might even be a good idea to assume that they will worsen over time.

WHAT DO YOU MEAN, "PROFITABLE"?

The analysis in this chapter has assumed a venture-happy world, where you can access arbitrarily large amounts of capital. Limiting the conversation to this perspective is myopic, to say the least, ignoring businesses that founders have built through bootstrapping. Another perfectly rational way to handle CPA management for your business would be to refuse to take on outside money and to aim either to break even (including—shudder—your fixed costs) or for a profitability target (paying yourself dividends from your profits).

In these cases, you would start with your monthly cash flow before a single dollar is spent on marketing. What contribution margin do you earn in a month? What are your fixed costs? Did your working capital increase (sucking up more cash) or decrease that month? Where are your accounts receivable and accounts payable? (We've moved from the high-finance IRR to actual accounting.) Once you've netted all these cash flows, you see what's left over. If that number is negative, you're in trouble. If that number is positive, you have a marketing budget! That residual becomes what you can spend on marketing, and you spend all of it as efficiently as possible. (If that residual is very large, you should still constrain it based on an IRR model—no reason to buy unprofitable customers just because you have the budget for it.)

If you had a minimum profit target or a limit on how much cash you were willing to burn in a period, you could use those numbers similarly. Work backward from your limit to determine what marketing budget it will accommodate, and as long as there are customers that you can acquire profitably based on your IRR model, acquire them all. It might go without saying, but this approach allows for slower growth than just acquiring every profitable customer you can, and your business might not be strong enough for you to achieve your target no matter how small you make your marketing budget. I could set my lower profit limit at $100 million per month, but it doesn't mean I'm going to find that much money in my bank account.

OPTIMIZING FINANCIAL PERFORMANCE

Now that you know how to calculate a CPA based on your LTV, your primary task in running your company is to keep CPA as low as possible and LTV as high as possible, like the team at Scentbird did. *Day to day, these should be your two most important goals for your business.* Remember that experimental mindset we talked so much about earlier in the book? This is where you should be directing it most. We've touched elsewhere in the book on specific marketing tactics you can use to build your business. Let's now bring them together here in the context of CPA and LTV, with some additional tips thrown in. To lower CPA, do the following:

- Try out multiple channels, keeping and scaling your winners and killing off your losers.

- Be opportunistic, looking for deals on advertising spots.

- Experiment heavily with creative, especially in Facebook and Instagram, where creating new ads is cheap.

- Try going after new audiences within each channel. On television, should you advertise on Lifetime or HGTV? Should you target Sweetgreen fans? Warby Parker fans?

- Tweak all elements of your marketing funnel. Do you drive to a landing page? A blog post? An earned media piece? A quiz? What happens if you make a quiz multiple pages? A single page? What if you add a countdown clock? What if you drive to a full product catalog versus a single product page?

- Experiment with pricing. Should you offer a free trial? Special discounts? Free shipping/handling? These are all powerful for driving CPA lower, though you'll pay for them in lower lifetime value. The trick is tracking whether the net impact is positive.

- Improve or adjust the product to be more compelling to new customers.

To improve lifetime value (and the margins that underlie its calculation), do the following:

- Regularly reexamine every leg of your supply chain. Talk to other DTC companies to make sure the pricing you're getting is strong. Get bids from other vendors and bring them back to your partners if the pricing you're getting seems off.

- Be a good partner to your partners. Regularly communicate your own needs and see if you and they can arrive at creative solutions together that save you money without costing your partner. For example, using smaller, tighter packaging might reduce bulk, making shipping cheaper for you without adding complexity for your supplier.

- Substitute variable costs for fixed costs. Creating your own manufacturing or fulfillment center capacity allows you to take a lot of the costs that your partners are probably building into what they're charging you (logged as variable costs) and move them into the fixed column. This might impress investors and acquirers, who, as we've seen, are focused on variable costs. But don't go down this path unless the business case is really compelling apart from the optics. Otherwise, stick to external partners.

- To improve margins, try giving key long-term partners equity (if they'll accept it) in exchange for product/services at cost. By sharing the pie, you're not taking on a massive fixed cost base, but you're getting the benefits as if you had.

- Increase prices to improve margins, but watch out for a hit to how many visitors to your site are choosing to buy and/or stick around. If retention is an issue, try lowering prices. See which of these pricing decisions (raising or lowering prices) has the greatest positive impact on overall LTV and CPA.

- Tweak products to make them more attractive to existing customers based on data or customer feedback. If folks are asking for bigger sizes, consider offering them. If some products are popular and others aren't, add more products like the popular ones and kill the duds.

- Add additional products to complement your core offerings, presenting them to customers in discount bundles (although beware of the margin hit in bundling).

- Buy higher-quality customers by killing free trials, referral programs, affiliate marketing, and so on. Keep in mind, of course, that boosting retention can often hurt CPA, and vice versa.

- Remind customers with declined credit cards to update them.

- Consider blocking prepaid cards or lower-quality credit cards.

- If you're in a single-order business, retarget your customers on email and perhaps on other channels, presenting new offers and products to encourage more orders.

MONEY TODAY FOR MONEY TOMORROW

Whether you use IRR or the 3:1 ratio, quantifying customer value, pegging your CPA so as to meet profit requirements, and taking steps to lower CPA and boost LTV are vital to obtaining capital. From an investor's standpoint, your business is like an oil-drilling operation, with each customer you acquire a little well that you're drilling. The lifetime value is the oil that comes out. Companies that can operate as cheaply as possible on fixed costs, can drill the greatest number of wells as cheaply as possible, and can get the most oil per well are going to enjoy the greatest access to capital. And they should: these companies provide the highest return on each dollar invested. Further, they generate the most cash, so their future funding needs are smaller per dollar of future profit. On that basis, they are the companies most likely to be appealing to acquirers or the public markets. So model your company's customer value, and like the team at Scentbird, do everything possible to keep CPA low and LTV high.

(THE NAKED TRUTH)

If you want to kill it selling naked, you have to square your CPA with your LTV. That is, you have to run your business so that the money you pay to acquire customers amounts to only one-third of the lifetime value of those customers. At least, that's how the venture capitalists think of it, and to most founders, their opinions matter. If you're running a subscription business, the problem with this ratio is that it doesn't account in a useful way for the fact that money today is worth more to you than money you receive in the future. Is it really such a bad idea to acquire a customer if you pay 50 percent of LTV, say, as opposed to 33.3 percent? Maybe not. Another way to come at this relationship between CPA and LTV is the concept of internal rate of return, or IRR. You specify the desired rate of return, and since you know the other variables, you can determine the CPA you need to meet or beat in order to operate profitably. Take steps to wrench as much lifetime value out of each customer as possible, and to lower your marketing costs. That's the path to the investment dollars you'll want in order to grow.

(**CHAPTER 11**)

BEWARE THE DUMPSTER FIRE

IN EARLY 2015, Simon Enever and Bill May performed a soft launch of Quip, their subscription oral care brand. Spending nothing on advertising and relying on public relations to get the word out, they sold a few thousand units of their newly designed electric toothbrush during the first week, with additional sales flowing in later. A nice start, but nothing earth-shaking. Then, a couple of months later, Bloomberg News ran a story on Quip that generated interest from a large manufacturer. Striking a partnership with that company, Simon and Bill focused for several months on solidifying their supply chain and other operational details while also managing their existing customer relationships. They didn't arrange for any more media during this time, planning to relaunch their brand later that fall with advertising support and the help of a small team.

In October, they kicked off this second launch. Attracting customers with their first Facebook advertising, they took pre-orders for merchandise that would be shipped several weeks later, in late November. Advertising continued in November, with customers placing preorders for a second shipment date just before Christmas. If you wanted to give your special someone a sleek new electric toothbrush as a holiday gift, this was your chance. For Simon and Bill, this second round of preorders was critical. Their success with investors—and possibly their continued existence as a company—rode on having a strong Christmas season, attracting thousands of new customers, and generating positive buzz. Keenly aware of the stakes, the two worked around the clock for weeks to handle issues as they arose and keep the business operating smoothly.

By early December, thousands of orders had streamed in, and it seemed that Quip was headed for success. Two weeks later, however, just days before their second shipment was supposed to go out to customers in order to arrive by Christmas, disaster struck. Their new logistics vendor called to say that it had filed import forms with the FDA incorrectly. As a result, thousands of electric toothbrushes shipped from their manufacturer were being held up at the local airport pending FDA clearance. If Simon and Bill couldn't get these brushes released, they'd miss their shipment date and thousands of preorder customers would go without their toothbrushes on Christmas. "We're there like, 'Our business will end if we cannot get our first shipment to customers at Christmas,' " Simon remembers. "It was that bad. It was everything that we'd built up towards that year."[1]

Simon and Bill jumped into action, calling anyone they could think of to resolve the issue. "You're calling phone numbers," Simon says, "no answers are coming back, then you're told, 'Yeah, it could take three days or it could take three months,' and you're like, 'Well, we won't have a business in three days, let alone three months.' " Not knowing what else to do, Bill even drove down to the airport where the shipment was being kept to see if it would help. Through numerous conversations with FDA and customs officials, they described their predicament—they *needed* those brushes released. They pestered and cajoled and pleaded and begged. Finally, the officials agreed to release the goods to Simon and Bill, just in time for them to process the shipments and send them out for Christmas delivery. "I don't know how we pulled through," Simon says, "but I think we were just so annoying and we were so persistent that we forced them to kind of just understand how minor the error was, but how huge an impact it would have on our business. And it was literally just [our vendor] listing our old manufacturer's name on the forms instead of the new one. That one detail trickled down to this huge issue that would have ended our company."

After months of work and several weeks of twenty-hour days, the launch was a success. By mid-2016, the company was headed toward 100,000 in unit sales. By 2017, with sales continuing to rise, Quip had raised $10 million from investors in Series A funding. By 2018, the company had sold its one-millionth toothbrush and landed a partnership with Target to sell its products at retail. That same year, Quip took on another $50 million in funding across two separate rounds.

Looking back on their near-fatal miscue, Simon drew a lesson about vendors: as helpful as they might be, you can't expect them to mind the details as well as you do. Simon certainly has a point. Although I'm a big fan of turning to vendors for almost everything (see Chapter 6), I do recognize that they aren't perfect. Mistakes happen, sometimes with life-or-death ramifications for the company. But there's a bigger lesson here. A successful launch of a direct-to-consumer firm (or any company, for that matter) may well be exciting, but it's also horrifically, almost overwhelmingly stress-inducing.

Talk to founders of digital start-ups, and you'll find that many have horror stories like Quip's. Some, like Warby Parker, Allbirds, and Candid, stocked out of product at launch and had to wait months to get back into the market. Sofía Vergara's underwear company, EBY, generated so much traffic that the site crashed, costing the business hundreds of sales. Honest Co. often had thirty-minute hold times on their phone lines as their business exploded in size—a worrisome situation, since long hold times tend to garner unfriendly attention from regulators. These are relatively positive scenarios. Another, less positive one—and all too common—is attracting initial customers, but at a scary-high cost that your business simply can't sustain.

If you think you'll do better than the founders of these companies because of your diligence, prior experience, and proficiency at planning, rest assured, you won't. You should expect utter chaos in the early days of your launch—a total, horrific dumpster fire. Prepare not to sleep. Prepare to exist in a perpetual crisis mode. Prepare to be pushed to your absolute limits. I'm not trying to frighten you—but yeah, I sort of am. Rapid growth is a real bear. If you haven't launched yet, now is the time to sleep in, stock up on antidepressants, and develop some basic self-care habits that you can fall back on under pressure. The only thing more stressful than having no customers is having thousands or tens of thousands of them knocking on your door all at once.

THE PRE-LAUNCH STATE OF BLISS

Picture an elderly gentleman or lady sitting in a quiet, wood-paneled study before a crackling fire, calmly reading a newspa-

per while occasionally sipping a cup of tea. That's you in the
period before launch. You regard your business in a detached
way. For all the work you've done, everything remains a
hypothesis—a very nice, relaxing, orderly hypothesis. You've
mapped out your business's operations. You have a model with
CPA and LTV targets and a projected month-by-month customer acquisition growth curve. Your entire world is a bunch
of projects in spreadsheets, and those spreadsheets are logical
and easy to follow.

Your day-to-day is also pretty steady. First, you're working
with your agency to get your brand and website done. You
opine like Solomon the Wise on which creative direction they
should pursue, and you bust your agency's chops if they're not
completing their deliverables. If they do fall behind by a couple
of weeks, no big. Your launch is delayed, and you look a little
amateurish in front of your investors. So what? You're also
building your day one team during this pre-launch period. Filling your key roles—engineering, customer support, legal, benefits and payroll, marketing, and so on—with either freelancers
or full-timers is pleasant enough. Since the business hasn't
launched, none of these people have any real work to do, and
you're evaluating them, in essence, based on whether they seem
congenial. Since lots of people are congenial, they seem excel-
lent at their jobs, and you feel proud of your team. Besides
marketing and team building, you're working to get inventory
to your fulfillment center—not so stressful, given your present
lack of customers.

Overall, nothing has started yet, so nothing can be broken.
You're working at a decent pace, with no particular sense of
urgency. You spend your days futzing with Facebook, your
website, your pricing strategy. Maybe you go for a little walk in

the afternoon to grab a cup of coffee. Maybe you dawdle over lunch. Life is good.

HELLO, CRAZY

Once you hang up that figurative "Open for Business" sign, everything changes. Bye-bye, calm. Hello, crazy. When you have customers, you have to service them, and your whole system now has to stand and deliver. What most entrepreneurs, if not all of them, find is that their systems only sort of stand and only sort of deliver. Guess who has to scramble to patch holes and put out fires. You!

At Hubble, our site went live on October 17, 2016, although we didn't start running ads until the next day. We were shocked, and giddy, to get three customers in those first hours. As we turned on our Facebook ads, though, the number of customers per day grew. We notched three, then three again. We attracted six more customers, then ten, then nine, then twenty-three. I remember coming in each morning and updating the count on the whiteboard. When press hit on November 1, traffic on the site spiked.

Unfortunately, this onslaught of customers tested our system in ways we hadn't imagined. To our chagrin, our system started breaking down. Every day, every week, some new issue popped up that we had to deal with immediately, or risk repercussions to the business. Here's a partial list of mishaps:

- We ordered the wrong inventory distribution because we hadn't anticipated how many customers would need which power of correction for their contact lenses.

- The information technology link between our fulfillment center and our site kept breaking, so customer orders weren't being processed.
- Our fulfillment center hadn't anticipated the volume of orders that came in, so they ran a backlog, sometimes of several days.
- DHL had just opened a new warehouse in Hebron, Kentucky, and kept losing packages or delaying their delivery.
- Our customer service team fell way behind on tickets.
- Bugs all over our site prevented customers from completing orders, particularly on tablet devices.
- Our marketing held up well, feeding customers into our system and creating chaos everywhere else.
- Our freight forwarder overcharged us by tens of thousands of dollars, and we didn't notice for months.

While many of these issues weren't as serious as Quip's near-deadly toothbrush shipping miscue, they all demanded immediate attention. In each case, we had to scramble to improvise solutions.

THE DAILY BLUR

If there's anything I wish I'd had going into Hubble, it'd be a sense of what to expect—and not expect—during launch. No book chapter can prepare you for the experience. You might be bracing yourself for failure, but have you thought about the growing pains of success? Maybe not.

Bear in mind, I've covered so far just a few of the potential problems you might encounter during launch. Others include:

- Supply chain issues, like faulty products and slow shipping.
- Marketing issues, most notably a failure to attract customers at a low enough CPA. This is the piece most likely to break down, and when it does, it makes all other marketing-related issues irrelevant.
- Technology issues, such as a website crashing due to high traffic volume, or glitches of one sort or another.
- Finance issues, like a failure to meet your customer acquisition or lifetime value targets, or inadequate capital to fund your business.

All of these problems require your immediate attention. If you're growing so fast that you're running short of capital, for instance, you can slow down a bit, but flatlining growth is hardly the exciting story you want to bring to VCs. Better to stay financed well enough to keep the party going (easier said . . .). But that in turn means meeting with investors on an urgent basis and putting together a compelling pitch at the same time as you're helping out with customer service tickets, yelling at your suppliers to correct problems with your products, getting on the phone with your attorneys to resolve a legal question, and working with team members or contractors to fix bugs on your site. Eight hours of sleep each night? Don't plan on it. And you might go through weeks or months of this before the frenzy of the launch dies out and your business stabilizes.

AN ISSUE THAT PROBABLY ISN'T: BRANDING AND DESIGN

When businesses struggle, founders often blame it on their brand, site design, and packaging. Some are so convinced that their branding and design suck that they go back and redo these items. Not only does this cost a lot, but it can delay your plans by weeks or months. Branding and design are hardly ever the big problem. If your business isn't working, dig into the marketing funnel. If you can't make headway, then at some point you'll want to consider whether your business just might not be viable.

Some people find this daily blur invigorating. I found it miserable. Besides customer service and other assorted issues, I spent the bulk of my time dealing with marketing. For months on end, I was glued compulsively to our marketing dashboards: the livestream data in Facebook Ads Manager, Google Analytics (traffic tracker for your site), and Shopify. (This never really ended—I have all those screens open right now while I work on this chapter.) Doing marketing solo was not good for my sleep or my sanity, but it was essential. Although our marketing agency had assigned a manager to our account, I became keenly aware of gaps in her performance. I noticed, for instance, that our advertising spend between midnight and eight in the morning yielded hardly any customers. To remedy the situation, I began going in at midnight and manually turning down our advertising spending, and then turning it up at seven in the morning.

As the weeks passed, I made more tweaks to our account manager's work. I would move budgets around during the day based on what was working or not and on how our overall spend was doing. I'd brainstorm new audiences and try cycling back in old ones that had gone stale. I'd tweak copy, and even though I lack any creative ability, I'd sometimes, in an act of desperation, start playing with images using free Photoshop-type tools I found online. It wasn't that our account manager was incompetent or unmotivated. She had a life and was juggling six clients. I, meanwhile, was obsessively watching our Facebook ads eighteen hours a day. After a couple of months, we decided to fire the agency. Then we fired another. And another. And another. Then we did it ourselves for a while before we eventually found partners we trusted.

On one level, I'm glad I spent so much time on marketing. Whenever I talk to pre-launch e-commerce founders, I always tell them to devote themselves to learning how to do their own marketing. Other founders told Ben and me the same thing, and we desperately wanted to ignore them because, as I argued earlier in this book, doing your own marketing sucks. But even if you don't intend to manage your own digital spend indefinitely, dealing with it for some meaningful stretch of time will put you in a much stronger position to interview and manage internal hires or external partners. Watching the marketing numbers is also the easiest way to spot problems like site outages, problems with your site's checkout function, Facebook glitches, and so on (reviewing customer service tickets also works here). That said, my obsession with marketing severely damaged my quality of life for months. And it wasn't just marketing, but rather the constant feeling that some part of our business was either broken or about to break.

Have you ever experienced extreme, unending stress and sleep deprivation over a prolonged period? If so, how did you deal with it? Giving some thought to this in advance can help make the ride just a little bit easier. If you know what to expect, you might not be quite so miserable when the worst does materialize, and you might take some time to put in place measures that worked for you in the past (although you'll still probably be pretty miserable).

GET A PRESCRIPTION

As hard as the launch was, I must admit that I was part of the problem as well. I've always been an anxious person, and my family tree is full of anxiety disorders. During my sophomore year of high school, I muddled through a prolonged bout of insomnia. Each night, I went to bed at 10:00 P.M. or so, watching the clock tick off hour after hour. My panic increased as I calculated how little time was left until my alarm would go off, and how awful I'd feel the next day.

I plowed through my high school anxiety on my own, but with Hubble, I needed help. I didn't seek it out during the first few months, because the workload was so hard that I could convince myself that my anxiety was situationally based and would abate as our launch period came to an end. About six months into it, however, as operations at Hubble began to stabilize a bit, I still didn't feel any calmer. I'd wake up at 6:00 A.M., pointlessly watch all the subscription orders for the day run through, and then struggle to get out of the apartment before noon because I was trapped in front of the Google Analytics screen monitoring potential customers who were about to buy. I told myself that if I just sat there and waited for a good stretch of new customers, then I would feel calmer and could go about my day. Of course, the wave of calmness never came.

My husband, Mark, had been begging me to see a psychiatrist for years. Now I finally did. Things weren't suddenly perfect, but the medication I was prescribed diminished my anxiety, and I felt like I got a bunch of time back in my day. When we were at dinner with friends and family, I could hold myself back from checking my phone every five minutes. I started setting new personal records on my daily runs and bike rides, and I even began playing tennis again. It's true that life calmed down for the whole team at Hubble around this time, so I probably would have felt somewhat better no matter what. Still, medication helped make the challenges we faced more manageable. Even more important, it felt good to deal with my mental health problems head-on.

> If you experience extreme anxiety or depression during the launch period, don't hesitate to get medicated or to sign up for therapy. A lot of founders feel uncomfortable seeking out help from a mental health professional. They're constantly in sales mode—pitching investors, recruiting new hires, signing clients— and can be embarrassed by what feels like weakness. But I have to believe that feelings like what I experienced those first few months after Hubble's launch are pretty common in the start-up community, and it would be better if we could talk more openly about them and get the help we need.

CHANGE UP YOUR GAME

Many founders find it hard to rip themselves away from their computer screens. A friendly reminder: in the run-up to your launch, and even amidst the mayhem, please don't forget to take care of yourself. This unpleasant sprint will last longer than you think you can handle. You aren't selfish for carving out time for yourself. Please, *please,* put down the laptop and the phone for an occasional afternoon. Go for a run. Watch a movie. When you get back to work, your mind will be fresher and sharper.

Also, be prepared to adjust your work routines to maximize your productivity. If you usually tap at your computer at a café late at night, is that necessarily the best approach? Maybe, but maybe not. Simon Enever recalls how he used to stay up until two or three in the morning to get his work done. During Quip's launch, when he was staying up even later, he realized that his attention was fading and the quality of his work diminishing at such a late hour. So he made a radical move: he started going to bed early and getting up at 4:00 A.M. to begin his workday. Since nobody else was up then, he found that he could work uninterrupted for a good five hours while he was fresh and rested. By eight at night, he'd be tired, but not as utterly exhausted as he had been while staying up late. After allowing himself an hour to have dinner and watch a little TV, he'd be ready to turn in. And he could do so guilt-free because he was working so much more productively in the mornings.

You can't know what kind of arrangement will work best for you until you've gone through an experience like the launching of a business. Just go into it with an experimental mindset, realizing that you might need to change long-standing habits. You'll be quicker to make the necessary changes, and thus better able to sustain the torrid pace without driving yourself too crazy. I benefited enormously by giving myself some time during the day to take a nap if I needed it or to crash early some nights if I was flagging. Most days, I went without this extra sleep, but just knowing that I'd built in room for an extra hour or two of sleep here or there helped me deal with my long-standing sleep anxiety. This in turn allowed me to improve my sleep quality night after night, and to perform better.

As you're playing with your own habits, pay attention to how you're treating your team. Everyone else is likely working extremely hard as well, and probably without the kind of up-side that you will enjoy. As tired as you may be, serve as a sounding board for them. Listen to their gripes. And when they pose questions about how the company is doing, be open and honest with them. Don't puff up your results to keep them excited and driving hard. People aren't stupid. They'll see through any bullshit you throw their way, and they'll come away resenting you for your dishonesty. In this respect, it helps to work with friends and family at the start, as I did (and do) at Hubble. Chances are, they're less afraid to call you on any bullshit they feel you're pushing on themselves or others.

WHEN THE FIRES DIE OUT

As hard as the launch phase is, it does eventually end. By the summer of 2017, we found ourselves going a few hours without anything massive breaking, then whole days and weeks. Hubble still wasn't perfect, but it started to feel more like a real company and less like a dumpster fire. We didn't have to wake up in the morning bracing ourselves for the crises that had accumulated in our inboxes overnight.

We could also step back and appreciate what we'd accomplished. Our revenue had grown from $550,000 in March

2017 to $750,000 in April, then $1 million in May, $1.3 million in June, $1.6 million in July, and $2 million in August. New monthly subscribers had grown as well, from three thousand in November 2016 to ten thousand in February, twenty thousand in May, and thirty thousand in August. Retention continued to beat our expectations, and our subscriber base soon crossed one hundred thousand. Because we hit new volume tiers in our supplier agreements, our margins expanded. And, in a virtuous cycle, higher margins increased what we could afford to pay for a customer, fueling further growth. On the strength of this performance, we were able to raise an additional $16.5 million in February 2017, and another $10 million in August 2017. As painful as our launch phase had been, at least our investors were happy.

I've complained a lot about the launch experience, and in truth I feel uncomfortable about that. We've been incredibly lucky with Hubble, and any griping from me is ungrateful. But I also want to be honest. Compared to what other people endure to build their careers, eight or nine difficult months isn't so bad. Nevertheless, the pain founders experience upon launching their businesses is real. Rapid growth is both fun and unpleasant. Given founders' reluctance to discuss their mental health, it's important to open up a conversation about the pain of the launch, even at the risk of annoying readers with my self-pity. As I said, no book chapter can fully prepare you for the experience; most of this you'll have to figure out on your own. But I hope that I've at least oriented you to the challenges you'll encounter and the emotions you'll feel. You might be bracing yourself for failure, but have you thought about the growing pains of success?

If the answer is no, don't let this chapter freak you out too much. As tough as it is to launch a direct-to-consumer business, you can still give it a go, even if you fall back on a bit of pharmaceutical help to get through it. If Ben and I can do it, so can you. As we've found, what awaits you on the other side—a sustainable, established business—is worth every bit of the effort.

THE NAKED TRUTH

After all the time you've spent preparing, the time has finally come to launch your business. Are you ready? Most likely not. Thousands of consumers beating down your door to buy your product is every founder's dream. It's also, it turns out, a bit of a nightmare. Your operational plans sounded good in theory, but now you're putting them to the test. Will they survive pressure? Be prepared for stress like you've never experienced it before. We're talking twenty-hour days spent dealing with every variety of issue, from website glitches to inventory shortages, potential lawsuits to lost packages. Some of these miscues will be minor, but then again, you might well find yourself like Simon and Bill, racing to your local airport and begging for the authorities to release your goods so as to save your company. Take your anti-anxiety medication, go to your therapy sessions, and for God's sake, take a mental health day (or couple of hours) every now and then. Do what it takes to survive. If you make it through to the other side, you'll face new challenges, but you'll finally also have a moment to survey what you've built, and hopefully you'll feel that it was all worth it.

CHAPTER 12

GROW YOUR OWN WAY

BY THIS POINT in the book, you're familiar with some of the core executional aspects of selling naked—how to develop an idea, win over investors and partners, set up back-end operations and paid marketing, develop a financial model, and maybe even launch somewhere along the way. I've emphasized the experimental nature of selling naked, urging you to embrace the unknown, test new tactics you might dream up, and learn from your mistakes. All along, I've tried to provide you with a structure for experimentation, so that you don't feel entirely lost, disoriented, or alone.

While the principles I've offered might help you get a direct-to-consumer business up and running, they almost certainly won't suffice to sustain or grow that business. In part, that's because the "rules" of direct-to-consumer are always changing, and the opportunities that exist at any given time don't last very long. I can share the basic knowledge that every successful founder takes for granted, but beyond that, you can't just copy what the last folks did and expect the same result. To stay alive and grow, you must linger on the outer edge of selling naked, pushing just a bit past what others around you are already doing. And if you manage to get on the edge, you have to keep pushing past what you've done previously in order to stay there.

That's what Ben and I have done at Hubble. By the summer of 2017, we'd managed to turn Hubble into a growing business by doing what's described in this book. With the dumpster fire of our launch comfortably extinguished, we had a bit of time to think about our future. As we saw it, Hubble would either fail or succeed over time. If it did succeed, it was possible we could replicate this model in other consumer categories. Ever the optimists, we decided to scope out categories in which we could develop similar businesses. We selected about sixty of them and ran Facebook lead ads for new direct-to-consumer business concepts. Our goal was simply to see which concepts consumers seemed to like the most.

Two of the most promising areas, it turned out, were the adult incontinence product and baby stroller categories. Two friends of ours, Will Herlands and Eric Osman, had been playing around with starting businesses in these categories as CEOs. Exploring the supply chain, we found that in both of these categories, supply was fairly limited, which meant that any business wouldn't be immediately overrun by copycats. In adult incontinence products, we envisioned selling a premium product that looked and felt like ordinary underwear but was more affordable than similar products then available. One independent supplier offered much better quality than the rest and was willing to sign an exclusive agreement with us. With all of this legwork in place, Ben and I helped raise money for these two businesses, working with the team of investors that had helped us with Hubble: Rick Heitzmann at FirstMark, Josh Kazam at Two River, and Len Potter and Drew Tarlow at Wildcat. Soon the founders of these businesses were off and running.

We didn't have a playbook for expanding our model. Spotting an opportunity, we experimented and charted our own course. In late 2017, we pushed our efforts in a second direction. Thinking about our businesses to date, we realized that none of them were the biggest in their respective industries, and that as a result our margins were lower and we offered consumers fewer SKUs. That got us thinking: the manufacturers out there that did have massive scale, as well as long-standing relationships with mass retail outlets, were struggling mightily with digital business. Maybe we could partner with them, merging our digital know-how with their superior product and distribution capabilities to create new businesses. We began communicating with a couple of large consumer packaged goods companies, eventually inking a deal with one of them to incubate direct-to-consumer businesses for them.

As we saw earlier in the book, the big, branded suppliers increasingly want to get into digital direct marketing, even though they continue to sell the bulk of their product at Walmart, Target, and other conventional retail outlets. Since they don't own the checkout at these retail outlets, they can't access the consumer data that would allow them to optimize their online marketing the way businesses like Hubble can. Businesses like McDonald's and Starbucks don't struggle with this problem as much. They own their own supply chain and retail distribution networks, and they can use the data they

collect to push discounts and other offers to you via their online apps. But for manufacturers, there really isn't a great solution, aside from the fairly cumbersome receipt capture services
mentioned in Chapter 1.

For the large brands, selling naked still makes sense, since
these brands can likely use the digital channel to drive more
business to their retail channels and optimize their overall
marketing spend. To make money, these companies need to
sell premium products online at higher price points than they
do at the mass retail outlets. (The margin on a $3 tube of tooth-
paste just isn't enough as a standalone to justify the costs of
shipping and Facebook marketing.) As of this writing, Ben and
I are helping large manufacturers do exactly this. We're learning a lot about these manufacturers and their needs, and we've
also been able to help them navigate what for them is a truly
foreign world. These manufacturers are not used to running
retail businesses and managing the functions that come with
that, like handling consumer data and communications. We've
shared our know-how, and also helped these companies adapt
their current policies and business practices to fit the demands
of selling naked. It's too early to know if our efforts will succeed. If not, we'll back off and find some new way to push beyond our existing playbook.

> Don't get too comfortable selling naked. Push into new terri-
> tory, whether it's an idea for improving your existing business
> or for developing an entirely new one. Instead of casting about
> for rules or "best practices," accept that they don't exist and
> instead focus on asking as many questions as possible. What if
> we adopted a totally new pricing strategy? What if we struck a
> deal with a new kind of marketing partner? What if we created
> a new type of retail store for our brand? What if we targeted a

new kind of consumer? Think of creative, cost-effective ways to run tests for these ideas. If some of the tests confirm that you're on to something, then push it further, making up your own "best practices" as you go.

STAY ALERT TO NEW OPPORTUNITIES

Another way to generate questions that might lead you to potential opportunities is to keep your eyes and ears open. The sharper you are at detecting relevant trends, and the more creative you are in thinking about the possible implications of these trends for your business, the more interesting questions you'll come up with and the more tests you'll run. New business opportunities will unspool from there.

What do some of these trends look like? As of this writing, in early 2019, we're tracking a number of developments that might impact the direct-to-consumer marketplace. A few are described here.

NEW ADVERTISING PLATFORMS

Our primary advertising vehicles, Facebook and Instagram, are always changing. A few years ago, Facebook News Feed ads were new. More recently, Facebook improved targeting and budgeting for video ads on its site and began allowing advertisers to see ads that others are running. Going forward, new advertising opportunities might emerge, such as placements on Instagram Stories and WhatsApp. Beyond Facebook and Instagram, what new platforms are on the horizon? Will any existing channels—Twitter, Pinterest, Snapchat, and so on—scale up their ad delivery capabilities? If so, new opportunities for targeting customers at lower CPAs might arise.

By the same token, ad inventory might decline, posing a risk to direct-to-consumer businesses. Younger consumers love videogames, spending hours on their favorite platforms. Yet most of those offerings don't host advertisements—they're subscription-based. What if younger consumers become so enthralled with Fortnite and other massive multiplayer games that they decide to reduce the time they spend on advertising-based social media platforms? Will games companies develop new advertising opportunities—for instance, by creating in-game "billboards" that traditional brands can buy, or avatar Shopify stores within games in which brands might appear? Or will opportunities to reach consumers diminish? Likewise, new augmented-reality and virtual-reality devices are on the horizon. Will they offer advertising opportunities? Just as big traditional brands like Procter & Gamble and Nike relied on television advertising to grow, brands that sell naked rely on paid social media advertising. If that declines, existing direct-to-consumer business models could face a tougher environment in which to operate.

INFLUENCERS

Kylie Jenner has amassed one of the world's largest Instagram followings, and she's monetized it via Kylie Cosmetics, a direct-to-consumer business that has grown to hundreds of millions in revenue on the back of flash product releases of small-batch production. In China, a number of influencers have followed a similar path to profit, particularly in categories like apparel and cosmetics, where contract manufacturers are abundant and it's possible to ramp up production quickly if a product takes off.[1] These businesses don't need much venture capital, since with flash sales they're not holding much inventory.

Founders of direct-to-consumer businesses can work with influencers in a variety of ways. They can pay influencers to tout their brands, or they can give equity. Many founders choose the former, since it's hard to squeeze sufficient value out of an equity grant. How many social media posts will the influencer pump out? Probably not enough to justify parting with a chunk of your business. Entrepreneurs might also try to co-found companies with influencers.

Does the presence of influencers spell opportunity for your business? You bet.

ACCESS TO CAPITAL

Monitor any trends that might affect your access to capital as you grow. Lately, VCs have approached direct-to-consumer companies more cautiously. They still like that these companies can scale up quickly, but they worry that selling naked doesn't allow firms to grow to such an extent that founders can make an exit and the investors can reap a big payday. They're demanding more of founders—specifically, quicker paths to profitable growth. And they're favoring serial entrepreneurs who already have a track record of success.[2] At the same time, brands like Native, MVMT, and Leesa are showing that entrepreneurs can bootstrap their businesses, parting with little or no equity, and still find a path to exit.

Investors are starting to service bootstrappers, giving them access to capital with new types of financing. Clearbanc, for instance, will provide entrepreneurs with up to $1 million in financing per month, charging a flat fee for the capital instead of a percentage return, and recouping their loan by taking a portion of future revenues from the business. Manufacturers are also stepping in to provide capital, cutting more deals in which they either buy a piece of a founder's business, provide working capital (via generous payment terms), or provide products to the business at cost. If they don't take equity and then recoup their investment during an exit, manufacturers can make money by seeing their sales volume grow as the business expands.

DIRECT-TO-CONSUMER INCUBATORS

Ben and I aren't the only ones out there who have sought to act as incubators. Courtney Reum, co-author of the book *Shortcut Your Startup,* left a career in consumer product investment banking at Goldman Sachs and, in partnership with his brother Carter, started the alcohol brand Veev. Several years into it, they found that they were more excited about consumer technology brands, including direct-to-consumer start-ups. After selling Veev, they created M13, a platform for creating and scaling consumer technology start-ups that applies a playbook approach of repeatable best practices.

As Courtney tells us, he and Carter felt that many founders didn't have all of the information they needed to launch their businesses most efficiently and, as a result, were wasting a lot of time, energy, and money replicating operational solutions that already existed. So the two created a playbook for going to market more efficiently, including lists of best-in-class vendors to handle the full range of business functions. Recognizing that the two could advise only a limited number of companies directly, they were building out a platform for doing so at scale. "Our hope," Courtney says, "is that if we do this well enough," founders "will never make a bad decision because everything that is in our playbook is highly vetted." M13 also has a venture fund focused on digital consumer businesses, one of the country's largest, as well as a brand development studio that works with "some bigger corporates to help create brands. Our first partnership is with Procter & Gamble."[3]

If incubators such as M13 succeed and more of them pop up, they could pose a threat to companies that sell naked by crowding the market with more brands. Because they mobilize shared infrastructure, knowledge, and resources, incubators (hopefully) operate more efficiently than individual businesses do, and consequently they don't have to demand the same economics of each brand. If you have twenty brands instead of one, each of the twenty can be weaker as a business than the one, and the incubator overall will still perform better. We've seen a similar dynamic play out in the hedge fund space. A decade or two ago, independent hedge funds abounded, but today they are cratering. That's because giant platforms have arisen that support hedge fund managers who previously would have been independent. By pooling resources and performance of their members, these platforms can help operators achieve more.

If incubators take off, founders will feel more pressure to work with them instead of operating independently. If you did want to stay independent, the quality and originality of your products would really have to shine. My guess is that incubators won't take over the space, since pooling operational functions and knowledge probably won't give them that much of an advantage over individual operators. But again, that's just a guess.

DIRECT-TO-CONSUMER MARKETING PLATFORMS

Today, hundreds (or more) of direct-to-consumer brands jostle for consumers' attention. Most of these brands look the same visually, not least because they often use the same branding and design agencies. They share similar or overlapping consumer bases; a similar focus on price and value; a similar focus on a single category (with possible extensions into nearby adjacencies); and, first and foremost, a similar reliance on Facebook or Instagram as their dominant customer acquisition channel. As investors and founders have recognized, the presence of so many similar brands can overload consumers. If you purchase from multiple brands, you can't easily search among all of them at once, and you don't earn discounts for buying from several of them. You also have to enter your account information every time you place an order with a new brand.

To solve this problem, some have proposed that a big company buy up dozens or hundreds of brands and roll them up into a single, big megabrand. Economically, that wouldn't make sense. Start-up brands that sell naked become merchandising experts in their categories. Hubble knows a lot about the needs consumers have when buying contact lenses, the pain points they experience, and how to sell these products on Facebook. All the founders appearing in this book possess similar expertise. Putting a bajillion of us under one brand and operating us in a centralized way isn't the same as mobilizing the expert knowledge we've painfully built up one product at a time. If you had a big enough team at your megabrand to amass all of this expert knowledge, you might eventually succeed, but that would be expensive, and you would be reinventing a part of the wheel that already exists. Further, many niche direct-to-consumer brands appeal to specific consumer values. Andie, for instance, aims to empower women, while Keeps wants to destigmatize hair loss. It would be hard for one big, corporate brand to stand for both female empowerment and openness about men's hair loss and still seem authentic in the eyes of niche consumers, even if this brand had access to all of the relevant consumer insights. Companies also tend to falter when they maintain presences in too many categories, as they don't have as much reputational skin in the game in each one.

There's another solution to watch out for: a platform that *federates* direct-to-consumer brands, like Etsy does for crafts-people. Brands could retain their own marketing budgets, customer data, and teams to build expert knowledge in their category, while their participation on the platform would allow them to prospect together on Facebook and Instagram to drive down costs. Brands would each have their own "store" on the platform, with the "stores" appearing to consumers as part of a single "mall." The platform would amass aggregated traffic and other data from all of its participating merchants, but the relationship with each individual merchant would be balanced: since both the platform and the merchant would see customer data, both would be able to optimize marketing. Contrast this arrangement with traditional e-commerce marketplaces like Amazon, which don't share enough data for merchants to optimize marketing for Facebook, Google, and others; to attribute sales to different traffic sources; or even, in many cases, to know who their customers are.

Such a platform could focus at least at first on "founder-led" brands, thus appealing to consumers with a coherent identity. The platform could draw brands by coordinating activity among them, something each of the brands is poorly positioned to do itself. Negotiating on behalf of many brands to build operational capabilities, the platform could deliver lower prices for creative services and shipping, could operate some customer service and logistics flows more efficiently, could obtain more favorable credit card merchant rates, and could make it easier to work with influencers, publishers, and media buyers. The platform could also benefit brands by creating affiliate revenue between them (if your brand buys traffic and another brand converts it into a customer, you make money instead of being scalped by a free rider). The platform would be well positioned to facilitate cross-brand promotions (buy product X and get 10 percent off product Y), which is hard to pull off without shared checkouts across brands. Finally, the platform could serve brands as an important resource for data and benchmarking.

Stay alert to the possibility of a digital "mall" for brands that sell naked. As of this writing, we're testing whether the market would support such an offering—we might have an answer by the time this book hits the shelves (keep an eye out for BZR and its CEO, John Shi). More generally, track any trends that might prove relevant to the direct-to-consumer space. How could your business profit? And how might you respond to minimize any potential risks? Draw on your broader community here. What new developments are others seeing? How might these affect your business in the months and years to come?

ALWAYS BE EARLY

As of this writing, Dollar Shave Club remains the most lucrative sale of a digitally native company. You could argue that the economics of that deal never made sense, and that the acquisition didn't work out well for its acquirer, Unilever.[4] But before you hate on Dollar Shave Club too much, consider this: it was early. Dollar Shave Club was the first direct-to-consumer company to understand the potential of YouTube viral videos to move product. It was the first direct-to-consumer company to aggressively utilize Facebook's mobile ad inventory. It was the first direct-to-consumer company to target consumer packaged goods companies as opposed to technology companies as buyers. It was the first on many fronts, and one of the first digital direct-to-consumer brands, period. Many founders would go on to copy Dollar Shave Club, but as the first mover, it made the most of the market opportunities that existed.

Your job is to be early, too, in as many areas as possible. Stay alert to what's happening, and never stop thinking. Every day, rack your brain for the next great idea, big or small, that nobody has thought of. Opportunities exist, but you need to seek them out. Is constant experimentation and innovation a lot of work? You bet. You're never "done," much as you might sometimes want to be. The market is always evolving, faster than you'd like. But that's the fun of it. And consider this: Just a couple of years ago, my partner, Ben, had a good idea and we decided to test it out using simple, cheap methods on Facebook. From that came an actual business. The rules in this book made a huge difference, but so did our determination to constantly reinvent elements of our business and, after a point, to venture beyond our existing business.

I can't promise that your business will achieve similar or better results. But I do know one thing: if you apply the principles in this book, you'll at least stand a fighting chance. And, if nothing else, you won't be bored.

(THE NAKED TRUTH)

The first eleven chapters have covered a range of practical issues related to starting a direct-to-consumer company. This chapter is about the end game, or at least the part of the game that emerges once you've successfully planned, set up, launched, and established your digitally native brand. If you're looking for rules to follow at this stage, you've come to the wrong place. You have to chart your own path. As you operate your business, keep asking questions. Turn those questions into experiments, and hopefully you'll turn at least some of those experiments into opportunities. To generate an endless stream of questions, scrutinize your own assumptions about your business, and track the trends. Influencers, new advertising platforms, incubators, new funding models, and direct-to-consumer marketing platforms might all give rise to the "next big thing"—or maybe they won't. Stay alert, and stay engaged. Don't let the uncertainty scare you. Be early in as many areas as possible. Stay out on the outer edge of this space.

ACKNOWLEDGMENTS

FIRST OFF, I want to express my heartfelt gratitude to the team at Hubble. Our work is what inspired me to write this book—every day we learn cool and interesting stuff together. Thanks as well to Ben, my friend and partner. We've worked together on a half-dozen businesses so far, and we haven't worn ourselves out yet. Here's to a dozen more!

I'd also like to thank my writing and publishing team for this project. Roger Scholl and the whole team at Crown Publishing/Currency believed in this book from the beginning, even when I was busy pitching against it by making the argument that I had no idea what I was doing. My agents, Todd Shuster and Justin Brouckaert at Aevitas Creative, were indispensable; they wisely pushed me to cover this bonkers new space we're all trying to build together. And, of course, thanks to my collaborator, Seth Schulman: we made it through a proposal, dozens of interviews, and plenty of work on this manuscript itself. You were patient with me as I tried to shift directions every five minutes, and you focused me throughout on what would actually make for a compelling book. To the extent we landed there, all credit goes to you.

Thanks to my family and friends, and especially those who helped us get Hubble off the ground: Paul Rodgers; my mom, Amy Genkins; my husband, Mark Severs; and Dan Rosen, who today is still putting up with us at Hubble.

Thanks to all the founders (of both brands and agencies) and other industry leaders who generously agreed to be interviewed for this project.

Thanks to our investors and our board: Rick Heitzmann at FirstMark; Josh Kazam at Two River; Len Potter and Drew Tarlow at Wildcat; Ellie Wheeler at Greycroft; Dr. Brian Levy; and Kejia Sun. I am grateful as well to everyone else on our cap table who is always there with time, thoughts, and introductions, and who have staggered me with their faith that we aren't totally incompetent.

Thanks to Will Herlands at Willow, Eric Osman at Mockingbird, Michael Feinberg at ResolvedCX, Melanie Travis at Andie, and Renata Black at EBY. I learn so much from you guys and have greatly enjoyed becoming involved in your businesses.

And thanks to Mildred. You don't let being a dog stop you from turning up at Hubble every day to help keep the trains running.

NOTES

INTRODUCTION

1. In 1997 alone, QVC logged $2 billion within the space of a year. David Rohde, "Ex-Hosts to Sue QVC Network, Charging Bias," *New York Times,* December 30, 1998.

2. Philip Inghelbrecht (co-founder of Tatari), interview with author, August 28, 2018.

3. Randall Rothenberg (president and CEO of the Interactive Advertising Bureau), interview with author, September 17, 2018.

4. Jack Haber (former CMO at Colgate), interview with author, August 15, 2018.

5. Ken Fenyo (McKinsey consumer market expert), interview with author, August 27, 2018.

6. Scott Galloway (professor of marketing at New York University's Stern School of Business), interview with author, September 11, 2018.

7. Jim Stengel (former Procter & Gamble CMO and respected marketing consultant), interview with author, October 25, 2018.

8. David Kidder (co-founder and CEO at Bionic), interview with author, September 12, 2018.

CHAPTER 1: DON'T BULLSHIT YOURSELF ABOUT DIGITAL BUSINESS

1. Material in this section comes from an interview with John Fiorentino (founder of Moon Pod) on September 7, 2018.

2. This is basic math. Let's say I have $10 million revenue per month on my subscription business, and 10 percent of that churns out every month. If I acquire enough customers to add $1 million of revenue, I'm not growing—I'm flat. The $1 million I acquired offsets the $1 million that churned off. At some point, the amount of revenue I need to add to keep my overall revenue flat costs more than it's worth, and I've hit my ceiling. Of course, I can push that ceiling upward by taking steps like adding new products and selling offline, but absent some new tricks, I've plateaued.

3. Lauren Johnson, "When Procter & Gamble Cut $200 Million in Digital Ad Spend, It Increased Its Reach 10%," *AdWeek,* March 1, 2018.

4. A couple of decades ago, the vast majority—some 90 percent—of advertising inventory available for purchase by brands were brand-building spots on television and radio and on billboards. Today, brand-building spots account for only 50 percent of available inventory, with the remainder of the inventory taking the form of digital direct response. So brands need digital direct-response strategies just to deploy their entire marketing budgets, since not every major advertiser can crowd into just 50 percent of the inventory.

5. Jason Guerrasio, "MoviePass Said a New Strategy for Working with Theaters Would Boost Revenue, but Its Finances Show Otherwise," *Business Insider,* August 15, 2018.

6. For a description of its complete profit model and how it worked (or failed to deliver), see Nick Vega, "This Is How MoviePass Plans to Make Money with a $10-a-Month Unlimited Plan That Seems Too Good to Be True," *Business Insider,* August 20, 2017.

7. John Quelch and David Harding, "Brands Versus Private Labels: Fighting to Win," *Harvard Business Review,* January–February 1996.

8. Krista Garcia, "Amazon Doesn't Dominate Private-Label Sales (Yet)," eMarketer, June 6, 2018.

9. Although whether Netflix can make the economics of its original content work remains to be seen, as the billions in annual investment accounts for a disconcertingly high portion of its revenues.

10. Sona, "27 Ways to Motivate Shoppers Who Research Online to Buy," Mine What, November 21, 2014. The 14.3 percent figure is from 2018: Fareeha Ali, "US Ecommerce Sales Grow 15.0% in 2018," *Digital Commerce,* February 28, 2019. See also Alberto Cavallo, "More Amazon Effects: Online Competition and Pricing Behaviors," Harvard Business School, September 7, 2018.

CHAPTER 2: DEMONSTRATE DEMAND

1. This account is based on two telephone interviews with Melanie Travis (founder and CEO of Andie), on May 11 and September 4, 2018.

2. Sophia Edelstein (co-founder and CEO of Pair Eyewear), interview with author, October 1, 2018.

3. Ryan Kim, "Report: 40 Percent of Mobile Ad Clicks Are Fraud or Accidents," GigaOm, August 31, 2012.

4. I have one hundred ad impressions to serve. I know that five of those are to users who regularly buy from ads and ninety-five are to users who never buy from ads or even pay attention to them. One advertiser says it is going to grade the ads against sales on an e-commerce store it owns. The others just say they want the cheapest impressions possible. Which one are you going to give the valuable impressions to? Right now, the upstarts are shrewdly buying the most valuable impressions, which is why the incumbents are buying the junk. Unfortunately, the upstarts are buying these valuable impressions for products with more limited distribution.

5. Of course, this logic can cut both ways. Sometimes the incumbent retailers ignore channel conflicts to get young brands with greater perceived cachet onto their shelves.

CHAPTER 3: TELL A GREAT STORY

1. Adam Heitzman, "8 Wacky Entrepreneur Stories to Inspire Your Own Business Success," *Inc.,* March 15, 2018.

2. In a SAFE, investors contribute funds, receiving in turn the right to purchase stock down the road subject to certain restrictions. Convertible notes are different: investors contribute money, receiving shares in the company during a future equity sale. SAFEs are in general simpler and more streamlined than convertible notes, offering reduced protections for investors. In these respects, they are more founder-friendly than these notes.

3. Bo Burlingham, *Small Giants: Companies That Choose to Be Great Instead of Big* (New York: Portfolio, 2007).

4. Brad Stone, *The Upstarts: Uber, Airbnb, and the Battle for the New Silicon Valley* (New York: Little, Brown, 2017).

5. Renata Black (co-founder of EBY), interview with author, September 17, 2018.

6. Eric Osman (founder and CEO of Mockingbird), interview with author, August 17, 2018.

CHAPTER 4: COMPENSATE EXPERTS AND PARTNERS

1. Craig Elbert (co-founder and CEO of Care/of), interview with author, August 29, 2018.

2. "Ten Jobs You Didn't Know Needed Licenses," Fox Business, May 10, 2012.

3. Carolyn Rush (VP of creative strategy at Worn Creative), interview with author, August 27, 2018.

4. Demetri Karagas (co-founder of Keeps), interview with author, May 21, 2018.

5. David Heath (co-founder and CEO of Bombas), interview with author, October 22, 2018.

6. Eric Osman (founder and CEO of Mockingbird), interview with author, August 17, 2018.

CHAPTER 5: WORRY ABOUT THE PIE EXPLODING

1. Noam Wasserman, "The Founder's Dilemma," *Harvard Business Review*, February 2008.

2. Renata Black (co-founder of EBY), interview with author, September 17, 2018.

3. Valentina Zarya, "Female Founders Got 2% of Venture Capital Dollars in 2017," *Fortune*, January 31, 2018; Gary Stockton, "Statistics and Obstacles Facing Women Entrepreneurs," Experian, January 29, 2018.

4. That is, according to Demetri Karagas's description on the social media network LinkedIn, accessed April 29, 2019, which is subject to change.

5. Demetri Karagas (co-founder of Keeps), interview with author, May 21, 2018.

6. Connie Loizos, "Secondary Shops Flooded with Unicorn Sellers," *TechCrunch*, February 18, 2016.

7. Eliot Brown and Greg Bensinger, "The Latest Path to Silicon Valley Riches: Stake Sales," *Wall Street Journal*, November 19, 2017.

8. Oren Charnoff (principal at Hanaco Ventures), interview with author, May 14, 2018. See also Brad Stone, "Silicon Valley Cashes Out Selling Private Shares," Bloomberg, April 21, 2011.

9. Stone, "Silicon Valley Cashes Out."

10. See "Abingworth Raises $315m for ABV VII 12th Life Sciences Fund," PR Newswire, July 9, 2018.

11. See https://www.abingworth.com, accessed May 3, 2019.

CHAPTER 6: USE THIRD-PARTY TOOLS

1. Courtney Reum and Carter Reum, *Shortcut Your Startup: Speed Up Success with Unconventional Advice from the Trenches* (New York: Gallery/Jeter, 2018).

2. David Heath (co-founder of Bombas), interview with author, October 22, 2018.

3. Oisin O'Connor (founder of ReCharge), interview with author, September 5, 2018.

4. Michael Feinberg (CEO of ResolvedCX), interview with author, October 11, 2018.

CHAPTER 7: FRAME THE DIGITAL OFFERING

1. Sophia Edelstein (co-founder and co-CEO of Pair Eyewear), interview with author, October 1, 2018.

2. "Pair: Sunglasses for Superheroes," *Rockin' Mama Life* (blog), October 25, 2017, http://www.rockinmamalife.com/pair-sunglasses-superheroes. This text appeared on the company's site as of 2018.

3. Berkeley Lovelace Jr., "Half the Number of Online Ad Clicks Are by Mistake, Says a Silicon Valley Veteran," CNBC, April 26, 2017.

4. Anna Hensel, "Facebook Users Can Now See All the Active Ads Run by a Page," VentureBeat, June 28, 2018.

5. James LaForce (CEO and founder of LaForce), interview with author, August 30, 2018.

6. Renata Black (co-founder of EBY), interview with author, September 17, 2018.

CHAPTER 8: CUT THROUGH THE METRICS BULLSHIT

1. Jake Kassan (CEO of MVMT), interview with author, November 7, 2018.

2. Roberta Naas, "Movado Group to Acquire MVMT Lifestyle Watch and Accessories Brand," *Forbes,* August 16, 2018.

3. John Fiorentino (founder of Moon Pod) interview with author, September 7, 2018.

4. Nick Shah (co-founder and COO of Ampush), interview with author, June 5, 2018.

5. Nick Greenfield (founder of Candid), interview with author, November 26, 2018.

6. Adam Lovallo (co-founder of Grow.co and founder of Thesis), interview with author, September 25, 2018.

CHAPTER 9: KNOW WHAT A CUSTOMER IS WORTH

1. Simon Enever (co-founder of Quip), interview with author, November 2, 2018.

CHAPTER 10: PULL YOUR FINANCIAL MODEL TOGETHER— AND USE IT!

1. Sergei Gusev (co-founder and COO of Scentbird), interview with author, October 18, 2018.

CHAPTER 11: BEWARE THE DUMPSTER FIRE

1. Simon Enever (co-founder of Quip), interview with author, November 2, 2018.

CHAPTER 12: GROW YOUR OWN WAY

1. Lauren Hallanan, "How Chinese Influencers Created the Kylie Jenner Business Model," *Forbes,* September 6, 2018; Hilary Milnes, "How Influencer Zoe Zhang Drives Retail Sales on Alibaba's Taobao," *Digiday,* April 3, 2018; Angela Doland, "China's Influencers Don't Just Push Brands—They Create Their Own," *Ad Age,* February 7, 2018.

2. Hilary Milnes, "'More Like Reality': In 2019, Hot DTC Brands Face Pressures to Prove Profitability," *Digiday*, January 2, 2019.

3. Courtney Reum (co-founder of M13), interview with author, October 26, 2018.

4. "Dollar Shave Club Sales Flatline Immediately After $1B Unilever Acquisition," 1010Data, September 25, 2017; Paresh Dave, "Dollar Shave Club Succeeded with Razors, but the Rest of the Bathroom Is a Challenge," *Los Angeles Times*, September 1, 2017.

INDEX

Abingworth, 115
add-ons, 188
adult incontinence products,
    246–47
advertising
    algorithms and cleverness of,
        144–45
    costs to run on Amazon, 25
    Facebook clicks, 210–11
    getting most valuable ad
        impressions, 48, 265n4
    lead ads, viii, 40–42
    managing, on Facebook, 129
    for mobile devices, 153–54
    native ads, xvii–xviii
    new opportunities, 249–50
    search engine, 175
    starting simple, 156–57
    tailoring, using digital feedback
        loops, xii, 10
    tinkering with to increase
        effectiveness, ix, 36
    using quotations from earned
        media for, 148–49
affiliate partners, 155–56, 175
Alba, Jessica, 5
algorithms, 10, 144–45
Allbirds, 231

Allswell Home, 21
Amazon
    advantages to, of direct-to-
        consumer sales, xii–xiii
    capitalization of, 111
    hybridization of, xvi
    number of products sold, 12
    optimization of marketing
        without selling products,
        23
    private brands of, as threat to
        traditional brands, 24–25
    sacrifice of short-term
        profitability for long-term
        profitability, xvi
Amazon Web Services (AWS), 121,
    124
AndieSwim.com, 30–33, 44–45,
    61, 86–88, 150, 154, 255
Assembled Brands, 59
attorneys, 82–83
average order value, calculating,
    187–89

baby stroller sales, 246–47
Betterment, 148
Bieber, Justin, 3

Black, Renata, 70–71, 105–6, 124,
    158–59
blogs, 149, 174
Blue Apron, 147–48
Bombas, 123, 127–28, 135–36
Bonderman, David, 79
Bonobos, 75
bootstrapping, 9, 18–19, 251–52
Boston Consulting Group (BCG),
    52
bounce rate, 168
branding, 83–84, 107
budget allocation, 129, 133
Burlingham, Bo, 59

CAC (customer acquisition cost),
    170
Campaign Monitor, 124
Candid, 231
capital, raising. *See also* equity-
    sharing; funding; pitching idea
capture sites, 42
Care/of, 75–78, 152, 153, 155
"channel conflict," 19–20
Charnoff, Oren, 109
Chewy, 5
Christensen, Clayton, 47–48
Clearbanc, 59, 251–52
Cogan, Ben, vii
    background, viii, 16, 52
    early success of Hubble, viii–ix
    idea for Hubble, 53
Cogan, Bruce, 72
Colgate, 43
collaboration, 16, 50. *See also*
    experts
compensation for employees, 130
compensation for experts
    with equity, 86–88
    at Hubble, 78
    by large corporations, 88–90
    with revenue-sharing agreement,
        85–86
    up-front, 85
compensation for third-party tools
    and services, 133–35

competition, 8, 60
consumers. *See also* customers
    base focus and marketing
        channel, 175
    channel diversity and, 223
    cost of making customers, 163
    cross-selling to, 10
    importance of understanding,
        158–59
    lead ads and, 41
    limit to amount of information
        absorbed by, 139–41
    marketing to, as individuals, x–xi
    younger, buy from direct-to-
        consumer companies, xix
contribution margin, 190–92
convertible notes, 58, 266n2
corporate bosses, pitching to,
    19–24, 64–69
CPA (cost per acquisition)
    importance of, 170
    IRR and, 214–17
    LTV and, 157, 173, 198, 207–13,
        216, 227
    methods of decreasing, 208–9,
        223–24
    metrics that contribute to,
        171–74
    monitoring, 133, 170–71, 172
    optimizing by channel, 174–76
    pushing to limit implied by
        model used, 220–21
    scale and, 176, 179
    summary, 184
    targeting, 179–81
CPC (cost per click), 168, 171
CPM (cost per thousand
    impressions), 168, 171
CPV (cost per view), 168
credit card processing fees, 195–96
crowdfunding
    demands of, 43
    examples of direct-to-consumer
        companies using, 4, 32–33
    for MVMT, 162
CTR (click-through rate), 168, 171
"the curiosity gap," 152

customers
building loyalty, 21
cost of making consumers, 163
expectations of, 7
first as best, 203
importance of improving
shopping experience for, 61
importance of relationships with,
10–11, 150–51, 158–59
offering new products directly to,
20, 21–22
ongoing feedback loop with, to
collect data, x–xi
outsourcing customer service to
third parties and, 125–26
quality of, 225
retention patterns, 145, 148,
201
CVR (conversion rate), 168, 171

data analytics, 11–12
"day job" keeping, 15
"decision fatigue," 154
DeepMind, 63
DeJoria, John Paul, 52
demand-related metrics. *See also*
specific metrics such as CPA
discovering source, 165–67
importance of, 163–64
types of, 168
design options for start-ups, 49
digital direct response marketing.
See digital feedback loops
digital feedback loops
advantages of, x–xi, 27
closing using loyalty apps, 23–24
daily rituals of, 11–14
described, x
hybridization of traditional
brands and, 22
lead ads and, viii, 40–42
other names for, xiii
tailoring advertising using, xii, 10
traditional brands and, xviii,
23–24
without selling products, 23

digital platforms. *See also specific*
platforms such as Amazon
cost of marketing on, 25
Google, Facebook, and Amazon
lock on digital marketing,
xvii–xviii
as threat to traditional brands,
24–27
direct brands, xiii
direct mail marketing, 175–76
direct-to-consumer companies. *See*
also hybridization; subscription
businesses; *specific companies*
absence of "rules" and "best
practices," 245, 248
constant need to change/
experiment, 50, 246, 248–56,
259
crowdfunding examples, 4, 32–33
difficulties faced by, 7, 8
ease of starting, 8
as epochal shift in distribution
channels, xiii
examples of, vii, ix–x
launching versus making stable
and successful, 6–7
reasons for failure of, xiii–xiv
simplicity of online experience,
141–42
size limitations, 8
as skunkworks within traditional
companies, 47–48
strongest success indicator, 168
testing idea for, viii–ix, 31–32,
36–40, 51
younger consumers buy from, xix
direct-to-consumer incubators,
252–54
direct-to-consumer marketing
platforms, 254–56
discount plans, 23–24
Disney, xvii
distribution and distributors
cutting out, 19–20
direct-to-consumer companies as
epochal shift in distribution
channels, xiii

distribution and distributors (*cont'd*):
  explaining, to potential investors,
    60–62
  options for start-ups, 48
Dollar Shave Club, 61, 64, 189,
    257
drop shipping, 193–94

EBY, 70–71, 105–6, 158–59, 231
e-commerce, as increasing in-store
    sales, 22
Edelstein, Sophia, 36–38, 139–41
Elbert, Craig, 75–78, 152, 153, 155
emails for marketing, 149–51, 175
Enever, Simon, 185–87, 203–4,
    228–30, 240
equity-sharing
  as builder of more valuable
    company, 103–6
  case for, 98–102
  control and, 102–3
  equity as risk and, 97–98
  example of Andie.com, 86–88
  example of Hubble, 104
  in exchange for product/services
    at cost, 225
  resources to fight competitors
    with and, 111
  SAFEs, 58, 266n2
  selling secondary, 108–11
Evercore, 108
experts
  connecting with, 92–93
  example of Hubble, 78–80,
    86
  example of Keeps, 106–7
  importance of, 76–78, 81
  as providing legitimacy to
    investors, 91
  range of, needed, 82–84
  summary, 95–96
  tips for getting needed, 90–95
experts, compensating
  with equity, 86–88
  at Hubble, 78
  by large corporations, 88–90

with revenue-sharing agreement,
    85–86
up-front, 85

Fab, 18
Facebook
  ad clicks, 210–11
  ad revenue, 10
  algorithms to tailor ads to
    individual consumers, 10, 144
  data on viewers becoming
    customers, 165
  effectiveness of, 174, 175
  lead ads on, viii, 40–42
  managing ads on, 129
  traditional brands establishing
    performance marketing
    capability with, xviii
Federal Trade Commission, 82
federated brands platform, 255–56
feedback loops. *See* digital feedback
    loops
Feinberg, Michael, 126, 131–32
Fenyo, Ken, xv
Fiorentino, John
  Good Ones blog, 4
  Gravity Blanket and, 4–5, 6, 15
  Justin Bieber and, 3
  strongest success indicator, 168
  venture capital and, 4
fixed costs, 218–19, 224
Fortune 500 companies. *See*
    traditional brands/companies
freelancers, 125–26
free trials, 147–48, 156
freight forwarding costs, 193–94
fulfillment center costs, 194
funding. *See also* equity-sharing;
    pitching idea; venture
    investors/capitalists (VCs)
  alternatives to VCs, 59
  company valuation and, 112–13
  crowdfunding, 4, 32–33, 43,
    162
  experts and, 106–7
  gender bias in, 106

obtaining by doing preparatory
    investigations, viii–ix, 31–32,
    36–40
risk and, 117
SAFE compared to convertible
    notes, 58, 266n2
subscription businesses, 145–46
by traditional big companies,
    113–16

Galloway, Scott, xvi
gender bias in funding, 106
Genkins, Amy, 72
Gillette, 43, 120
Gilt, 18
GitHub, viii
Goldberg, Randy, 128
Goldman, Seth, 52
Good Ones (blog), 4
Google
    ad revenue, 10
    algorithms to tailor ads to
        individual consumers, 10
    data on viewers becoming
        customers, 165
    DeepMind and artificial
        intelligence, 63
Gravity Blanket, 4–5, 6
Greenfield, Nick, 177–78
Greycroft, 79–80
Groupon, 156, 175
growth equity funds. *See* venture
    investors/capitalists (VCs)
Gusev, Sergei, 207–9
Gutentag, Steve, 107

Haber, Jack, xiii
Harry's, viii, 52, 64
Hastings, Reed, 12–13
Heath, Andrew, 128
Heath, David, 91, 123, 127–28,
    135–36
Heitzmann, Rick, 79, 247
Herlands, Will, 246
Hewlett-Packard, 52

Honest Company, 5, 188–89, 231
Honest Tea, 52
Hubble Contacts
    customer activity rates, 200–201
    environment at time of pitching,
        64, 142–43
    equity-sharing, 104
    examples of information obtained
        from digital feedback loops, 27
    experimenting after launch by,
        45–46
    experts and, 78–80, 86
    exploitation of competitors'
        vulnerabilities, 143–44
    founders, vii
    funding, viii
    idea for, 53
    IRR and, 218
    launches outside U.S., 119
    launch in U.S., ix, 233–34,
        238–39, 241–42
    managing anxiety and depression
        during launch, 238–39
    marketing budget allocation
        changes, 129
    relationships with customers,
        159
    research for, and involvement of
        author, 53–54
    success of, viii–ix, 7
    third party tools and services
        used by, 121
    ventures prior to, 16, 18
Huggies, 22–23
Hulu, 49–50
hustling, tips for, 17–18
Huyett, Kate, 127, 128
hybridization
    as answer for traditional brands/
        companies, xvi–xix, 22, 26–27,
        248
    creation of digital feedback loops,
        22
    effect of, on legacy business,
        64–66
    removing as much risk as
        possible, 44

Ibotta, 24
Indiegogo, 43, 162
influencers, 250–51
Inghelbrecht, Philip, x
The Innovator's Dilemma
    (Christensen), 47–48
Instagram, xviii, 174, 175
inventory management costs, 195,
    196
investors. *See* venture investors/
    capitalists (VCs)
IRR (internal rate of return)
    CPA and, 214–17
    described, 215
    fixed costs and, 218–19
    methods to improving, 224–25
    targeting, 219–21

Jet.com, xvi–xvii
joint venture partnerships, 85–86

Kalanick, Travis, 103
Karagas, Demetri, 88, 90, 106–7
Kassan, Jake, 162–64, 182–83
Kazam, Josh, 79, 247
Keeps, 88, 106–7, 255
Kickstarter, 4, 33, 43
Kidder, David, xix
Kimberly-Clark, 22–23
Kondamuri, Nathan, 37–38,
    139–41
Kylie Cosmetics, 5

LaForce, James, 148–49
LaPlante, Kramer, 162–64
launch stage
    Hubble experiences, ix, 119,
        233–34, 238–39, 241–42
    managing stress and sleep
        deprivation, 237–41
    marketing, 236–37
    potential mishaps, 228–30,
        233–35
    summary, 244

versus making stable and
    successful, 6–7
lead ads, viii, 40–42
learning mindsets, importance of,
    34–35, 44, 50
Levy, Brian, 79
life balance, 124
LinkedIn, 77, 92, 93–94
liquidation preferences, 112
liquidity events, 109
lobbyists, 82
Lovallo, Adam, 180, 181
loyalty programs
    starting digitally, 22–23
    using apps to "close the
        [feedback] loop" for non-
        distribution traditional brand,
        23–24
LTR (lifetime revenue), importance
    of, 170
LTV (customer lifetime value)
    calculating
        for single-order businesses,
            198–200
        for subscription businesses, 169,
            200–203
    calculating revenue average order
        contributes, 187–91
    components of, 170
    CPA and, 157, 173, 198, 207–13,
        216, 227
    as determinant of marketing
        costs, 204–5
    importance of, 187
    maximizing, 186, 208, 209
    summary, 206

M13, 252–53
manufacturing costs, 192–93
margin
    areas making biggest impact on,
        171
    contribution per order, 190–92
    defined, 170
    special offers and, 188
marketing. *See also* advertising;

demand-related metrics; *specific metrics such as* CPA
  allocation of budget for, 118, 129, 133
  branding and, 83–84, 107
  costs, 13, 25, 204–5, 217–18
  data analytics, 11–12
  establishing relationships as key, x–xi, 10–11, 150–51
  free trials, 147, 156
  learning how to do own, 237
  in *Mad Men* era of 1960s, 9–10
  membership as holy grail, 10–11
  optimization of, without selling products, 23
  profit per dollar of, 168–69
  referral programs, 147–48
  scaling up, 157–58
  selling directly to consumers optimizes current digital, 20
  "spray and pray" approach, x
  summary, 161
  third-party tools and services and, 125
  tweaking of, 236–37
  without advertising, 228
marketing channels
  blogs, 149
  determining most successful, 165
  direct mail, 175–76
  direct-to-consumer platforms, 254–56
  emails, 149–51, 175
  federated brands platform, 255–56
  importance of diversity, 177–78, 223
  influencers, 250–51
  social media platforms, 141, 144–45
  traditional media, 20, 157, 264n4
  visuals, 155
marketing data. *See also* digital feedback loops
  from capture sites, 42
  feedback loop with customers, xiii, xviii

from lead ads, 41
methods of obtaining digital, xi–xii
obtaining, and short-term unprofitability, xv
from preorders, 43
through proto-versions of inventory-less store, 42–43
Maveron, 107
May, Bill, 185–87, 228–30
McDonald's loyalty app, 24
middleman, companies eliminating, vii, ix–x
mobile phones, optimizing site for, 141, 142, 151–55
Mockingbird, 71, 94–95
money-back guarantees, 147
Movado, 163
MoviePass, 20–21
Musk, Elon, 55
MVMT watches
  funding, 18–19, 162, 163–64, 182–83
  success of, 163–64
  transaction range of, 9

native ads, xvii–xviii
Native deodorant, 9, 18–19
Netflix
  number of movies and TV shows in listings, 12
  as producer of original content, 25–26
  product offerings at beginning, 55
  steering consumers to cheaper productions, 12–13
  value of, 198–99
network, using your, 71–72, 92
nonprofit arena, 17–18
NovaQuest, 116
Nurislamova, Mariya, 207–9

O'Connor, Oisin, 127
omnichannel retail, described, xvi

One Kings Lane, 18
opportunity costs, 197, 215, 221
"opt-in" versus "opt-out," 154–55
Organ Preservation Alliance, 18
Osman, Eric, 71, 94–95, 246
Outbrain, effectiveness of, 174
outsourcing. *See* third-party tools
    and services

Packard, Dave, 52
Pair, 37–38, 139–41
Palantir, 55
partnership option, 47–50, 265n5
Paul Mitchell hair care brand, 52
payback concept, 212–13
payment terms, 192, 196–97
peak scale, 218–19
performance marketing. *See* digital
    feedback loops
Pinterest, effectiveness of, 174
pitching idea
    amount of information to share,
        57
    to corporate bosses, 64–66
    draw on network, 71–72
    example of Hubble, 64
    example of Uber, 61–62
    expectations when, 58
    explaining how business is
        unique, 61
    identifying minimally viable
        product business could sell,
        55–56
    importance of crafting narrative
        to audience, 59–60
    as iterative process, 69–71
    maximizing chances of success,
        63
    need for experts and, 91
    not to most desired investor at
        beginning, 70
    number of slides and type of
        information included, 56–57
    professionally but not too slickly,
        56
    questions typically asked, 60–61

sharing credit, 67–69
    as storytelling, 54
    summary, 72–74
    to VCs, 62–64
podcasts, 174, 175
Potter, Len, 79, 247
pricing options, 145–46
private-label products, as threat to
    traditional brands, 24–26
procrastination trap, 118–21, 138
products
    market structure of industry, 60
    offering new, directly to
        consumers, 20, 21–22
profitability
    margin from direct-to-consumer
        selling versus traditional retail,
        66
    profit-sharing agreements and,
        85–86
    reduction while traditional big
        companies build direct-to-
        consumer businesses, 113–14
    sacrificing short-term for long-
        term, xv–xvi
    targeting, 221–22
public signage, 177
purchase funnels, 142

questionnaires/quizzes, using,
    152–53, 154, 155, 167
Quip, 185–87, 228–30, 240

radio, 175
Rebrov, Andrei, 207–9
ReCharge, 124
referral programs, 147–48
regulations, checking at beginning,
    39–40
repurchase rates, 199
reputation and risk, 99–100, 103–4
ResolvedCX, 126
Reum, Carter, 121, 252–53
Reum, Courtney, 121, 252–53
revenue retention, 201–2

risk
cannibalization of legacy
business, 64–66
case for spreading, 98–102
equity as, 97–98
large companies' retention of
minority stakes in start-ups,
115–16
large corporations' compensation
to experts and, 88–90
maximizing chances of success in
pitch, 63
minimalizing, 44, 47, 117
reputation and, 99–100, 103–4
selling secondary and, 110
VCs and, 62–63, 111
Rodgers, Paul, 72
Rosen, Dan, 72
Rothenberg, Randall, xiii
Rush, Carolyn, 84

SAFE (simple agreement for future
equity), 58, 266n2
sales tax, 193
SavingStar, 24
Scentbird, 207–9
search engine advertising, 175
search traffic, 143
"selling secondary," 108–11
serial entrepreneurs, 64
Severs, Mark, 72
Shah, Akash, 76–78
Shah, Nick, 173
Shapiro, Jerry, 88
shipping costs, 193–95
Shopify, 80, 121, 124
Shortcut Your Startup (Reum and
Reum), 121, 252–53
Shuster, Todd, 92
single-order businesses
calculating LTV for, 198–200
peak scale for, 218–19
retargeting customers, 225
Snapchat, effectiveness of, 174
social media, 141–45, 250–51. *See
also specific platforms*

SoftBank, 108
Sony, product offerings at
beginning, 55
SpaceX, 55
special offers, 188
Spotify
effectiveness of, 175
number of songs, 12
steering consumers to music with
lower royalties to pay, 13
Sprout, 124
St. Shine, 40, 79
Starbucks, loyalty app, 24
start-ups. *See also* direct-to-
consumer companies; experts;
experts, compensating;
hybridization
hustler mentality, xix
issues of product distribution and
design, 48–49
narrow product offerings at
beginning, 55–56
partnership option, 47–49,
47–50, 265n5
products sold by, as good enough,
14
start-ups, tips for starting
1. start part-time, 15
2. collaborate with others, 16
3. think of venture as pathway to
future opportunities, 16–17
4. hustle, 17–18
5. bootstrapping option, 18–19
questions to answer, 39–40
Stella Connect, 124, 126
Stengel, Jim, xviii–xix
Stitch Fix, 152
Stone, Brad, 61–62, 109–10
stress, managing, 237–41, 244
Stripe, 121, 124
subscription businesses. *See also*
specific companies
affiliate partners and, 155–56
calculating LTV, 200–203
cost of replacing customers, 9,
264n2
customer quality, 169, 227

subscription businesses (*cont'd*):
  free trials, 147
  funding, 145–46
  growth limits, 8
  for movie tickets, 20–21
  peak scale for, 218
  retention deals, 186–87
  retention patterns, 145, 148, 201

Taboola, effectiveness of, 174
Target, 9
Tarlow, Drew, 79, 247
taxes, 193
television, effectiveness of, 174
ten Brink, Rachel, 207–9
Thiel, Peter, 55
third-party tools and services
  advantages of using, 122–24
  commitment length, 132
  communicating with, 134
  compensation for employees and,
    130
  continual evaluation of in-house
    versus, 135–37
  continual testing effectiveness of,
    132–33
  core team size and, 130
  freelancers as, 125–26
  internal management of, 127–28
  life balance and, 124
  for marketing, 125
  relationships and payment
    arrangements with, 133–35
  summary, 138
  used by Bombas, 123, 127–28
  used by Hubble, 121
  vetting vendors, 131–32
3:1 LTV/CPA ratio, 210–13, 216
time, value of, 123, 221
time-weighting, 212, 214
traditional brands/companies. *See
  specific examples such as*
  Walmart
  "channel conflict" issue, 19–20
  compensation for experts by,
    88–90

  difficulties of adapting to change,
    47
  digital platforms as threat to,
    24–27
  direct-to-consumer start-ups as
    learning opportunities, 46–50
  efforts of, to sell directly, xviii
  establishing performance
    marketing capability with
    platforms, xviii
  establishing skunkworks within
    company, 47–48
  extra costs of direct-to-consumer
    selling, 20
  funding direct-to-consumer
    businesses, 113–16
  getting boss to buy into selling
    naked, 19–24
  hybridization as answer for,
    xvi–xix, 22, 26–27,
    248
  hybridization's effect on legacy
    business, 64–66
  loyalty programs, 22–23
  profit margin from direct-to-
    consumer selling, 66
  using direct-to-consumer sales for
    new offerings, 20, 21–22
  using in-house versus third-party
    offerings, 122
traditional media marketing, 20,
  157, 264n4
Travis, Melanie
  avoiding "decision fatigue," 154
  background, 30
  blog by, 150
  crowdfunding by, 32–33
  development of direct-to-
    consumer company, 31–32
  equity sharing with experts
    needed, 86–88
  experimentation and testing by,
    44–45
  idea for direct-to-consumer
    company, 30–31
  pitch by, 61
Twilio, 124

Twitter, effectiveness of, 174
Two River, 79

Uber, 61–62, 103, 108
unilateral pricing policy, 53
Unilever, 64, 257
upsells, 188
The Upstarts (Stone), 61–62

value-added tax, 193
variable costs, 192–96, 224
venture investors/capitalists (VCs).
     See also pitching idea
as bootstrappers' source of
     capital, 251–52
bootstrapping instead of, 9,
     18–19
capital for joint ventures with
     large companies, 114–16
expectations, 9
experts as providing legitimacy,
     91
increase in caution by, 251
increase in funds of, 110
percent of revenue as profit and,
     191
quantifying customer value and,
     198–99

questions of, 60–61
risk aversion of, 62–63, 111
3:1 LTV/CPA ratio and, 212–13
validation of business from
     earned media and, 148–49
want founders who are learners,
     34–35
Vergara, Sofía, 105
visuals, using in marketing, 155

Wall Street Journal, 108
Walmart, xvi–xvii, 21
Warby Parker, 37, 38, 52, 231
Wasserman, Noam, 103
Wealthfront, 148
WeWork Cos., 108
Wheeler, Ellie, 79
Wildcat Capital Management,
     79
Willow, 189
Wolk, Aaron, 128
working capital, 192–93, 196–97

YouTube, 175

Zendesk, 124
Zynga effect, 177–78

ABOUT THE AUTHOR

JESSE HORWITZ is a serial entrepreneur who in 2016 co-founded the e-commerce contact lens company Hubble Contacts, whose growth has exploded from 3,000 subscribers at launch to hundreds of thousands today. A graduate of Columbia University, Horwitz worked for Bridgewater Associates. He spent several years on the investment team for Columbia University's endowment, focusing on private equity, venture capital, hedge funds, and real estate. Horwitz consults with major Fortune 500 retail companies on how to adapt "selling naked" strategies into their own marketing and brand mix. He and co-founder Ben Cogan were listed in *Forbes*'s 30 Under 30 list. Hubble has been written about in *The New York Times Magazine*, *The Wall Street Journal*, and *Fast Company*.

Jessehorwitz.com